The Short Oxf

General Editor: Pa

The Seventeenth Century

Edited by Jenny Wormald

The Short Oxford History
of the British Isles

General Editor: Paul Langford

The Seventeenth Century

Edited by Jenny Wormald

OXFORD
UNIVERSITY PRESS

OXFORD

UNIVERSITY PRESS

Great Clarendon Street, Oxford OX2 6DP

Oxford University Press is a department of the University of Oxford.
It furthers the University's objective of excellence in research, scholarship,
and education by publishing worldwide in

Oxford New York

Auckland Cape Town Dar es Salaam Hong Kong Karachi
Kuala Lumpur Madrid Melbourne Mexico City Nairobi
New Delhi Shanghai Taipei Toronto

With offices in

Argentina Austria Brazil Chile Czech Republic France Greece
Guatemala Hungary Italy Japan Poland Portugal Singapore
South Korea Switzerland Thailand Turkey Ukraine Vietnam

Oxford is a registered trade mark of Oxford University Press
in the UK and in certain other countries

Published in the United States
by Oxford University Press Inc., New York

© Oxford University Press 2008

The moral rights of the authors have been asserted
Database right Oxford University Press (maker)

First published 2008

All rights reserved. No part of this publication may be reproduced,
stored in a retrieval system, or transmitted, in any form or by any means,
without the prior permission in writing of Oxford University Press,
or as expressly permitted by law, or under terms agreed with the appropriate
reprographics rights organization. Enquiries concerning reproduction
outside the scope of the above should be sent to the Rights Department,
Oxford University Press, at the address above

You must not circulate this book in any other binding or cover
and you must impose the same condition on any acquirer

British Library Cataloguing in Publication Data

Data available

Library of Congress Cataloging in Publication Data

The seventeenth century / edited by Jenny Wormald.
    p. cm.—(The short Oxford history of the British Isles)
  Includes bibliographical references and index.
    ISBN 978-0-19-873162-7 (acid-free paper)—ISBN 978-0-19-873161-0 (pbk.: acid-free
paper) 1. Great Britain—History—Stuarts, 1603-1714. 2. Great Britain—Politics and
government—1603-1714. 3. Monarchy—Great Britain—History—17th century. 4. Great
Britain—Civilization—17th century. I. Wormald, Jenny.
    DA375.S48 2008
    941.06—dc22   2008016740

Typeset by Laserwords Private Limited, Chennai, India
Printed in Great Britain
on acid-free paper by
CPI Antony Rowe, Chippenham, Wiltshire

ISBN 978-0-19-873162-7 (Hbk)
ISBN 978-0-19-873161-0 (Pbk)

10 9 8 7 6 5 4 3 2 1

General Editor's Preface

It is a truism that historical writing is itself culturally determined, reflecting intellectual fashions, political preoccupations, and moral values at the time it is written. In the case of British history this has resulted in a great diversity of perspectives on both the content of what is narrated and the geopolitical framework in which it is placed. In recent times the process of redefinition has positively accelerated under the pressure of contemporary change. Some of it has come from within Britain during a period of recurrent racial tension in England and reviving nationalism in Scotland, Wales, and Northern Ireland. But much of it also comes from beyond. There has been a powerful surge of interest in the politics of national identity in response to the break-up of some of the world's great empires, both colonial and Continental. The search for new sovereignties, not least in Europe itself, has contributed to a questioning of long-standing political boundaries. Such shifting of the tectonic plates of history is to be expected but for Britain especially, with what is perceived (not very accurately) to be a long period of relative stability lasting from the late seventeenth century to the mid-twentieth century, it has had a particular resonance.

Much controversy and still more confusion arise from the lack of clarity about the subject matter that figures in Insular historiography. Historians of England are often accused of ignoring the history of Britain as a whole, while using the terms as if they are synonymous. Historians of Britain are similarly charged with taking Ireland's inclusion for granted without engaging directly with it. And for those who believe they are writing more specifically the history of Ireland, of Wales, or of Scotland, there is the unending tension between so-called metropolis and periphery, and the dilemmas offered by wider contexts, not only British and Irish but European and indeed extra-European. Some of these difficulties arise from the fluctuating fortunes and changing boundaries of the British state as organized from London. But even if the rulers of what is now called England had never taken an interest in dominion beyond its borders, the economic and cultural relationships between the various parts of the British Isles would still have generated many historiographical problems.

This series is based on the premiss that whatever the complexities and ambiguities created by this state of affairs, it makes sense to offer an overview, conducted by leading scholars whose research is on the leading edge of their discipline. That overview extends to the whole of the British Isles. The expression is not uncontroversial, especially to many in Ireland, for whom the very word 'British' implies an unacceptable politics of dominion. Yet there is no other formulation that can encapsulate the shared experience of 'these islands', to use another term much employed in Ireland and increasingly heard in Britain, but rather unhelpful to other inhabitants of the planet.

In short we use the words 'British Isles' solely and simply as a geographical expression. No set agenda is implied. It would indeed be difficult to identify one that could stand scrutiny. What constitutes a concept such as 'British history' or 'four nations history' remains the subject of acute disagreement, and varies much depending on the period under discussion. The editors and contributors of this series have been asked only to convey the findings of the most authoritative scholarship, and to flavour them with their own interpretative originality and distinctiveness. In the process we hope to provide not only a stimulating digest of more than two thousand years of history, but also a sense of the intense vitality that continues to mark historical research into the past of all parts of Britain and Ireland.

Lincoln College   PAUL LANGFORD
Oxford

Contents

List of illustrations

List of maps

(All maps adapted from Morrill (ed.), *The Oxford Illustrated History of Tudor and Stuart Britain* (1996).)

List of contributors

KEITH BROWN is Professor of Scottish History and Director of the Scottish Parliament Project at the University of St Andrews. His research interests are on the early modern Scottish nobility and the history of the Scottish parliament, on both of which he has published widely. His more recent book is *Noble Society in Scotland: Wealth, Family and Culture from Reformation to Evolution* (Edinburgh, 2000). He is currently working on a book entitled *Noble Power in Scotland from the Reformation to the Revolution.*

TOBY BARNARD has been Fellow in History at Hertford College, Oxford, since 1976. He edited with Jane Fenlon *The Dukes of Ormonde, 1610–1745* (Woodbridge, 2000). His other books include *Cromwellian Ireland; A New Anatomy of Ireland: The Irish Protestants, 1641–1770; Making the Grand Figure: Lives and Possessions in Ireland, 1641–1770; Irish Protestant Ascents and Descents, 1641–1770; The Kingdom of Ireland, 1641–1760; Guide to the Sources for the History of Material Culture in Ireland, 1500–2000.* He is currently a Leverhulme Senior Research Fellow working on the cultures of print in Ireland. He is also an honorary member of the Royal Irish Academy.

JOHN MCCAFFERTY is a Senior Lecturer in History at University College Dublin. He is also Director of the UCD–Irish Franciscan partnership body: the Micheál Ó Cléirigh Institute for the Study of Irish History and Civilization. He is primarily an ecclesiastical historian whose interests centre on late medieval and early modern Ireland. Recent publications include *The Reconstruction of the Church of Ireland: Bishop Bramhall and the Laudian Reforms* (Cambridge, 2007) and, with Alan Ford, *The Origins of Sectarianism in Early Modern Ireland* (Cambridge, 2005).

CLARE MCMANUS is Reader in English Literature at Roehampton University, London. She is the author of *Women on the Renaissance Stage: Anna of Denmark and Female Masquing at the Stuart Court, 1590–1619* (Manchester, 2002), editor of *Women and Culture at the Courts of the Stuart Queens* (Basingstoke, 2003, and co-editor of *Reconceiving the Renaissance: A Critical Reader* (Oxford, 2005).

She is currently editing John Fletcher's *Island Princess* for Arden Early Modern Drama.

JOHN MORRILL, FBA, is Professor of British and Irish History at the University of Cambridge. His main research interests are in what he calls 'the creation of a British state system but not a British state' in the early modern period, and all aspects of the 'British Revolution' of the mid-seventeenth century which were the subject of his Ford Lectures in the University of Oxford in 2005, and which are being prepared for publication under the title *Living with Revolution*. His acclaimed life of Oliver Cromwell in the *Oxford Dictionary of National Biography* has just been published as a short book by Oxford University Press.

J. A. SHARPE is a Professor in the Department of History, University of York. He has published extensively on the history of crime and punishment, and latterly witchcraft, in early modern England. He is also author of *Early Modern England: A Social History* (London, 1997). His current research interests are in the operation of the legal system in the early modern Isle of Man, and the history of interpersonal violence in early modern England.

JENNY WORMALD is an Honorary Fellow at the University of Edinburgh. She was previously a Fellow in History at St Hilda's College, Oxford. Her original research was in late medieval and early modern Scottish history, an interest which she has maintained while moving into the wider field of 'British history', even if the phrase is still one which she finds hard to understand. She has published widely on both Scottish and British history. Most recently she was the editor of *Scotland: A History* (Oxford, 2005), to which she contributed the chapter on the seventeenth century.

Figure 1 Fenchurch Arch.

Introduction

Jenny Wormald

The seventeenth century was, historically, and is, historiographically, a mess—wherein lies its fascination. This is a book about that century, the 'short seventeenth century', squeezed between the 'long sixteenth', 1485–1603, and the 'long eighteenth', 1688–1815. And perhaps it is appropriate that it should be so. For these were eighty-five intensely crowded years. They began in 1603 with the accession of a foreign, Scottish, king, James VI, to the thrones of England and Ireland and the principality of Wales; they witnessed in the middle of the century civil wars within all three kingdoms, which resulted in the public trial and execution of another king, Charles I; they then saw the attempt to create a British republic, whose failure led to the restoration of the monarchy under Charles II, only to see it crash down again less than three decades later, in the so-called 'Glorious Revolution' of 1688–9 against James VII and II; and with a certain neatness, they ended with the accession of another foreign king, the Dutch William of Orange, this time foreign to all three, not just two, of his kingdoms. That might well appear to be quite enough to be going on with; for in contrast even to that most profound and often traumatic of events, the long-drawn-out Reformation of the sixteenth century, these were rapidly disturbing and sometimes violent episodes, abruptly shattering long-established assumptions and expectations and habitual patterns of conduct. Of course 'history' never stands still. But in these eighty-five years it moved at bewildering and sometimes kaleidoscopic speed. And in addition it poses a new and possibly insoluble historical problem. For with the advent of the union of the crowns, historians can no longer discuss the geographically component parts of the British Isles, and their interactions with one another. They have to face up to three kingdoms now joined together in that entity so utterly difficult to define, the entity vaguely called Britain. 'British History' has a new meaning; indeed, it is in this century that it might for the first time be said to have any meaning at all.

But what is 'British History'? Is there actually such a thing as 'British History'? At one level, yes, if only in the sense that since J. G. A. Pocock launched his famous 'British History: a plea for a new subject' in 1975, early modern historians have spilt a very great deal of ink on the subject, debating whether British History exists, is possible, should be practised, distorts, illuminates. Should it be approached holistically, episodically, or comparatively, or, as Glenn Burgess urged, in a combination of all three? Can any single historian possibly cope with the sheer weight of research and knowledge needed to embark on British, rather than English, Scottish, Irish, Welsh history? It is a fair question, and it is by no means unreasonable that there are historians who think that they should not try; not every part of historical investigation demands a 'British' approach, and imposing a 'British' straitjacket could undoubtedly be counter-productive. Moreover, it is a question which raises the old and chain-rattling spectre that British History will be Anglocentric history—'the history of England with the other bits tacked on'. And sometimes, indeed, it is.

Yet it is very hard for any seventeenth-century historian to write about any part of the British Isles without tacking the other bits on, or at least being aware of the other bits, and very few try it today. So perhaps it is time to bury Scottish, Irish, and Welsh fears of Anglocentricity. Indeed, when James VI became James I of England, he certainly regarded himself, initially at least, as king of Britain; the mid-century crisis which overwhelmed Charles I and his monarchy began in Scotland and was exacerbated in Ireland before, with considerably more doubt and dither, England came in on the act; and James VII and II, the last of the old-style Stuart kings, having been flung out of both England and Scotland, turned to Ireland for possible salvation. None of this suggests that non-English historians should feel the need to worry about Anglocentricity. Paradoxically, it was an English historian of Britain, and a leading exponent in the field, John Morrill, who would challenge another leading pioneer of British history, the English historian Conrad Russell, on the grounds that he used Scottish and Irish history as a way of explaining English history; witness the title of his book, with its discussions of Scotland and Ireland, but yet called *The Origins of the English Civil War*. It is certainly a novel experience to find English scholars being critical about Anglocentricity, and one which suggests that non-English scholars can relax, even if as yet perhaps too much from the sidelines. Moreover, Morrill's stricture is perhaps too severe; does it actually diminish British History when one of its most distinguished practitioners used his research into Scotland and Ireland to elucidate the English civil war which was for so long seen only in English terms? As Burgess has rightly pointed out, the way forward for British History is Scoto-, Irish-, Welsh-, as well as Anglo-centred British History; the more that this happens, the more we will have to draw on in understanding seventeenth-century Britain, as, in effect, historians of the various parts of the British Isles pool their resources and thus make possible the synthesizing of problems which had their own distinctive impact on the countries which made up Britain but yet affected the whole. That it is already happening is evident in the chapters in this book. The combination of the holistic, the episodic, and the comparative can prove fruitful—up to a point.

There is, however, another way of looking at it. Historians faced by new historiographical fashion, called into being by the undoubted existence of the multiple kingdoms of the British Isles, may be in danger of levelling out the problems of the age in their search for an overarching concept. The multiple kingdoms of the early-modern period tended to be deeply unpopular, provoking far more resistance and national touchiness than acquiescence; they were more divisive than unifying. The English had not yet settled comfortably into the habitual use of 'England' and 'Britain' to mean the same thing; at the beginning of the reign of James VI and I, they were far more frightened about the loss of the name 'England', and the king had to assert by proclamation the title of king of Great Britain when it had been refused him by his first English parliament of 1604. Yet there was already a hint of that future reassuring solution; when James wanted to talk about 'the empire of Great Britain', he was told that the title had already been hijacked, for it had been used for England in the last years of Elizabeth's reign. The Scots, initially jubilant about having given England a king, and mindful of gains to be made from the richer southern kingdom, were, within four years of the union of the crowns, worrying about being relegated to the status of a province; their overt example was Spain, but it is very likely that they had Ireland in mind. And the English view of the Irish as provincial, subordinate, barbaric, and, in the case of many of them, damned anyway, hardly encouraged Irish enthusiasm for its ill-defined links—was it a kingdom or was it a province?—to its conquering neighbour. Moreover, despite certain superficial similarities—structures of government in all three kingdoms, a common Protestant faith in England and Scotland—what were far more important were the profound differences, cultural, political, ecclesiastical, seen never more clearly than in the crises of the century when, despite a common enemy, in Charles I and James VII and II, the input of and reaction to these crises in the three kingdoms owed far more to 'national' tradition than to the multi-kingdom present.

This is hardly surprising, given that it was hard to find anyone, other than James VI and I, who really wanted to be 'British'—and even he was using it as a bargaining counter, with an eye to his 'ancient and native kingdom' from which he had departed, rather than an absolute ideology. Every king of this period knew perfectly well that he was ruling over three disparate kingdoms, whatever lip-service was initially and unsuccessfully paid to the concept of 'Britain'. And that was equally well known by his subjects in the three kingdoms. They could not actually be disentangled, so long as they were under one ruler. As John Morrill points out, the one occasion when at least the Anglo-Scottish union—though not that with England, Ireland, and Wales—might have been broken, after the execution of Charles I in 1649, came to nothing, for while Cromwell envisaged an English republic as the way out of several problems, Charles II and the Scots between them refused to return to the earlier independent kingdom of Scotland. Charles II was not going to settle for less than his father and grandfather, and the Scots might happily bully monarchs, but that did not mean that the English should kill them, and monarchy was certainly preferable to having a republic; Stuart kingship, mid-seventeenth-century Scottish style, was infinitely more the natural order of things than the vision of a jumped-up minor English gentleman, however much practical politics dictated that he was a power in the British land. The trouble is that, as so often in the seventeenth century, the various parts of 'Britain' were pulling in different directions. Very rarely did they—or more precisely, their ruling elites—pull together. How, then, do we approach the first century of 'Britain', or 'British History', other than with great caution?

It may now be time to stand back from both concepts, and think instead of invoking a different model. Whether 'Britain' or 'British History' have a reality, multiple kingdoms certainly did, and perhaps British historians, like their European counterparts, might bring the focus back more specifically onto them, so that the question becomes one not so much of British but of European significance. The British Isles, after all, formed only one of the many early-modern multiple monarchies. It also happens to be one of the few which has survived; and as another is the Spanish *monarchia*, this might suggest that it is worth considering the Spanish exemplar, despite vast differences in the experiences of the two. This is a huge subject. The relevant point to be made here is that 'Spain' is a convenient but very misleading term. There was indeed a Spanish *monarchia*. The Spanish monarch, like the British one, was the sole and personal unifying force. But 'Spain' as a political or economic entity did not exist. So should we not acquit the inhabitants of seventeenth-century Scotland, England, Ireland, and Wales of any more awareness of being, or desiring to be, 'British' than the inhabitants of Castile, Aragon, Catalonia had in being 'Spanish', and leave them to be what they actually were: inhabitants of the multiple kingdoms of the British Isles? Which has problems enough.

These problems were reason enough to ensure that most early-modern composite monarchies did not survive. Henri de Valois, elected king of Poland, much preferred, when he succeeded to the French throne as Henri III, not to try to create a multiple monarchy, but to sneak out of Poland and get back to France with all possible speed; and the attempt to create a single Polish-Swedish Vasa monarchy was equally short-lived. The multiple monarchy of Sweden, Norway, and Denmark had already partially collapsed back in 1523, when Sweden detached itself from the union of Kalmar. Even within the Spanish *monarchia*, itself riven by efforts to readjust the political balance between and economic input of its original kingdoms of Castile and Aragon, there were territories which simply wanted to get out; Portugal, taken over by Philip II in 1580–1, managed it in 1648, Catalonia, despite a massive revolt and some help from France, did not. Multiple monarchies could therefore have a dynastic or elective reality, but they can hardly be said to have been welcome. Monarchs who inherited more than one kingdom might have something to offer, as James VI did in resolving the grievous dynastic problem faced by late sixteenth-century England, as Keith Brown shows. And initially, at least, his Scottish subjects could not only rejoice in having given England a king, the last, paradoxical, act in the long history of English kings' efforts to annex Scotland, but look forward enthusiastically to tapping into English wealth and office; sadly for them, with the exception of a very few, the English ensured that they were very quickly disappointed. Moreover, whatever the dynastic relief of 1603, that resolution of an immediate problem was in the longer term outweighed by the unpalatable nature of Stuart monarchy, even in James VI and I's reign as far as his English subjects were concerned, and increasingly throughout their three kingdoms in the reigns of his successors.

Such things might be regarded as the standard problems of multiple monarchies: resentment of monarchs, rivalries between the composite kingdoms, and jealousy, especially of the dominant one by those which felt marginalized. In no case was there any obvious reason why the king's subjects in his various territories should like one another, plenty of reasons why they should not. That is perfectly evident in the case of England, Scotland, Ireland, and Wales. But the British composite monarchy had a particular problem, experienced only by two others and then on a much more contained scale: religious division. The Spanish *monarchia* had to cope with the partially Calvinist Netherlands, France, itself in any case less of a multiple monarchy, with the largely Huguenot territory of Béarn, reunited with France in 1616. It is in no way to play down the ongoing late sixteenth- and early seventeenth-century drama of the Revolt of the Netherlands, with its massive international impact, to say that at least it was chronologically finite, resulting in the splitting of the northern and southern Netherlands and the creation of the United Provinces. The case of France and Béarn was a much less bloody affair; the French crown allowed a measure of toleration to the Catholics similar to that offered elsewhere to Huguenots, and was prepared to leave the Béarnais estates to function without undue pressure or interference, with the ultimate outcome that in 1789 they agreed to join with the Estates General of France (even if they decided to do so at a moment when the France which they now fully joined was about to be utterly transformed). Neither, therefore, match the extreme difficulty faced in the British Isles, when one of the three kingdoms was, and would remain throughout the succeeding centuries, largely Catholic within a Protestant composite monarchy.

In the seventeenth century, this insoluble problem had a profound effect on the attempt to create a stable composite monarchy, let alone 'Britain' or—that exceedingly thorny question—a 'British' state. In his proclamation of 1604 by which he assumed the title of king of Great Britain, James VI and I pointed to shared experience: language, religion, which brought together two former enemies in a 'Ile [which] hath almost none but imaginarie bounds of separation without, but one common limit or rather Gard of the Ocean Sea'. It was a vision taken up by Ben Jonson, in the motto he devised for the first of the seven triumphal arches for James's ceremonial entry into London in 1604, 'Orbis Britannicus, Divisus ab orbe'—'the world divided from the world'. It was geographically somewhat more accurate than Shakespeare's famous invocation in *Richard II* of the 'scept'red isle',

> This precious stone set in the silver sea
> Which serves it in the office of a wall ...
> ... this England.

But it cut out Ireland. And indeed, the regal style James took in 1604, for all that he did not adopt a colonial approach to Ireland, also separates the British mainland from Ireland; he was 'King of Great Brittaine, France and Ireland'.

Leaving out of the reckoning the ludicrous inclusion of France, he did have a point; and three of the chapters in this book, by John McCafferty, John Morrill, and Toby Barnard, emphatically show why. The social contempt felt by the English for the Irish, their belief that the solution to Ireland was Anglicanization in law, dress, and manners, caused trouble enough in Anglo-Irish relations. But they pale into insignificance beside the attempt to bring together three kingdoms when in one there was the flourishing Counter-Reformation Catholicism from the 1590s, in sharp contrast to the floundering efforts to establish itself of the Protestant church of Ireland. It made utterly impossible, for example, the desired policy of stamping out religious division, that rare phenomenon, as Conrad Russell has pointed out, of a vision shared by Charles I and the Covenanters—the latter even invoking Bede on the point—despite the fact that they themselves had profoundly different ideas about how it should be realized. Protestants could just about hope that other Protestants would see the light, even if it might take at least repression and possibly the sword to bring it about. Even this fragile and fleeting hope could never apply to Ireland.

Thus Russell and Morrill were surely right to see the problems of the British multiple kingdoms, to a far greater extent than anywhere else, as 'largely religious'. And this brings me to the third of the problems about the British Isles in the seventeenth century: the idea of the 'state'. Of all pre-modern historians, the Anglo-Saxonists seem most confident that England in their period was a state. The later medievalists are less certain. The early-modernists have a strong sense that 'kingdoms' became 'states' in their period, with their greater centralization, bureaucratization, and taxation, but can be hard put to it to define the concept, though the term 'the military-fiscal state' is much used. Michael Braddick, for example, has powerfully argued for successful state-building in England between the late sixteenth and early eighteenth centuries, accepting the idea of the military-fiscal state, but also rightly pointing to its crucial social dimension. Julian Goodare, equally rightly sensing profound developments in late sixteenth- and early seventeenth-century Scotland, urges an 'absolutist state', based on the changing nature of the relationship between an increasingly centralizing and taxing government and the nobility, but emphasizing that this is 'a process as well as a thing'. By contrast, Jonathan Scott has firmly pointed out that early seventeenth-century England simply did not have the resources to become a military-fiscal state. For him, 'the "evolution" of this [English] state during the seventeenth century occurred not as the result of its "success" but in the context of its collapse'; so it is to 'Anglo-Dutch statebuilding' that we must look. And Laura Stewart, to whom I am much indebted for discussion on this point, has identified the Scottish 'state' as being very limited in the early seventeenth century, but her own research into Scottish taxation suggests that its fiscal and military capacity was greatly increased in the civil war period. All agree, however, that the 'state' was not static but a progress. And the concept is very much complicated not only by the survival of local power centres in Scotland, but by the fact that Charles II and James VII and II were pushing power back into the localities in England. The progress, as Stewart points out, was not linear.

Of course the fiscal weakness of the British monarchy and its British territories are a key consideration here. But it is surely also possible to argue that its particular religious problem, beginning with the Reformation and surviving in strength throughout the seventeenth century, sustained preoccupations and obsessions within the British Isles which had little to do with the sort of state-building which is more readily detectable in Europe. In his remarkable book *England's Troubles*, Jonathan Scott insisted that seventeenth-century England must be seen in its European context, to predictably fascinating effect. England, and the other British kingdoms, did indeed react to the great European events. But the form of their reaction left them largely untouched by the huge stresses of warfare on an international scale which had so much to do with European state-building; that lay in the future. Meanwhile, this comparatively side-lined group of kingdoms struggled through their own internal religious and political problems and agonies. It is indeed ironic that the three rulers who were positively interventionist in Europe were the Scot James VI, the minor gentleman Oliver Cromwell, and, after 1688, the Dutch William III, the first continuing the tradition of his Stewart ancestors by pacific means, the other two by military ones, with the last hauling his British kingdoms decisively and finally out of their concentration on domestic affairs. Otherwise, with the brief and unhappy exception of the first four years of Charles I's reign, the vision of the inhabitants of the British Isles was largely bounded by the 'Gard of the Ocean Sea'.

So what about 'Britain' or 'British History'; multiple kingdoms; 'state-building', British-style: themes so crucial to the seventeenth century? With these problems the contributors to this volume wrestle.

The problem with which the contributors, and the general editor Paul Langford and Matthew Cotton of Oxford University Press, have also had to wrestle is the editor. For personal and health reasons, I have been unable to edit this book as quickly as I would have wished. In these stressful academic days, not least because of the pressures of the RAE, I want to record how deeply grateful I am for their tolerance, kindness, and understanding. It has been an immense pleasure for me to work with them.

The high & mighty Monarch CHARLES by y grace of GOD king of Great Brittaine France & Ireland Defendor of the Fayth. etc.

EDYNBURGH

C v. Dalen sculp.

Figure 2 Cornelius van Dalen, 'Charles I in front of Edinburgh', probably 1633 or 1641.

1

Monarchy and Government in Britain, 1603–1637

Keith M. Brown

Dynastic issues

The Stewarts were already an old dynasty when the biological failure of their recent Tudor sparring partners catapulted James VI to the throne of England in the spring of 1603. Such good fortune, however, was not unanticipated. Stewart monarchs had been heirs to the more dynastically fragile Tudors for most of the sixteenth century, since Henry VII married his eldest daughter, Margaret, to James IV in 1503. Mary, queen of Scots, had claimed to be the rightful queen of England from the death of Mary Tudor in 1558, and had been recognized as such by much of Catholic Europe. Her son, James VI, embodied the best Protestant claim to succeed Elizabeth I from his coronation in 1567, a claim that was strengthened enormously by Mary's execution twenty years later. Already the signing of an Anglo-Scottish league in 1586 had prepared the ground for James to take an important step forward in his path to the English throne. The English pension to which he now had access never amounted to formal recognition, but with the removal of his troublesome mother, James VI was king-in-waiting, however much his aged cousin, Elizabeth I, avoided the issue, and in spite of his own worries about lesser dynastic rivals or Acts of the English Parliament that might invalidate his claim. Even Elizabeth's knowledge of his covert support for the Essex conspiracy of 1601 did not stop the transformation of James's dynasty from being monarchs of Scotland into rulers of England, Ireland, and Scotland. Three hundred and thirty-two years after the Stewarts acquired their Scottish throne by outlasting the Bruces, James VI and I achieved an ambition greater than anything performed by those generations of English monarchs who had sought to bring Britain and Ireland under one ruler.

In England, there was widespread optimism at the start of a new reign, and general relief that the tired, old queen had gone, the myth of the Elizabethan golden age only gaining ground later when memories of her dithering and failure had faded. Opposition to James in 1603 was confined to the ineffectual Bye and Main Plots. Two years later, in November 1605, a band of desperate English Catholics tried to exploit the king's alien background in the Gunpowder Plot, designed to kill the royal family and the Scottish courtiers while simultaneously striking a blow against England's Protestant establishment. Guy Fawkes's failure, and the savage reaction to the plot, served merely to strengthen the bonds that had quickly developed between the English people and their new monarch.

The politics of any early modern royal dynasty could not avoid revolving around marriage and reproduction. Although James VI and I gave the English a sense of dynastic stability unknown since 1547, the Stuart dynasty had only recently acquired a measure of long-term biological security. James VI had no immediate family and, unlike his grandfather, James V, he avoided entangling himself in extra-marital sexual relationships so that there were no royal bastards by the time of his marriage in 1589 at the age of 21. His wife was Anne of Denmark, a younger daughter of Christian III, a powerful ally in the Baltic, a region of enormous importance to Scottish trade, and one that from 1603 would become of greater significance to England. Yet it was 1594 before an heir, Prince Henry, was born, Princess Elizabeth followed two years later, and a second son, Charles, in 1600. Other children were born to the marriage, but none survived into adulthood, and the fragility of family life was exposed when in 1612 the king's vigorous and militantly Protestant elder son died. The strained nature of the royal marriage made it unlikely that there would be another son

(Queen Anne died in 1619), leaving the dynasty's hopes pinned on the physically frail Prince Charles. Marriage in 1613 between the popular Princess Elizabeth and Frederick, elector palatine, strengthened the dynasty's connections with central European Protestantism. Unfortunately, Frederick's rash acceptance of the throne of Bohemia, to which members of the Imperial house of Habsburg were usually elected, led to war and to his expulsion not only from Bohemia but from his own territories on the Rhineland. The prolonged flirtation with a Spanish marriage for Charles that began in 1614, ending only in 1623, meant that he too was relatively old before contributing towards the longevity of the Stuart family. A year later, a marriage treaty was agreed on the rebound to Henrietta-Maria, sister of Louis XIII of France, but it did not take place until May 1625, two months after James VI's death. Once again the dynasty was hanging by a slender thread, Charles I and his homeless sister, Elizabeth of Bohemia. It remained so for another five years due to the sexually repressed nature of the new king, and his initially frosty relations with his wife. It was 1630 before a child, another Charles, was born. Thereafter, Mary and James followed, so that by 1633 the dynasty again looked biologically secure.

One factor that worked in the favour of the Stuarts as a royal dynasty was the absence of serious rivals. Throughout its long history as kings of Scots, the family had faced no challenges to its claim on the throne, and within Scotland's political community there was no rival to trouble James VI's hold either on the Scottish crown, or on his claim to that of England. Residual loyalty to his mother, Mary, faded after the defeat of her forces in 1573, and was ended altogether with her death in 1587. The only noble house that might rival the Stuarts was the house of Hamilton, the head of which, the duke of Chatelherault, had been governor of the kingdom during Mary's early minority. His heirs proved to be impeccably loyal, and James made a point of bringing the second marquis of Hamilton to London, creating for him a powerful position at court, but effectively removing him as a focus for discontent in Scotland. Charles I repeated this ploy with James Hamilton, third marquis of Hamilton, who was appointed master of the horse and became the king's close friend and adviser in the 1630s. Significantly, when Hamilton did return to Scotland in the following decade rumours quickly started up, unfairly accusing him of having designs on the throne. The other family with some claim to the Scottish crown was the house of Lennox, a junior and French branch of the royal Stuarts. As with the Hamiltons, James insisted that the second duke of Lennox accompany him to England, placing his cousin in charge of the bedchamber and bestowing on him English titles and gifts. Far more than the Hamiltons, the Lennox Stuarts became Anglicized. The only remaining rival, Arabella Stuart, might conceivably have been placed in James's way in 1603, and it was claimed that Sir Walter Raleigh and his friends intended to do just that. The discovery of the Main Plot in June of that year revealed some English opposition to the new king, but its plotters had more against the dominant Cecil faction at court than against James, and they were easily rounded up and imprisoned. Arabella was not implicated, but she was closely watched, being politically neutralized by the placing of obstacles in the way of her marriage. When she did marry in secret in 1610, she was imprisoned in the Tower of London where she died three years later.

In any political system the individual character of those who govern matters greatly; in monarchies this is particularly true. The man who became king of three kingdoms in March 1603 was the most seasoned ruler to succeed to the English crown in centuries. He would need that experience since his inheritance was a difficult one. England had for too long been engaged in a war with Spain that had lost any sense of direction, there was widespread discontent with the church, the crown had massive financial problems, and parliament had decades of accumulated grievances it wanted the new king to address. Ireland was in an even worse state, having endured years of malign administration and rebellion. James VI brought to his new office some twenty years' experience of governing Scotland. In that time he had made mistakes: he occasionally demonstrated poor judgement in dealing with nobles and servants, he could be financially irresponsible, and he interfered in church affairs more than was necessary. These were errors he would make again after 1603. Yet in attaining an acceptable level of political stability by the mid-1590s, James had already demonstrated great skill. In important matters he was patient, taking the long-term view, as one would expect from a man who had waited most of his life for Elizabeth I to name him her heir; he was inclined to seek peaceful compromises, both in international affairs and in his dealings with individuals; he was aware of the need to reward good service, even when he could not afford it. These traits too continued to characterize his rule after 1603. While his verbosity and love of debate often got him involved in unnecessary political controversy, James was a deep-thinking intellectual who wrote books on kingcraft and witchcraft, and he engaged in religious dispute passionately and with reason. The king was a hard, if erratic, worker, the temptation of the chase often drawing him away from government for long spells. He was gregarious and familiar with his nobles, but contemptuous of the common people. This was the character of the 37-year-old man who became king of England and Ireland in 1603, and nothing he did over the next twenty-two years would have come as a very great surprise to those who knew him.

Charles I was of a different character entirely, and as a mature man of 25 when he became king, he was unlikely to change in office. The key to his nature was a deep-seated insecurity expressed in authoritarian directives. A small man in height and in mind, he stuttered and fought to overcome a sense that no one took him seriously until the day he became king, having been overshadowed by his elder brother, and then by James's favourites. Charles lacked his father's intellectual breadth and flexibility, having instead a sly cleverness; he was obsessed with order, from the etiquette of his court to church ritual; he found compromise almost impossible, seeing it as an indication of weakness, and was unable to comprehend the need to make short-term concessions in order to achieve long-term goals; his friendships tended to be brittle and although he did inspire loyalty, he usually succeeded in arousing suspicion. Above all else, his views on kingship were rigid and impractical. Yet Charles I was certainly not a bad man. He had a very strong sense of family, he was quietly pious with a strong sense of conscience to guide him, he worked assiduously and efficiently, the personal courage he would later display in the face of death was demonstrated in his 1623 journey to Spain, and his determination to tackle head-on some of the issues his father had skirted around was not entirely foolish. He also loved art, being a knowledgeable connoisseur as well as a great collector, and his concern with good taste and decorum did him no harm.

British union

The possibility of a regal union had been around for most of the sixteenth century, allowing plenty of opportunity for people to think about what form it might take, and how it should be interpreted. It is, therefore, surprising that ideas about Britain were so vague in 1603 and that a British agenda was so unprepared. To James VI and I, who had himself proclaimed king of Great Britain and Ireland in October 1604, it appeared both sensible and straight-forward. God had restored a unity to Britain lost in the distant past, and it was the divine purpose to create a Protestant empire ruled by a British king. It followed that there should be a British court, church, and parliament, that the functions of government and administration should be fused, the laws united, a common iconography adopted, a single coinage and economic policy devised, and that, with the aid of shared political loyalties, religion, and language, a British people would emerge. This was James VI and I's vision; it was shared by almost no one else. All the mumbo-jumbo in the world, which is what much of British ideology rested upon, could not overcome the deep-seated resistance of national identity in England and Scotland, or bind together the fractured communities of Ireland. Even the very name Britain aroused resentment, and the English especially refused to recognize the king's proclaimed title. The idea of Britain made for interesting intellectual diversifications, appealing to a sophisticated mind like James's, but it had no roots and no prospects, as was apparent long before the 1607 session of the English parliament brought hostility to the king's agenda into the open.

Not surprisingly, the extent of institutional union that flowed from the personal union was minimal, and the regal union amounted to not much more than three kingdoms sharing one king. Of course, the political relationship between England and Ireland was different from that between England and Scotland, or Ireland and Scotland. The kingdom of Ireland, created by Henry VIII in 1541, was a subject territory of the English crown, its parliament was carefully monitored by the English privy council, it was governed by an English lord deputy. English officials like Sir Arthur

Chichester and Sir John Davies in the 1600s through to Sir Thomas Wentworth in the 1630s saw themselves as progressing a deliberate policy of Anglicization. Davies, for example, exploited the common law and the absence of parliament to undermine the position of the Old English community, while eroding the foundations of Gaelic society, using the courts to attack tanistry and gavelkind. Irish lawyers were excluded by law from practising on the grounds of their Catholicism, although the shortage of lawyers made it impossible not to employ them. In 1628, the crown finally agreed that Irish Catholics could practise law, on condition they took the oath of allegiance and spent five years at the inns of court in London. Consequently, by the 1630s many in government thought that assimilation was working. Meanwhile, the Scots were encouraged to collude with the English in Ireland, acquiring seats in the Irish parliament, offices in the Dublin administration, positions in the church of Ireland, being granted monopolies, and joining enthusiastically in the plantation of Ulster. Whatever the intentions of English administrators, in Ireland it was a British programme that unfolded, and it was in Ulster that British terminology was most widely employed.

James VI and I did nothing to disturb England's relationship with Wales, and the creation of his eldest son, Henry, as prince of Wales in 1610 was a popular means by which the Welsh were drawn to the Stuart dynasty. James was inclined to see the 1534 union of England and Wales as a reasonable basis for an Anglo-Scottish settlement, one that would incorporate Scotland into a greater England, and it was this 'perfect union' the English found most palatable. Naturally, the Scots saw neither the Irish or the Welsh models as acceptable, favouring something between a loose personal union and a federal arrangement that was difficult to fit into English constitutional ideas. The result of these incompatible views was mutual suspicion, hence the king's attempt to achieve a union of parliaments in 1604 foundered. Thereafter, movement towards institutional union was meagre. The English and Irish parliaments repealed laws hostile to Scots, there was experimentation with free trade until crown fiscal needs resulted in the reimposition of tariffs in 1610, the personnel on the two privy councils overlapped slightly, the church of Scotland was shunted towards a reflection in outward form of the church of England, and there was a single royal court, the most significant institutional link between the political elites of the king's diverse domains.

That court setting was the best hope for James's vision of a British people, an environment in which his union of 'hearts and minds' might be nourished. Certainly under both James and Charles I the court was international. The Scots held a disproportionate number of important court offices, especially before 1617, and most significantly in the bedchamber, but thereafter the rise to prominence of George Villiers, duke of Buckingham, shifted the balance of power away from them. Yet, even in the 1630s, key offices in the household, like the master of the horse and the captaincy of the guard, went to Scots. Early in James's reign, this imbalance was a cause for understandable English resentment, although it was never expressed in the kind of aggressive discontent that might have forced the king to choose between old friends and new allies. In a wider sense, as a point of contact, the court performed an integrative function, drawing nobles from all three kingdoms to a setting in which they competed for royal favour, while also socializing and intermarrying. A British aristocracy did not yet emerge from the different nobilities, but those Scottish nobles with English titles, wives, offices, and incomes, like the third marquis of Hamilton, were having to juggle more than one identity. Similarly, Randal MacDonnel, earl of Antrim, was in the 1630s an Irish Gaelic warlord and a British courtier, linked by marriage to the Villiers family. Here too, however, the level of integration did not overcome the primary loyalty to national identities.

Below this level of a noble elite, a British consciousness never permeated, except perhaps among a few clerics determined to use Britain as a vehicle for driving forward their ecclesiastical agenda. Scots born after James's 1603 accession were judged by the English courts in the important Calvin's Case of 1608 to have the same legal rights as English-born subjects. However, this decision intimated more about the king's prerogative powers than about national identity that was shaped by deeper geographic, political, religious, and cultural factors than could be legislated in any court of law. A sense of English national consciousness was widely shared, even if in a domestic context it often appeared to be overridden by an acute sense of localism. Scottish national identity was no less secure, although in this case the powerfully competing lowland and highland versions of it generated a tension that could be both creative and destructive. In the Orkney and Shetland Isles a Scandinavian identity even survived, in spite of ever more aggressive policies adopted by the Scottish crown. Irish identity was more problematic, being compromised by layers of settlement and conquest, creating in the process layered communities of Gaels, Old English, New English, and Scots, each suspicious of one another. Nevertheless, all these forms of national and regional identity were more durable and widely understood than the contrived British identity being promoted by the crown.

Where the Stuart crown did evolve domestic policies that were a product of its British ambitions, rather than its English, Irish, or Scottish nature, was at the peripheries. The unification of political authority in 1603 resulted in two clear territorial shifts in power. On the one hand, the Anglo-Scottish border ceased to be a semi-military zone, becoming instead the 'middle shires' James VI had predicted, terrorized into an acceptable degree of law and order by coordinated policing on either side of the former frontier. Secondly, the Gaelic world of the Scottish highlands and Ireland found that it could no longer exploit the division between the two English-speaking kingdoms. Peace in Ireland in 1603, the abortive colonization of Lewis in 1605, the flight of the Irish earls in 1607, the 1609 statutes of Iona binding the west highland chiefs to Edinburgh's version of civil society, and the beginning of the plantation of Ulster in 1610, all flowed from the fact that London and Edinburgh were able to develop a British solution to the Gaelic problem.

Foreign policy

Most obviously, foreign policy was decided by the king and imposed on all his kingdoms, there being no sense in having competing policies for each constituent domain. Both the Tudor and Stuart monarchies of the sixteenth century made imperial claims, and in the 1540s the former had sought to embrace Scotland under its imperium. James VI and I attempted to harness those energies to something much more ambitious, to his vision of Great Britain as one of the mighty empires of Christendom that would provide the Protestants of Europe with a counterpoint to the Holy Roman Emperor, leading in time to a reconciliation of these two confessional communities. It was typical of James's supreme self-confidence, and even before Elizabeth's death, he was positioning himself to take on this role, courting Scandinavian and German good will. That theme of empire was encouraged by the fact that James ruled over three kingdoms, and by Britain's geographic isolation, an isolation that was sea-bound, hence the extension of the claim to imperial sovereignty over the surrounding waters. The empire's 'civilizing' responsibility was extended out from the western highlands of Scotland to Ireland by deploying its core Protestant population as colonists. Imperial rule also took root in North America where Jamestown was founded in 1607, with other colonies following on: Newfoundland in 1610, Bermuda in 1612, Nova Scotia in 1620, Barbados in 1627, and the Leeward Islands a year later. A series of aggressive and speculative English trading companies were established in these years, including the East India Company which set up a trading base at Surat in 1607.

Yet at the heart of Jacobean foreign policy was Europe, and the king's determination to establish peace as a prelude to the creation of some form of reunified Christendom, hence the ending of the Anglo-Spanish War as early as 23 June 1603. James was no coward, having campaigned in the field against his own rebels, but he disliked war intensely, and was unenthusiastic about martial activities other than riding. Instead, he believed that disputes between states could best be solved by rational discussion among rulers and their diplomatic representatives. The king had no interest in pursuing an aggressive and costly foreign policy, and was reluctant to militarily defend Protestant interests where they were under threat. Instead, there was a series of treaties with Spain, France, and the United Provinces between 1604 and 1608, and an almost desperate effort put into negotiating a Spanish marriage for Prince Charles. Essentially, James imposed a Scottish foreign policy on England that proved to be of enormous benefit to all Britain. As king of Scots, James had no real continental enemies and, in spite of the tensions created by religious differences, the Scots were largely friendly towards France and Spain. Fortunately, there were many in England who also realized that there was no point in further prolonging the war with Spain. Instead, James hoped to create a diplomatic balance of power in Europe, hence the Spanish marriage negotiations that dragged on unsuccessfully from 1614 to 1618.

The outbreak of war in central Europe in 1618 signalled the beginning of the end of James's hopes for peace. At the risk of arousing deep-seated anger in England, where there was suspicion that the king was leaning towards a Catholic policy (especially in the light of growing Arminian influence at court), and where there was a revival of nostalgic Elizabethan triumphalism, James resisted providing military aid to his exiled son-in-law, Frederick, whose Palatinate territories were over-run by Imperial troops in 1620. The Spanish marriage proposal was hopefully revived in 1622–3, but Spain's demands again proved too high. Only after he ran out of diplomatic options did James agree to take sides. Yet even at this stage he refused to adopt the militant 'blue water' strategy advocated by Prince Charles, Buckingham, and their uneasy allies in the English parliament.

Charles I initially pursued a much more populist, aggressive foreign policy, attacking Spain in 1625, and then stumbling into war with France in the following year in spite of his recent marriage to Henrietta-Maria. Even before fighting began, the huge cost of military aid to the Dutch and in Germany created domestic tensions as the English parliament proved unwilling to adequately fund a war. Political crisis was soon looming as British military power proved embarrassingly ineffectual, especially as it was placed in the incompetent hands of Buckingham, whose expeditions to Cadiz in 1625 and La Rochelle in 1627 served only to expose the hollow pretensions of the Stuart monarchy and the English parliament that had egged it on. The disastrous series of military bunglings, and the demands for men and money, heightened factional conflict at court and in an English parliament that demanded war while refusing to provide the means to fight one. Resentment increasingly focused on Buckingham until his timely assassination in August 1628. War also added to popular discontent in Scotland where, in spite of the supply of greater taxes than ever before, there was no appetite for fighting the old ally, France. When peace was made with France in April 1629, and Spain seven months later, it represented a recognition that, until the issue of finance was tackled, Britain lacked the military power to intervene in the Thirty Years' War. That option had been reluctantly conceded by the king in order that he might dispense with his troublesome English parliament which was closing in on other royal prerogatives as the price of supply. Throughout the 1630s, therefore, Charles I sat on the sidelines, a peripheral figure in European affairs, unable to halt the advance of Catholicism, or to stem the rise in French power.

The court

The Stuart court of the early seventeenth century stood at the very centre of the political life of the three kingdoms. For James VI the step from his small, intimate, and often hard-up Scottish court to the magnificent grandeur of the new British court was, perhaps, the single biggest change in his fortune. There were more people employed in running the king's household in London than there were directly employed by the crown in administering the kingdom of Scotland. However, James did not simply slide into the Tudor court like a new tenant, he altered what had been a rigid structure formed around an old woman to a more fluid system around a dynamic man in his prime. The court became more open at its outer edges, while simultaneously maintaining at its centre a tightly managed and Scots-dominated bedchamber. Here, James retreated with his old friends and servants, men like Sir George Hume, earl of Dunbar, and Sir Thomas Erskine, earl of Kellie. Outside the bedchamber lay the privy chamber, still heavily dominated by Scots for much of the reign, and beyond that the rest of the household and court. While the personnel changed under Charles I, significantly reducing the Scottish contingent, and the political role of the bedchamber was less marked after Buckingham gained entry, the essential structure did not alter. Here was the locus of political fortune for the aspiring and ambitious elites of the multi-kingdom monarchy ruled over by James VI and I and his son. Even the greatest of magnates, or the highest ranking officers of state, sought an entry to the court and to its inner sanctums, pressing their suits on the king's most trusted servants. No English secretary of state, no Scottish lord chancellor, no Irish lord deputy was appointed to the bedchamber of either king, but none could afford to neglect the men who provided him with private counsel and intimate service.

If the structure of the court altered little under these two Stuart monarchs, the tone was sharply divergent. James's court acquired an exaggerated reputation for being raffish and licentious, a place of drunken feasting, violent quarrelling, voracious greed, and seedy sexual encounters, encouraged by the king's own homosexual leanings. It was epitomized in the fall in 1615 of Somerset, accused with his wife of murdering Sir Thomas Overbury who had opposed the countess's earlier divorce from the second earl of Essex. Here, it seemed, everyone could be bought, and the king indulged a feverish atmosphere of intense competition for money, titles, and offices. The meteoric rise of George Villiers from relative obscurity in 1615 to a dukedom eight years later on the strength of his physical attractiveness and of the king's emotional dependence on him, indicated just what was possible. Buckingham also further devalued the currency in royal patronage, selling honours and engaging in more blatant corruption, thus placing greater strains on the unspoken web of social obligation that bound court life together. By contrast, Charles I's court was tasteful, restrained, ordered, the feeding frenzy of the Buckingham years was toned down after his death, and the central message of the elaborate and expensive masques of the 1630s was the sacred marriage of the king and queen reigning peacefully over a pastoral country. The king had constructed his own imagined world, dangerously out of touch with reality. Meanwhile, public perceptions, especially in English puritan and Scottish presbyterian circles, continued to see the court in their imaginations as a symbol of political corruption and religious decay.

The lure of the court was access to patronage. Even those who appeared to be critics of it were often positioning themselves to acquire a foothold there. Hence the apparently inexplicable transformation of Wentworth into a peer and president of the council of the north in 1628. Offices, pensions, and all form of rewards were dispensed by the king, and to be considered at all one had either to be physically present at court, or to have a patron there who would speak on your behalf. Some of the most lucrative offices were based in the court itself, offices like keeper of the privy purse, or groom of the stole, and even lesser household officers, like the gentlemen of the privy chamber, were able to exploit their proximity to the king to enrich themselves with pensions, old debts, wards and marriages, or monopolies. All sorts of patronage was fought over in the great arena of the court, from Scottish offices of state, to English peerages, to Irish land grants. In 1630, the future position of the depute treasurer of Scotland was not settled in Edinburgh, but in London after the two sides in the dispute arrived there to engage in private lobbying and mutual vilification. No one could expect to stay in office long once his credibility at court was on the wane, and the repercussions from the fall, or death, of a great patron, like the earl of Salisbury in May 1612, could be momentous for his many clients.

Under James VI and I management of patronage was chaotic, with the same office or grant often being made to more than one individual. The king's unwillingness to disappoint, his tendency to make promises he could not keep, his scant regard for cost, all heightened expectation, creating an unstable level of competitiveness. This was not entirely unhelpful to the king, but it placed a strain on the system, and on James himself who had to bear the constant pressure from supplicants pressing their suits, even in the privacy of the bedchamber where royal servants took on the role of interested patrons. It was only with the rise of Buckingham to a position in which he monopolized the flow of patronage that the king was able to free himself from this daily grind. Corruption was rife, and was expected, although political careers could still be cut short if such practices were exposed. Hence the fall from power of the English lord treasurer Suffolk in 1618, or in 1621 of Sir Gideon Murray of Elibank, the Scottish treasurer depute. Even more dramatically, the sordid story of sexual betrayal and murder that brought down Somerset demonstrated that even a royal favourite was not immune to changes in fortune. Buckingham introduced a new level of venality to court life, but after his death in 1628 Charles I tried to impose greater control over patronage. He instigated a degree of economizing, and the rapid accumulation of office and wealth that had been a feature of his father's reign dried up. Nevertheless, the interdependence of riches and court influence remained, allowing men like the third marquis of Hamilton to acquire political leverage greater than most crown officers of state, and the opportunity to make a fortune. The struggle for resources and for the king's ear gave rise to factions, self-interested alliances of nobles, officers, and royal servants, brought together to achieve particular ends. While James did permit political debate at his court, the divisions there often lacked any real ideological cement. He had presided over a factious court in Scotland before union, and he employed the same tactics of dividing in the hope of ruling in England. He also allowed one faction to achieve its ends if it appeared to serve his own purposes, as was the case in 1603 when Sir Walter Raleigh was destroyed. Kinship connections were important, for example the English Howards and the Scottish Erskines formed tight-knit clienteles, and geographic factors might also be significant, with national and local rivalries being played out at court. In the 1600s, the Scots never formed a coherent political lobby, and a powerful individual like Dunbar had many enemies among his own countrymen. Wentworth's Yorkshire enemies dogged him at court throughout the 1630s, and the Irish-based entrepreneur Richard Boyle, earl of Cork, was able to mobilize the lord deputy's New English enemies in the final attack on Wentworth in 1640–1.

It would be mistaken to imagine that these power struggles were only over patronage. Policy also shaped alliances, sharpening the contest, and creating a bridge between court, parliaments, and localities. The Howards' advocacy of a pro-Spanish foreign policy, Buckingham's championing of Arminian ideas, or the attitude of rival Scottish courtiers to the 1625 revocation, all had an impact inside the court and elsewhere. Mostly, the key to political success lay in winning the game at court, no policy being imposed on kings by those without a powerful position there until the Scots rebelled in 1637.

Only if the court is envisaged in the narrow sense of the royal household can the privy councils of the three kingdoms be seen as distinct from it. More often than not, conciliar office was acquired through court patronage, and different councillors belonged to rival court factions. The fall of Robert Ker, earl of Somerset, in 1615 had repercussions for the composition of the councils of England, Ireland, and Scotland. Nevertheless, the different councils that administered Britain did represent alternative power centres to the bedchamber, or to the parliaments when they met. By 1603, James VI's Scottish privy council was a mature and settled body that contained many petty jealousies, but was no longer riven by the political divisions of the early 1590s. Until the end of his reign, the king made few dramatic changes, placing great trust and confidence in men like Chancellor Dunfermline, Treasurer Mar, and Archbishop Spottiswoode to get on with his business. The council's deft touch, and its willingness to tell the king when he was wrong, ensured that absentee government did not mean that Scotland was neglected, and government in the years 1603 to 1625 was unquestionably the most successful since the early sixteenth century. In some respects James behaved in the same manner in England, continuing Elizabeth I's councillors in office, although he soon doubled the number to create a large body more like his Scottish council, and leaving Sir Robert Cecil with a handful of other experienced men to get on with managing his affairs. He never allowed himself to be wholly the prisoner of any faction so that, even when the Howards were in the ascendancy following Cecil's death, their enemies continued to serve as councillors alongside them. In comparison, the Irish privy council was less independent and less conciliar, being more the creature of the lord deputy. Hence the enormous impact that Wentworth was able to make in a relatively short time in Ireland, something that would have been impossible in Scotland where even the highest ranking officers of state could never hope to dominate their colleagues.

With the rise of Buckingham, the Scottish privy council did begin to experience some meddling in its affairs, but here Buckingham allied himself with powerful Scots at court, rather than imposing his clients on the council as he did in Ireland. The real shock to the political equilibrium established by James in Scotland only came after his death when Charles I set about remodelling the relationship between the privy council and the court of session, undermining his father's experienced but admittedly elderly councillors, and refusing to take advice, insisting instead in converting it into a body to carry out his bidding. By the mid-1630s it was filled with men entirely dependent on the king: crown-appointed bishops, career officials, or courtier nobles with huge debts like the sixth earl of Morton. In England, James VI and I's tolerance of faction as a means of managing his privy council ensured that it was drawn into court and parliamentary disputes. This continued after Buckingham's rise, and in the early 1620s attacks on him in parliament were encouraged by other councillors like the earls of Southampton and Oxford. After the experience of the 1626 parliament the king began to remove the duke's rivals, replacing them with his allies and clients. This created a more efficient body of councillors, but one less able to provide a range of advice, and by 1632 there was almost no dissent from Charles's views, including on the vexed question of pursuing a pro-Spanish foreign policy.

Parliaments

Stuart kings had to deal with three parliaments, each different in composition and procedure, each requiring distinct management. The arrival on the scene of a new legislature at Jamestown, Virginia, in 1619 was an intimation of the enthusiasm among the subjects of the Stuart monarchy for such deliberative bodies. However, it is easy to overestimate the significance of parliaments in the political history of the period. The Irish parliament was a pale shadow of its English counterpart, its form barely concealing the fact that as a consequence of Poyning's Law it was heavily influenced by the privy council in London. When in 1626–8 the crown entered into negotiations with its Irish subjects for increased revenue in return for concessions on religion, the Irish parliament was not summoned. Instead Lord Deputy Falkland negotiated with an assembly of nobles and gentry at Dublin, an indication that the Irish parliament was seen as only one of a number of possible means of consulting the political elite. Outwardly the Scottish parliament was more distinct from the other two, each of which had separate houses of lords and commons, having instead one chamber made up of three, or four, estates of bishops, peers, shire commissioners and burgh commissioners, as well as the officers of state. The entire thrust of the Scottish parliament was to get business done quickly so that sessions were short, debates were minimal, and there was only one reading of proposed legislation before the full meeting of parliament. The hard work of taking forward articles (bills) to parliament and working out the detail of legislation was carried out in a delegated committee of the lords of the articles. This was in sharp contrast to the English house of commons that was prone to unnecessarily prolonged debate, factionalism, and irrelevance. Nor did the Scottish parliament have a monopoly in creating law in Scotland where conventions of the estates could enact temporary legislation. The English parliament was the most complex body, its highly evolved procedures creating a more institutional self-consciousness, its ninety county seats especially were highly prized in the status-conscious world of the landed elite, and, of course, it represented the most powerful of the king's three kingdoms. For that reason alone, it mattered more, and its deliberations over union in 1604, the great contract in 1610, relations with Spain in 1624, or grievances in 1628, all created problems for kings far greater than anything achieved by the Irish or Scottish parliaments.

While the prestige of all three parliaments was very considerable when in session, none of these assemblies sat continuously, and most of the time parliaments played a peripheral role in the political lives of the three kingdoms, especially in Ireland. In England, a parliament sat in each year from 1604–7, 1610–11, 1614, 1621–2, 1624–6, and 1628–9; in Scotland a parliament sat in 1604, 1606, 1610, 1612, 1621, and 1633, although conventions of the estates also sat in 1617, 1625, and 1630; in Ireland a parliament sat only in 1613–15 and 1634. In the thirty-five years from 1603 to 1637, there was no parliament in England on twenty of them, in Scotland there was no parliament or convention on twenty-six of these years, and in Ireland, parliament only met on four years. In fourteen of these years there was no legislative assembly sitting anywhere in the king's domains, the longest period being from 1635 to the post-revolutionary Scottish parliament of 1639. Like most early modern rulers, therefore, the Stuarts increasingly preferred to avoid the summoning of representative bodies, their chief purposes for doing so being to negotiate taxation, or to pass legislation favourable to the crown, like the creation of a royal supremacy in the Scottish church in 1610. All three parliaments also had a judicial role, but this was rarely used by the crown, and it might even be turned against it in England after 1621 when the English Lord Chancellor Bacon was impeached, the first such action for 161 years. However, it is worth remembering that most of the legislation passed by any of these parliaments was initiated by private members.

Political ideology, especially in England, was divided on the extent to which the king stood above the three estates, or had his authority legitimized by the concept of king-in-parliament. In Scotland, the argument about political sovereignty focused less on parliament, although in practice its crucial role in legitimizing authority was recognized on all sides. For kings it was important to win those arguments, and James VI and I entered personally into the fray, describing the Scottish parliament as nothing more than the king's 'head court' and the English parliament as the king's 'Great council'. Aside from this rhetoric, the real battle was one of parliamentary management. The crown's control of its parliaments differed greatly, although in all three kingdoms the king's prerogative powers included the right to summon, prorogue, and dismiss parliament. Without question, the Irish parliament was the easiest to pack with members sympathetic to royal policies. Already by 1613 the 100 Irish Catholic members in the commons found themselves outnumbered by 132 Protestant New English members. The Irish parliament also met under the watchful gaze of the lord deputy, a role Wentworth fulfilled so ably in 1634 when it granted six subsidies of £50,000. Besides, even if legislation had been enacted against the wishes of the king, it required the approval of the English privy council. In Scotland, the presence of officers of state and bishops provided the king with a core of dependent votes in the unicameral chamber. Royal patronage usually delivered significant support among the peers, who could be topped up with new creations, and the crown interfered in the selection of shire and burgh members. The most significant instrument of management available to the crown in Scotland was the lords of the articles that was increasingly stuffed by royal nominees. This relatively large and not unrepresentative body ensured that little business was discussed in open parliament that did not have its approval, and in some respects the role of the full assembly was reduced to approving decisions already taken in the committee of the articles.

In England, where James made considerable efforts to understand how parliament operated, the king had a much more difficult job. Here royal ministers, who were usually concentrated in the lords, had to work hard at getting business through the two houses that had acquired considerable powers of scrutiny. In 1604, for example, the house of commons succeeded in forcing the king to partially back down in his efforts to have disputed elections settled in the courts, a move that would have made parliament subject to a lesser authority. Elections too were less easily manipulated, and the electoral process was open to a much larger constituency in the shires than was the case in Ireland or in Scotland where there was a negligible interest in contesting parliamentary seats. Perhaps as many as one in three of the adult male population of England could participate in elections, and while at least a quarter of the seats in the commons were in the gift of peers sitting in the lords, and up to two-thirds of the membership of that house was drawn from the landed nobility, popular issues like anti-popery did figure in electioneering. There is significant evidence that in England ordinary people, especially in London, debated national political affairs. It was the crown's inability to adequately manage English elections in the 1620s that contributed to Charles I's decision in 1629 to dispense with parliament for what would become the eleven-year 'personal rule'.

There was no concept of loyal opposition to the crown in the early seventeenth century. Kings were offered different advice from interested parties, but the focus of discontent was the king's ministers, never the monarch who would have to decide when to ditch unpopular servants. It was Charles I's determination to stand by Buckingham that made his relations with his English parliament so tense for much of the 1620s. However, while the English parliaments of that decade might have been particularly awkward, all three parliaments provided forums within which royal policies were opposed. Prior to 1603, James VI regularly suffered setbacks in his Scottish parliaments, or conventions, most commonly over taxation. After the regal union, the king's enhanced status and patronage, and the growing influence of the lords of the articles, saw royal control tightened. Scottish ministers were also better placed than their English counterparts in that they sat in the unicameral chamber, and there were few of the damaging feuds among councillors that occurred in the English parliament. However, the cooperation of the Scottish parliament could never be taken for granted, and in 1621 James's ministers were severely tested by opposition to his financial and religious policies. In 1633, even the presence of a bad-tempered Charles I, personally noting the names of dissenters, did not prevent nervous expressions of discontent at his fiscal and religious proposals. In Scotland, it was usual for the king to get his way in the end, but the price was a store of resentment that would find expression in those parliaments of 1639–41 that dismantled royal authority.

The infrequency of Irish parliaments indicates the crown's surprising nervousness over its ability to control them, and certainly on the two occasions a parliament was summoned the lord deputy was embarrassed. When in 1613 it met for the first time in twenty-eight years, the Catholic members staged a walk-out in protest against the crown's manipulation of the speakership. Following the prorogation of the parliament, a petition of grievances was taken to London that contributed to the removal of Lord Deputy Chichester two years later. In 1634 Sir Piers Crosby, an Irish privy councillor, led a successful attack on a relatively innocuous crown bill, irritating the lord deputy and earning him seven years of harassment and victimization that continued until Wentworth's fall from power.

It was the English parliament that proved most difficult for Stuart monarchs, and James VI and I, who was prone to becoming involved in damaging political debates, lectured English members on the merits of the Scottish estates where he claimed he was more able to get his way. The first parliament of the reign, in 1604, was poisoned from its outset by the virulent opposition to the king's plans for parliamentary union, and until its dissolution in 1611 was dogged by tension over long-accumulated grievances like wardship and purveyance. The Addled Parliament of April–June 1614 returned to the theme of impositions with court factions using the opportunity to attack their rivals, clogging up business and preventing anything being done. Similar factionalism characterized the parliaments of the 1620s, with royal ministers being attacked by their own colleagues—Bacon in 1621, Cranfield in 1624, Buckingham in 1625–6—the functioning of government undermined by the withholding of adequate supply, and the staging of sterile arguments over legal points ostensibly about the royal prerogative. More often than not, these were tactical devices aimed at disabling rivals, and in 1624 even Prince Charles manipulated parliament to destroy Cranfield who was opposing his war plans in council. Yet within the English parliament there were growing, if exaggerated, fears that it was the last bastion of representative government in a Europe where authoritarian kings were enhancing their own authority. There were also real issues of substance that divided members, for example John Pym's attack on Arminian influences at court in 1625 reflected an ideological struggle similar to that already evident in the Scottish parliament four years earlier. When in 1628 Charles I conceded the petition of right (that he subsequently tried to renege on) in return for supply and an end to the attacks on Buckingham, it was clear that parliament was applying itself to reducing the royal prerogative. Following the dramatic climax during the 1629 session when members held Speaker Finch down in his chair while the commons passed three resolutions against innovations in taxes and religion, Charles I decided to do without further counsel from this awkward and meddling assembly for the foreseeable future.

Finance

All European rulers of the sixteenth and seventeenth centuries experienced profound financial problems as the means of funding government failed to keep pace with the growth in its functions and the rising cost of its activities, especially war. As king of Scotland, James VI was poorer than most contemporary monarchs, but Elizabeth I's penny-pinching sprang from the same deep-rooted difficulties of trying to lubricate the machinery of government from the depleted resources of the crown's ordinary income. While James VI and I was much richer than he had been before 1603, he inherited along with Elizabeth's heavy debts a knowledge that the English crown could barely meet its ordinary expenditure far less the costs of war. Furthermore, in order to raise extraordinary income his officials had to wrestle with a politically costly tax system that was undermined by massive tax evasion. Unfortunately, James did not fully appreciate the limitations of his new kingdom's fiscal structure, and even if he had grasped the weakness of the English crown's position, he could not afford to be parsimonious. As a married man with a family, his household was much more expensive than that of Elizabeth I, and James had a keen awareness of the need to be generous to his new English subjects as well as rewarding his old Scottish friends. Therefore, while the prodigality of his court might not have been financially prudent, it was politically necessary. Within a few years the crown's English debts had risen to £597,337 as the king's generosity ran out of control, spending in 1609 exceeded half a million pounds, and the alienation of crown lands was so extensive that James had to be persuaded to agree to make no further grants.

Meanwhile in Scotland, the years immediately after 1603 saw much of the king's debt cleared, and royal income was largely converted into pensions. Absentee government was cheap government, and when the king's progress to Scotland in 1617 cost £200,000 Scots (£16,666 sterling) the advantages of his being elsewhere were brought home to a privy council worried that the fiscal position of the crown was becoming more precarious again. However, just as the financial reforms introduced by the Octavians, eight men appointed in 1595 to put the king's finances in order, had been wrecked by courtiers, the same self-preservation undermined repeated efforts from 1617 by Treasurer Mar and his successors to cut expenditure. Attempts to reduce spending elsewhere invariably met with the same stiff opposition from courtiers faced with cuts in their pensions and gifts. Until 1618 the Howards successfully blocked any investigation in England, and Cranfield's subsequent review of expenditure there and in Ireland ended in his impeachment six years later. In all three kingdoms, therefore, the problem of an inadequate income could not be addressed by reductions in expenditure, and the crown was forced into putting more and more pressure on those who might generate additional income.

Without regular taxation, the crown's political manœuvrability was extremely limited, hence the many successful efforts to maximize those income streams that were available to the king. Under James VI and I the use of impositions, the selling of monopolies and titles, searching out old debts, and the revival of feudal rights were all exploited. Nevertheless, by 1617, even before the full effect of Buckingham's impact on royal finances had been felt, and at a time when England was still at peace, the debt stood at £726,000, approaching a doubling of the Tudor legacy. Faced with the even greater costs of funding a war, Charles I extended the range of operations, for example, the commission for defective titles was established in 1628. Similar tactics were employed in Ireland where the customs were farmed in 1613 for £6,000, and in the 1630s when Wentworth's policy of 'thorough' substantially increased royal revenues. While the Scottish revenue was relatively insignificant in terms of overall income, there too officials were increasingly obliged to squeeze feudal casualties, and to engage in dubious and unpopular financial practices, like the selling of monopolies and the coining of base money in 1633.

The dilemma facing the crown was that the alternative means of raising money, taxation, carried high political risks. In Ireland and Scotland this was less significant than in England where parliament was better placed to force concessions. When in 1628 Irish Catholics agreed to provide the king with £120,000 in return for the 'graces', relaxing the enforcement of the oath of supremacy, guaranteeing landed security, and not enforcing recusancy fines, the agreement was simply ignored by the crown after the money had been paid. Nevertheless, making Ireland a net contributor to the British monarchy was not easy, and it was only at the end of the 1630s that Wentworth was able to provide the king with a surplus. However, his methods of extracting that money infuriated the New English whom he squeezed hardest. Already in the 1590s, the Scots had become used to paying more, if irregular, taxes, although there was considerable resistance in the conventions of 1599–1600 when supply was denied. The union bonanza made Scottish taxes superfluous until 1606 when reality set in among royal officials. Thereafter, taxes were granted by succeeding parliaments and conventions, providing an annual supplement to royal income in the region of £100,000 Scots (£8,333 sterling), a low if adequate sum until economic and political conditions deteriorated from around 1617–18. The 1621 parliament averted a crisis in royal finances when, in addition to a generous land tax, it introduced a raft of new taxes on consumers of basic goods like coal and salt, while income on interest was also taxed. Yet Charles I still inherited heavy debts of around £159,000 Scots (£13,250) against an ordinary income of £223,930 Scots (£18,660), and this was before the impact of war, so that almost all the tax collected from the 1625 grant went to servicing the debt. Even after the restoration of peace, the crown's commitments to creditors like William Dick of Braid and its pensions bill exceeded the ordinary income, making it dependent on taxes and further loans to stave off bankruptcy. At the same time, the crown's involvement in unpopular economic policies, currency manipulation, tariff reform, and a common fishery policy that was designed by the court to exploit Scottish resources all aroused hostility.

But it was English taxes that mattered most. Here the stumbling block was parliament's determination to use the leverage it had over the granting of supply to make the king give up the more unpopular ordinary sources of income like impositions and feudal dues. In 1606 Bate's Case extended the royal prerogative over duties, allowing the king to levy these without parliament's consent, and two years later a new book of rates raised impositions over a greater than ever range of imports. Nevertheless, the shortfall in income remained substantial. Salisbury's far-reaching efforts in the great contract of 1610 to negotiate a deal exchanging regular taxes of £200,000 per annum and the clearing of crown debts for the surrender of feudal rights foundered as the king grew increasingly suspicious that he would lose out on the deal. This absence of regular taxes was an irritant in peacetime, forcing the king into more borrowing and fiscal devices like the forced loan of 1611, or the sale of honours. More importantly, it left the crown woefully short of what was required to conduct a war, as Charles I discovered in the mid-1620s. It was estimated in 1621 that effective intervention in Germany would cost half a million pounds: the English parliament voted to provide £140,000 towards a campaign (that in Scotland granted £33,000 over the next four years), although the parliaments of 1624, 1625, and 1628 did grant further supply. However, the conditional nature of the grants—the 1625 parliament granted two subsidies of tonnage and poundage for one year—only heightened the discomfort of the crown. Charles I was driven down the road of introducing a highly controversial forced loan, bringing in £240,000 in 1627 and proving a more effective means of raising revenue than taxation. However, the political cost was high, and it was challenged at law in the Five Knights Case of that year, establishing the principle that the king could imprison without trial those refusing to pay. All this merely heightened distrust and indignation, the crown's revenue-raising tactics being condemned by parliament in 1628, adding to the rupture with the house of commons in 1629. Meanwhile, crown debts during the war grew to a staggering two million pounds. While Charles I was able to demand and get more taxes from his reluctant Scottish and Irish parliaments in 1633 and 1634, he had instead to resort to ship money in England, a highly effective local tax that netted £800,000 between 1634 and 1638. First introduced to coastal counties, collection was soon extended to inland counties, offering yet more ammunition to those arguing that the crown's financial exactions were illegal. However, there was little opposition to it before 1639 when England found itself sucked into the king's Scottish problems. The avoidance of war, a tightening up of expenditure, and the efficiency of alternative revenue-raising schemes like impositions (worth £250,000 per annum by 1640), the revival of forest laws, and knighthood fines, meant that taxation had become less important to the crown. Hence there was less and less need to summon the English parliament.

Local government

The contact between the king, his court, the parliaments, and the multitude of localities that made up his three kingdoms was both personal and institutional. As a Scottish king, James VI based himself between Edinburgh, Linlithgow, and Falkland, but he made regular forays further afield, to put down rebellion in the north-east, to conduct judicial raids on the borders, or to visit his nobles in the west. After 1603, he visited Scotland only once, in 1617, failing miserably to keep his promise to return every three years. Charles I was just as reluctant to revisit his homeland, making a belated and short journey to Scotland in 1633 to attend his coronation and preside over parliament. Both royal visits proved to be disappointing to the Scots, demonstrating the extent to which communication between them and their kings was being strained by distance. Arguably, Charles I's 1633 Scottish progress was not merely counterproductive, but was crucially important in solidifying opposition to his policies. Ireland was ignored altogether, the Stuart dynasty having no more desire to go there than had their Tudor predecessors. Wales too was not considered worthy of a royal presence. Yet if James VI and I and Charles I were reluctant to step outside of England, they were also unwilling to be seen by many of their English subjects. The only occasion northern Englishmen saw their kings was *en route* to and from Scotland. Even in those counties around London where the royal family hunted and visited a handful of courtiers, neither king was keen to court popularity with the kind of prodigious progresses favoured by Elizabeth I. For the overwhelming majority of their subjects, even among the political ranks, these kings were distant figures who lived far away at court, and that view was much the same in Perthshire, Galway, Glamorgan, or Yorkshire.

In the absence of the king himself, he was represented in the localities by royal officers. These men were largely drawn from the ranks of the hereditary, landed nobility, a body that is best understood as encompassing the titular peerage and the untitled English or Anglo-Irish gentry, Scottish baronage, and the chiefs of Gaelic society. It was not impossible for men whose origins were lower down in the social order to acquire local office, but it was unusual, and by the time they reached office they would already have possessed the wealth and social connections that bound them to the nobility and its values. The earl of Cork might have been born as the son of a mere Canterbury gentleman, but his business acumen allowed him to carve out a huge interest in Ireland where his wealth and authority eased him into noble society long before he acquired his first title in 1616. Only in towns were magistrates likely to be commoners, although here too the nobility intruded wherever possible. Of course, there was an enormous range of status and power within the nobility from great territorial magnates like the earls of Argyll, Ormond, Pembroke and Northumberland, to minor parish gentry and lairds. Nevertheless, local society throughout Britain and Ireland was governed by noble families linked to one another by bonds of kinship and clientage, and sharing a common set of core values about lineage, honour, and the attributes of a gentleman. Even in more remote localities, like north Wales, or the western highlands of Scotland, the gentry and clan chiefs were being drawn into the wider world of national politics and culture. There was no class conflict within this governing elite, but there was intense and bitter rivalry between families over control of local patronage, whether it be the parliamentary seats of English counties, the distribution of plantation estates in Ireland, or the privileges of regality courts in Scotland. If the contest for that patronage was the stuff of local politics, influence over its distribution was what gave the crown leverage in the localities. Meanwhile, the court brokers who acted as the conduits between the king and the localities provided the vital connection between factional conflict at court and in those localities. In Ireland, the rise of Buckingham was reflected in the appointment in 1615 of his client, the obscure Sir Oliver St John, as lord deputy, replacing the Howard-backed Sir Arthur Chichester. Soon Villiers connections extended throughout the kingdom, fuelling the colonization scheme in Connacht from 1624.

If the thousands of threads that connected this great web of nobles and their families to the king was complex, the administrative structure through which royal power flowed was rudimentary and relatively simple. Superficially, all three kingdoms shared a similar system of local government with the country divided up into counties, or shires, presided over by royal officers such as lieutenants, sheriffs, justices of the peace, and, in the towns, mayors (in England and Ireland) or provosts (in Scotland). Yet this common Norman inheritance disguised significant differences. In Ireland, local government was regulated by the lord deputy in Dublin who struggled to impose a colonial administration of New English settlers, but was forced to make Irish appointments by the lack of manpower. Nevertheless, Sir John Davies, appointed attorney general of Ireland in 1606, was able to oversee a level of intervention in local Irish communities that would have been inconceivable for crown officers in England or Scotland. Even without formal colonization, the exploitation of the law and the wealth of the New English community had a huge impact on landholding, for example in Sligo where around half the land changed hands in the eight decades before 1641. Arguably the single most impressive example of government flexing its muscles in the early seventeenth century was the successful organization and implementation of the colonization of half a million acres of Ulster, a region until then of robust Gaelic dominance that was changed irrevocably.

In English local government the key figure for the crown was the lord lieutenant, an office usually granted to great peers who acted as the king's eyes and ears in the provinces. The administrative responsibilities of the annually appointed sheriffs—usually drawn from the gentry—were so burdensome that few wanted that office, particularly at the time of parliamentary elections since the sheriff could not stand for parliament, depriving him of the honour of winning one of the county seats to Westminster. It was justices of the peace who made up the core of men, also of gentry status, who dominated local judicial business. James VI and I made considerable efforts to improve the quality of these local magistrates, and from 1625 their greatly inflated numbers were culled in order to improve efficiency. That this should coincide with a time when their workload increased enormously was probably unhelpful, and Charles I also irritated local communities by demanding greater accountability, interfering in the militia, and trying to force the gentry to stay on their estates. Lacking its own paid local officials, the crown had no choice other than to work with families already dominant in the localities, and initiatives that signalled interference aroused what often appears to have been unreasonable hysteria about the threat to local liberties.

Authority in Scotland was even more centrifugally devolved. There, royal influence was minimal at a local level. Lieutenants were appointed by the crown, but only for limited periods and with specific military remits that often left their authority compromised by the rights of hereditary jurisdictions. Most sheriffs were in hereditary hands in 1603, and while the crown did have some success in pursuing a policy of purchasing, or occasionally forfeiting, sheriffdoms, twelve of the thirty sheriffdoms were still in private hands in 1637. Commissioners of the peace, modelled on the English justices of the peace, were introduced in 1609, but the office was largely innocuous, being confined to very minor policing issues. Real power in the Scottish localities lay in the deeply entrenched hereditary franchise courts of the nobility. Barony courts gave every noble judicial authority over the economic and minor law and order affairs of his own estate, while in the regality courts lords exercised quasi-royal power including the rights of 'pit and gallows'.

The second half of the sixteenth century had seen a string of rebellions throughout Britain. English rebels met with no success at all under the Tudor monarchy that dealt mercilessly with those who disputed its authority, from the unfortunate tenants on the Darcy estates in 1569 to the earl of Essex in 1601. By contrast, Irish rebels enjoyed a great deal of success, stretching the resources of the crown to its limits, and exposing the inadequacies of the Tudor state in fighting a protracted land war. Yet at the end of the day, the Irish failed in all their objectives, and it was James VI and I's great fortune to find the earl of Tyrone ready to submit at the very moment he acceded to the Irish crown in 1603. In Scotland, the crown's authority was dramatically overturned at the Reformation in 1560, and again in 1567 when Mary was forced to abdicate. Civil war, rebellions, and coups continued to punctuate Scottish politics until 1594, and a powerful mix of Knoxian and Buchananite resistance theory was developed that found a ready audience among a broad spectrum of nobles, clergy, and evangelical Protestants.

In spite of the precipitate flight in 1607 of those earls engaged in treasonable dealings with Spain, the crown continued to see Ireland as the most likely location for rebellion to break out, due largely to recent history, the extent of Roman Catholicism, and fear of Spain. However, the vigilance of English officials, combined with Irish rebel ineffectiveness, ensured that nothing of consequence occurred. Sir Cahir O'Doherty's rising at Derry in 1608 represented little danger to the government, and while fears continued to be expressed about a likely rising—Ulster in 1615, Leinster in 1629—it never materialized. There were tensions in Dublin in 1613 when the borough liberties were subverted by the crown, but on the whole the Gaelic and Old English accepted the waves of English and Scots colonists with remarkably little resistance, evidence of their political and military weakness rather than acquiescence. If colonization did create deep-rooted, visceral divisions in Irish society, there is little evidence of it before the rebellion of 1641, which is not to say that it did not exist below the surface of an enforced peace. The riots in Dublin in 1629 were provoked by the closure of Catholic churches and monasteries, a dangerous policy on which to embark, offering some indication of how far the Irish Catholic community could be provoked. Furthermore, while the rigours of Wentworth's 'thorough' policies of the 1630s maintained English rule, his personal unpopularity broadened opposition to include powerful figures within the establishment eager for an opportunity to bring him down.

Had it succeeded, the Gunpowder Plot of 1605 might have propelled the three kingdoms into crisis, but even if the king had been killed, it is unlikely that English Catholics would have been able to sustain an effective rising. English society also had little to fear from popular protests in the first half of the sixteenth century, the failed rising against enclosures in the Midlands in the spring of 1607 being the most serious outbreak of insurrection. Protests by people at this level in society were unheard of in Scotland, or in Ireland. Nevertheless, in spite of the overexcited nature of parliamentary politics in England, especially in the 1620s when the forced loan and the billeting of troops outraged local sensibilities, the country experienced only episodic expressions of discontent with Stuart government. Devon was not untypical of a local community in which the gentry succeeded in administering local government while at the same time defending their interests against external encroachments. In Cornwall, where local elites had strong bonds with the crown through the duchy of Cornwall and the stannaries, the gentry were divided on how to respond to royal policies. Religious discontent also fanned grievances, although the unease of a county like Essex with its significant Puritan community should not be considered typical.

On the surface, Scotland was very much at peace, and the minor rebellions on Orkney in 1612, Islay in 1614–15, and Caithness in 1620 were no more than irritations to the Edinburgh privy council. Yet by the later 1620s, under the surface of sullen obedience, the Scottish localities were drifting dangerously beyond the point where the crown's servants could exert influence. The revocation of 1625 was intended to bring about a redistribution of crown and former church lands that would address the real financial problems each institution faced, and to weaken the territorial dominance of the feudal superiors over their tenants. However, its dubious legality and the crass management of its introduction served only to alienate the entire landed community. The teind commission, established two years later as a form of compromise, resulted in an excessive degree of investigative activity by the crown into the legal and economic foundations of landed society, inciting wide levels of non-cooperation and further resentment against the king. The Five Articles of Perth in 1617 and the liturgical policy of the mid-1630s all met with deliberate and highly effective obstruction. Conventicling also spread after the initial furore over the Five Articles, fuelled by evangelical revivals in the 1620s, and Charles I's provocative policies. It would certainly be mistaken to suggest that the crown's power in all three kingdoms was disintegrating evenly, or inevitably, but by the 1630s erosion in Scotland was accelerating, and the connection between events in each country would prove disastrous to the king.

The crown's harsh response to criticism was also inflammatory, leaving its opponents with fewer and fewer options other than rebellion. In England, the imprisonment in the Tower of London of Sir John Elliot in 1629 until his death three years later, the incarceration and mutilation of William Prynne in 1633–4 for attacking stage plays, the whipping and pillorizing of John Lilburne in 1637 for printing without licence, all sent clear messages that the king would not tolerate criticism. In Ireland, Lord Mountnorris was court-martialled and sentenced to death in 1635 after he organized opposition to Wentworth's management of the customs system. Dissent was crushed in Scotland too, and the suspended sentence of death hanging over the second Lord Balmerino from 1634 was intended to frighten others away from indulging in protest.

Conclusion

How effectively did the Stuart monarchy rule its multi-kingdom possessions between 1603 and the outbreak of revolution in Scotland in 1637? As a dynasty it proved more successful in managing succession than its Tudor predecessor in England, both James VI and I's accession and that of his son in 1625 being smooth transitions of power. The Stuarts were also fortunate in having none of the Tudor fears about rivals, and they pursued intelligent marriage strategies for members of the dynasty. Furthermore, compared to the experiences of his own youth, the troubled events of his mother's reign, and most of her predecessors, James VI and I and his son Charles I were remarkably secure as kings of Scotland. No one disputed the Stuarts' right to rule in any of their kingdoms, and that in itself is an achievement worth noting, even if it was as much the product of good luck as skilful management. However, in endeavouring to weld the disparate Stuart inheritance into a unitary British state, James VI and I found that he could not drag his different peoples with him. Competing national identities, institutional conservatism, and narrow self-interest combined to defeat him. Although he never entirely gave up on his vision, James knew within a relatively short time of his arrival in England that there would be no British parliament. Nor was there any significant progress on legal, economic, or governmental union. Only in the reinstitution of episcopacy in Scotland did James see some hope for ecclesiastical convergence. Britain might be ruled by one king, but it would continue to be governed through three distinct political and administrative systems. What one can never know, of course, is whether it would have been better for everyone if James VI and I had got his way in 1604. Would a united parliament, a single privy council, a church of Great Britain, and an enlarged free trade zone have found a way to negotiate a more acceptable settlement between the monarchy and the political elites of the three kingdoms, avoiding the meltdown that occurred in the years after 1637? The suspicion is that it would have been of most benefit to the crown, and that the Scots would have been provoked into protest even earlier. However, in one respect the crown was able to function as a British monarchy, and that was in foreign policy. Here the Stuarts were remarkably successful for, apart from Charles I's adventurous foray into the Thirty Years' War in 1625–9, the three kingdoms were at peace throughout this period. James VI and I pursued peace by choice, Charles I by necessity, but whatever the motive the consequence for their subjects was that they were less affected by warfare than almost any other peoples in Europe over such a long period.

A settled dynasty, government that recognized the distinctiveness of the three kingdoms, and the avoidance of entanglement in costly foreign wars for the greater part of the years 1603 to 1637 all point towards political success. James VI and I also established a court that operated effectively as a point of contact for the political elites of England, Ireland, and Scotland. Raffish, chaotic, and factional it might have been, but the interaction between the king, his household servants, privy councillors, and the many suitors who came to London to lobby all produced something approaching a consensus on many issues. The king's encouragement of debate and his toleration of different ideas from his own meant that he was generally well informed and in receipt of good counsel. Even when Buckingham began to monopolize patronage, James remained receptive to contrary opinion from rival courtiers, or from his Scottish privy council, and, in spite of his outburst at the 1621 English parliament, he listened to what critics in the house of commons had to say. Under Charles I all this altered as step by step the king narrowed the range of counsel to which he was exposed. The London court was reshaped according to the king's conformist ideas, James's councillors were sidelined and replaced by more pliant men in England and Scotland, in 1632 Ireland was placed in Wentworth's iron grip, the English parliament was ignored altogether, the Scottish parliament was subverted, and the Irish parliament was bullied. By the mid-1630s Charles I was listening to a small group of advisers who told him only what he wanted to hear and who marched according to his tune, men like Laud, Hamilton, Wentworth, Cottington, Traquair, and the queen. The result, in hindsight, appears predictable, a king isolated and out of touch, even if one can understand why Charles thought it necessary to streamline the conduct of business in order to get things done. What is clear, however, is that the distinct manner in which these two kings employed their court made a difference to the kind of counsel they received. There was nothing about the multiple monarchy itself that made an absence of adequate counsel inevitable.

Was Britain badly governed? Undoubtedly there were men in all three parliaments who disagreed with royal policies, chiefly foreign policy, fiscal issues, the liberties of subjects, and religion. The question of how far Britain should placate Spain was divisive, especially in England in the 1620s, but while the war was managed incompetently there was no overwhelming groundswell of opinion ranged against James VI and I for pursuing peace, or against

Charles I after 1629–30. However, the crown's financial weakness in all three kingdoms was more serious. Not only did it reduce the king's ability to act quickly and flexibly, but a combination of an inadequate income and the inability of the political nation to address this issue forced both James VI and I and Charles I to devise unpopular and underhand methods of raising money. The crown manipulated impositions, forced loans, and ship money in England, the taxation of annual rents (interest on loans), management of the coinage, and the teind commission in Scotland, and the dishonest dealing with the Irish over the 'graces'. On the whole, the Scots responded to royal requests for relatively modest taxation with the least acrimony, the Irish with little choice, and it was the English who were the most obstructive. If the Stuart kings were guilty of financial sharp practice, their English parliaments were equally guilty of making unreasonable demands on the royal prerogative that neither James VI and I or Charles I could be expected to concede.

Here was the point where conflicting ideas about the freedom of the king clashed with the liberties of parliaments and local privileges. Once again, for all his overblown claims to absolute authority, James VI and I understood the practical necessity of compromise and the real limitations of his power, hence his grudging respect for the house of commons, or his tolerance of the hereditary jurisdictions of his Scottish nobles. By contrast, Charles I appeared to threaten the very existence of parliaments, he interfered in the localities, alienating the Old English in Ireland by trampling over their rights, infuriating landed society in Scotland with the revocation scheme, and offending local sensibilities in England by collecting the forced loan or trying to reform the militia. Of course, it is now difficult to argue that Britain was seething with discontent by the 1630s, there is too much evidence to indicate that in all three kingdoms many people were oblivious to any sense of looming political crisis, but there were many of the king's subjects irritated or angered by the government. The almost complete absence of rebellion in early Stuart Britain before 1637 might indicate that Charles I could have got away with it had he not mishandled the Scottish revolt so badly. But the Scots did revolt because of how they were being governed, and the fact that both the Irish and the English followed their lead in the way that they did suggests a depth of discontent that did not appear out of nowhere. Of course, missing from all the above is the issue that more than any other fired political debate, hardened divisions, and inspired men to take those dangerous steps that turned them from dutiful subjects into rebels: religion.

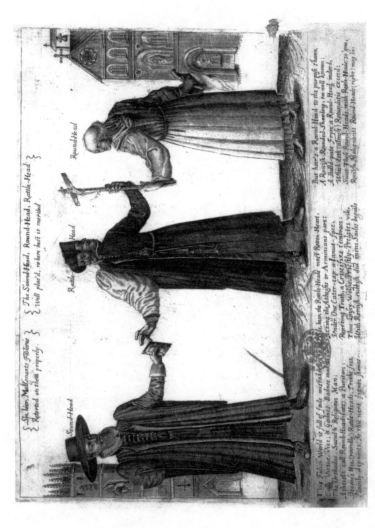

Figure 3 Sound-Head, Rattle-Head, and Round Head.

2

The Churches and Peoples of the Three Kingdoms, 1603–1641

John McCafferty

James VI and I and religion in the three kingdoms

The first two Stuart rulers of all Britain and Ireland were faced with many challenges arising from the quite different, but interlocking, pasts of both islands. The varieties of Christianity practised by their subjects presented particularly delicate and potentially, and sometimes actually, explosive problems of government. In Scotland, James VI and I faced and had faced a Reformation worked out while he was a child. It had been achieved without the crown and often against it. In England and Wales he faced a reformed church settled and, to some degree, fine-tuned by the dead queen. In Ireland there were not one but two church settlements. One had been exported there by his Tudor predecessors but it enjoyed limited success and little apparent chance of making further advances, even though James thought it might be otherwise. The other settlement was increasingly organized and directed by Rome. In 1625 Charles inherited a Scottish church rendered enticingly but deceptively similar to his English church. In England James had contented himself with buttressing Elizabeth's edifice while adding a few touches of his own. Charles I became the only Stuart king to live and die in the Church of England. In Ireland there were still two churches. Thanks to immigration the Church of Ireland now had considerably more adherents and had developed a more explicitly Reformed outlook than its English mother. The Catholic Church in Ireland had moved into line with Counter-Reformation theology and practice and enjoyed a resident hierarchy trained on the continent. It, too, claimed to be the *Hibernia Ecclesia*, church of Ireland.

In each kingdom and at the start of both reigns the crown, the political nation, and almost every subject found themselves grappling with a set of disturbing questions. What was the proper relationship between the monarch, the church, and by extension the Christian subject? How should the church be governed? What was the correct relationship between the crown and a subject who rejected the ecclesiastical settlement either because of its perceived incompleteness or because of its rejection of papal authority? What was the true role and function of the clergy? What was the right manner in which to distribute and use the accumulated property and revenues of the medieval church? Set at an angle to these delicate problems was another question that belonged both to the most abstruse theological calculations and to the chilling arithmetic of personal salvation. Who was the Antichrist? The answer to all of these religious questions and indeed the very degree of emphasis placed on them varied from kingdom to kingdom and within each realm.

On Wednesday 6 April 1603 James VI and I entered his new kingdom of England at Berwick. Having been received by dignitaries at the gates of the city he processed to the church where he heard 'a most learned and worthy sermon'. The preacher on this solemn occasion was Toby Matthew, then bishop of Durham, and future archbishop of York. Among the clerics in his Scottish retinue were the bishops of Dunkeld and Ross. The latter's son-in-law, also present, was John Spottiswoode, at that time minister of Calder but destined to be archbishop of Glasgow, of St Andrew, and lord chancellor of Scotland. The king and bishops sitting in Berwick church listening to sermons made a living tableau of the kind of ecclesiastical settlement he would offer to his subjects of Scotland,

Ireland, England, and Wales. The great snag was that many of these same subjects had their own ideas about how religion should be practised in those dominions. As he moved south reports reached the king of events in Ireland where O'Neill had finally surrendered, thus completing the military conquest of the whole island unwillingly embarked upon by Elizabeth. At the same time there was also news of a rash of revolts in the most prosperous towns and cities of Munster where the Catholic Old English inhabitants hoped to jostle the king into granting toleration of their faith. Others were hopeful too. The eyes of the puritans, the more intense, more evangelical Protestants of England, were raised up as well. Here was a king brought up in the Scottish Kirk, tutored by George Buchanan, and the writer of a paraphrase on the Book of Revelation and on the duties of Christian kings. On 28 April he was presented with a document purporting to represent 'more than a thousand of your majesty's subjects and ministers all groaning as under a common burden of human rites and ceremonies'. This 'millenary petition' quoted James himself and urged him to be a godly physician, a healer of the diseases of the church of England. Both actions, dramatic revolt across the Irish Sea and the judicious phrases and careful definitions of the petition, were designed to test the temper of the new ruler.

James resolved to do what he enjoyed most. He decided to talk. He arranged a meeting with chosen representatives of the petitioners at Hampton Court after the Christmas holidays. In the meantime he issued a proclamation which pushed the likely outcome of any conference in one direction. The king disliked the flurry of puritan petitions that descended on him during the late summer and early autumn. These confirmed his view that the godly supplicants were, in the main, obedient subjects but that hidden in their ranks was a factious and potentially anti-monarchical fringe. So long before the meeting at Hampton Court the king's winnowing fan was in his hand, as the tone of his proclamation of 24 October 1603 made clear. Those who hoped for a godly purge would be disappointed as both the constitution and doctrine of the Church of England were deemed to be 'agreeable to God's word and near the condition of the primitive church'. The only prescription the royal physician was prepared to offer was one for mild medicine to tackle proven ills. If this proclamation had been published twenty-three years later by Charles I there the matter would have rested but his father always preferred (and took pleasure in) palpable, personal displays of his royal supremacy.

The conference convened on 12 January 1604 and began two days later with a meeting of bishops and deans in the privy chamber. On Monday 16 January the king pitched four puritan spokesmen against two bishops and then rounded off proceedings with a plenary session on the Wednesday. All of the widely differing, often partisan, accounts of the affair point in one direction—James had lots of fun. He not only delivered himself of one of his most enduring aphorisms, 'no bishop, no king', but also managed to confirm the Elizabethan settlement and in doing so make it his own. Conjuring up an image of a Christian prince ruling by divine authority and supported by an apostolic order of bishops was at once a defence of the *status quo* in England and a herald of the shape of things to come in Scotland. Yet not all the traffic at Hampton Court was the one way. The godly did get a serious slap on the wrist but everyone was reminded that a godly prince might well choose to sanction some limited but significant reform. The character of the parishes was to be shifted decisively in favour of a preaching ministry. A number of customs, such as the use of the sign of the cross in baptism, surplices, and confirmation by bishops which were condemned as the relics of popery by the petitioners, while not taken away, were explained. Episcopal wings were gently clipped by a new requirement that senior clergy must be present at ordinations, suspensions, and deprivations of ministers.

Hampton Court made crystal clear the chain of command in the Church of England: the king, the bishops, the clergy, the people. The supreme governor was willing to argue, debate, encourage but he would not negotiate or haggle with churchmen or kirkmen. Richard Bancroft, the new archbishop of Canterbury, was entrusted with the task of drawing up a code of canons which had at its heart clerical subscription to the Royal Supremacy, the Book of Common Prayer, and the Thirty-Nine Articles. The winnowing foreshadowed in October 1603 became a reality when about 100 ministers who refused to subscribe after every persuasion were ejected from their benefices. As a result the great bulk of the clergy did conform, leaving only a few to set off on the high and rocky road to separatism. Once subscribed, however, clergy were generally free to pursue the bare minimum or the enthusiastic maximum conformity within their own parishes. Puritanism was now safely contained within the body of the Church of England and the king had laid the spectre of presbyterianism to rest both to his own satisfaction and that of his subjects who had feared a Scottish disciplinarian monarch.

The decisions taken in 1604 bore most intimately on the English church but the ecclesiastical blueprint established was also of significance in the king's native kingdom and in his newly conquered one. James had made clear his desire to see the 'kingdom of Ireland ... reduced to the true knowledge of God'. In the previous twenty years it had become clear that the established church was not going to capture the allegiance of the Gaelic Irish or the Old English descendants of the medieval colonists. The country was a nagging headache for the crown. It had to be governed. Good government depended on Old English cooperation which meant, in turn, that anti-recusancy laws with the bite of their English or Scottish counterparts could not be passed through the Irish parliament. Yet for many English or Scottish Protestants even tacit toleration of popery was a scandal. Ireland complicated English foreign policy also. In negotiations the kings of France or Spain were only too happy to bring up the sufferings of Irish Catholics. Any ensuing concessions went down badly in Britain and still worse with the growing Protestant population in Ireland. From time to time the headache intensified into a migraine. The fact that there were more Irish Protestants in Ireland as the century progressed was mainly the result of the Ulster Plantation, which was a combination of free enterprise and evangelical mission. Distribution of the forfeited lands of the Gaelic earls drew Scottish and English adventurers (though never in the anticipated numbers) to this first British colonial frontier. The scheme lavishly endowed the Church of Ireland and while there was little conversion of the native population the newer colonists began to rival the Old English in numbers and influence.

Hampton Court set the unmistakable seal of James's approval on princely Reformation in England. James VI made no secret of his desire to bring the crown back into the Kirk of Scotland and to give his countrymen the ample benefits of a supreme governor. He aimed to combat the view that the kirk and crown were utterly separate and the attendant belief that the kirk had the right to chastize or even discipline the crown. This had been most dramatically expounded in Andrew Melville's furious remark that in Scotland: 'Thair is twa kings and twa kingdoms ... thair is Christ Jesus the king, and his kingdom and his kingdome the kirk whose subject James the Saxt is, and of whose kingdom nocht a king, nor a lord, nor a heid but a member.' 'God's sillie vassall' knew that he had to clip the wings of the General Assembly of the Kirk and establish an equally clear chain of command in Scotland. He began the process in 1600 by securing parliamentary representation for bishops as ecclesiastical commissioners, thereby awaking the Scottish episcopate from its slumber. After 1603, charmed by the deference of his English bishops and buoyed up by the revenues and the authority of his southern crown, he moved faster. Two years later ten of the thirteen Scottish sees had bishops, though they were for the time being still more like glorified superintendents. A General Assembly held at Aberdeen in July 1605 had no royal licence and so provided the opportunity to force the issue of the relationship between crown and kirk. The following year a parliament in Perth restored bishops to their temporalities and formally acknowledged the authority of the crown over *all* estates. Scotland, like England, was to be one kingdom with one royal governor.

At the end of August 1606 Andrew Melville and other dissidents were summoned to London. This was to be no Hampton Court. The Scottish ministers were allowed no debate and favoured with no theological quips. They were there to listen. What they heard was a barrage of pulpit thunder equating the 'usurped' power of the pope with the 'pretended' power of presbyteries. Melville's exasperated denunciation of Archbishop Bancroft's vestments as 'Romish rags and a pairt of the beastis mark' earned him a sojourn in the Tower lasting until 1611. In the wake of this chastening display the powers and influence of Scottish bishops waxed, they were voted 'constant moderators' by the General Assembly in 1607 and in 1609 archbishops were restored to jurisdiction over their own courts. Twice English preaching teams were sent north by royal command to expound on the apostolic origins of episcopacy. Restored to a degree of permanent existence and in command of a jurisdiction technically parallel to the system of synods, presbyteries, and kirk sessions, the bishops were well on the road to becoming equivalent to their Irish and English counterparts. James kept up the momentum by establishing in 1610 two courts of High Commission whose wide powers included oversight of those who preached against the established order of the Kirk. That 'established' order was, of course, being gradually redefined. The 1610 General Assembly which was managed by Archbishop John Spottiswoode passed measures requiring clergy to swear an oath of obedience to the king recognizing the sole royal prerogative of calling assemblies and erecting a functioning episcopal authority in all the dioceses. In keeping with the emphasis on apostolic roots, Spottiswoode of Glasgow, Lamb of Brechin, and Hamilton of Galloway were consecrated in London by the bishops of Ely, London, Worcester, and Rochester. The three Scots went home to confer apostolic succession on their peers. This was no haphazard transfer of power and behind the solemnities of consecration great care was taken to avoid any impression of an English takeover. Neither of the two English primates, Bancroft of Canterbury nor Matthew of York, was present nor did Gledstanes of St Andrews go to England. Formally, at least, there was now an intrinsic parity between the three sets of bishops across the three Stuart kingdoms. One of these bishops, Andrew Knox, even held dioceses in two kingdoms simultaneously—the Isles in Scotland and Raphoe in Ireland.

James VI and I was at once wily and realistic. Although the pace of change in Scotland was dizzying for some and provoked apocalyptic rumblings in others, the political nation was not allowed to become overheated. The Kirk would not become a carbon copy of the Church of England. Synods and presbyteries and the local discipline of kirk sessions persisted and functioned. The new prelates were the king's creatures but they generally cooperated with the presbyteries. Just as in England, once some formal victories had been secured there was a latitude which bordered on *laissez-faire*. The king was theologically literate but judicious with it. Jacobean confessions of faith such as the Irish Articles of 1615 and the Scottish ones of 1616 were squarely in the Reformed tradition, proving that prelacy was not a step down the road to popery. The choice of English bishops was carefully considered to the point of being even considerate and the appointees represented a broad spectrum of theological opinion. The appointment of George Abbot to Canterbury in 1611 makes a nice example. Abbot loathed the papal Antichrist, defended apostolic episcopacy, and was also staunch in the Calvinism instilled into him as an undergraduate.

While ecclesiastical polity could be settled fairly satisfactorily and theological disputation managed, contained, or harmlessly fudged, liturgical change, that is, alteration in the mode of worship in the parishes, was a much tougher nut to crack. In England and Ireland the Prayer Book of 1604 was a mark of conformity whether read in full or in part. In Scotland the Book of Common Order was more of a pick and mix for ministers and there was no penalty for not using it. Furthermore, the Kirk had abrogated the older cycle of the liturgical seasons, flattening it out to put the emphasis on the week and on the Sabbath. At the Perth General Assembly of 1618 an attempt was made to nudge the Kirk into greater sacramental and liturgical congruence with the other two established churches. The Five Articles, which barely squeaked through, sought to bring in kneeling for reception of communion, private communion for the sick and dying, private baptism in cases of necessity, catechesis of children made subject to episcopal instruction and blessing (a kind of first cousin once removed from confirmation), and the celebration of Christmas, Good Friday, Easter, Ascension, and Pentecost. During James's only return trip to his native land in 1617, the English Prayer Book was used in the chapel royal and over the following years a series of proposed revised liturgies were drawn up based on Scottish forms. For many ministers and people Perth represented a step backwards, a setting up of old idols once more, and so the king met resistance. He backed off. Although even more adroit management was called for to see the Five Articles through parliament in 1621, it became clear, even from several hundred miles away, that the Scottish Privy Council and bishops were loath to embark on any serious attempt to enforce conformity. As it was, there had been a spate of open-air preaching campaigns and the development of conventicles—semi-detached voluntary congregations. Characteristically James was content to leave liturgical change on the statute book until the times were more propitious. In the same way the prayer books simply remained committee drafts. Leaving changes in worship to one side also made sense because of the anxious atmosphere about following the defeat of the Protestant forces led by the king's son-in-law in Bohemia. By the mid-1610s there was plenty of tinder lying about but James never permitted it to burst into flame. Yet he did leave it smouldering for an heir who preferred the bellows to the damper.

Catholic subjects and the papal Antichrist

The physical layout and the furniture of churches built in the reign of James VI and I are testimony to the centrality of the Word. New parish churches were often simple rectangular buildings constructed as auditoria where the use of removable communion tables moved the centre of gravity from the altar to the pulpit. Bishops were expected to preach and they themselves directed clergy as teams of preachers. Most Protestant clergy in Britain and Ireland had been trained up in a Calvinist, or more precisely, Reformed setting and the Irish and Scottish confessions reflected the temper of all of these ministers more accurately than the intricacies of the English Thirty-Nine Articles. There was however a sizeable group who stood entirely outside the loose conformities of the establishment. Their defining mark—though they themselves often vigorously debated its meaning—was their obedience to the bishop of Rome, the pope. Undoubtedly many people, including James himself when in the mood, were prepared to take the *politique* view and accept some distinction between political and spiritual allegiance. Some took the long view and held that Catholicism would fade away through the education of children and the imposition of civil disabilities. Another analysis of the recusant problem, and considered equally (if not more) rational by contemporaries, was to maintain that the pope was the Antichrist, 'that man of sin foretold in the scriptures' as the Irish Article 80 of 1615 put it. The Irish Convocation was simply giving expression to a belief that constituted a real ground for union of hearts and minds of most of the Protestant subjects of the Stuart monarchy. Catholics, then, no matter how decent and law-abiding, were servants of the great enemy of humanity, part of a vast international conspiracy. Scots,

Irish, English, and Welsh recusants had turned themselves into foreigners in their own lands and potential if not actual agents of Rome, France, or Spain. Protestant peoples and nations, on the other hand, were elect, chosen, destined. Popes or their apologists might claim the power to depose rulers and this was considered proof of their wicked usurpation of divine power. Yet a still small voice deep within Jacobean Protestant minds hinted that if the ruler was too lenient, prepared to countenance Antichrist or even appear to lead the churches back towards Rome, then the lesser magistrates, the particular beloved of Calvin's God, might have to help a king rediscover his mission. A firm rejection of Catholicism was considered not only to be the mark of the loyal subject but also to be the solemn duty of the anointed ruler.

James VI and I was not averse to the view that the eleven popes whose reigns overlapped his own long life were manifestations of the Whore of Babylon. For him belief in papal power to depose rulers was merely a Catholic version of Melville's two kingdoms. He laid the foundations of Chelsea College in 1609 as an institution to nurture a crack team of divines who would take up their pens in defence of royal supremacy and against Rome's own controversial writers. He did so himself in his bearish *Premonition to Christian Princes* of 1609. Overall his attitude to Catholicism was measured and those who hoped for *de facto* toleration were not entirely amiss. One aspect of his terrified reaction to the Gunpowder Plot is nicely indicative. On the one hand he tried to seek papal help in restraining overzealous Catholics making contact through Anglo-Spanish channels. On the other hand he joined with parliament in taking vigorous legislative action through the 1606 *Act for the better discovering and repressing of Popish recusants*. Contained in the Act was an oath of allegiance which raised the matter of the pope's deposing power in the starkest manner. The oath created divisions between English Catholics and the ensuing disputes also spread across the sea to Dublin. For his part James was drawn into a peppery exchange of pamphlets with Cardinal Bellarmine and the king was not afraid to apply (in *Triplici Nodo* (1608)) the scriptural prophecies of Antichrist to the papacy. But the strategy is familiar: to divide the moderates, the viscerally obedient, from the hardliners. Like English separatists and Scottish Presbyterians fervent papalists were welcome to choose exile from the king's dominions. The Gunpowder Plot was, in this respect, both an end and a beginning. It marked the end of what might be called Catholic activist politics and the start of a royal policy allowing tolerance but not toleration. Catholics were, however, subject to bouts of persecution or, legally speaking, prosecution triggered by the international situation, strains in domestic politics or in response to the discovery of a 'popish plot'.

In Ireland the fortunes of Catholics were determined by a greater set of variables than those of their British fellows. Loyal Old English recusants shared in the government of Ireland, though the long-term strategy was always to erode their power in favour of Protestant newcomers. But Irish Catholicism was far from monolithic and other voices were making themselves heard in this period. There was, particularly after the departure of leading Gaelic Irish nobles in 1607, a sizeable exile community abroad. Made up of dispossessed aristocrats, clerical students, and soldiers, the predominantly, though not exclusively, Gaelic Irish émigrés clustered in Flanders, Spain, and France and about the Irish colleges of Louvain and Salamanca, Rome and Madrid. While very few flirted with transferring allegiance to Spain (a legitimist position based on the marriage of Philip to Mary of England), exile writers, especially the Franciscans at Louvain, strove to build up a sense of a kingdom of Ireland as a Catholic *patria*. Many agitated for, plotted for, or dreamt of a full toleration and even of a revocation of Elizabeth's ecclesiastical settlement of 1560 with the added possibility of an Irish parliament unfettered by Poyning's Act. Neither James nor Charles was ever going to acquiesce to this extreme logic of multiple monarchy (it could be said that James VII and II did attempt it and paid the price) but there were, nonetheless, developments in Ireland which pointed alarmingly towards the creation of at least the veneer of a Catholic nation and away from the racial divisions of earlier centuries. Such recusant activity was, of course, gall and wormwood to the Church of Ireland which was hobbled in its efforts by minimal anti-recusant legislation and the frequent unwillingness of the crown to sanction intensive penal campaigns. Some viceroys did attempt enforcement and a priest and bishop were even executed in 1611, though on treason charges. However, skilled Old English courtiers more often than not succeeded in drawing the sting of even the most committed lord deputy. The prospect of a domestic explosion in Ireland was always unwelcome and that when combined with diplomatic considerations meant that the Catholic Church in Ireland continued to grow in strength and self-confidence throughout this period.

Rome's concern to defend and manage Catholicism *in partibus infidelium* was made manifest by the foundation of the congregation or department of *Propaganda Fide* in 1622. Protestant alarm at Antichrist's bureaucratic arrangements was, in part, justified by the shadow hierarchy developing in Ireland from the 1610s onwards. Twenty Catholic synods to enact the decrees of the Council of Trent are known to have been held between 1600 and 1640. Roman prelates were brazenly behaving as if theirs was the church by law established. Even as episcopacy was being drip-fed back into the kirk, Irish sees were filling up with papal appointees. The predominantly British bishops of the Church of Ireland looked on in bitterness as the abstract Antichrist of their university debates took flesh in the form of his emissaries in their own dioceses claiming the same title, the same dignity and jurisdiction, and hinting at recovery of same patrimony.

Ireland forced kings to blend foreign and domestic policy and when it came to religious matters the first ruler of all Britain and Ireland sought the imperial purple outside as well as inside his own realms. James VI and I did believe that the union of crowns was pregnant with possibilities beyond customs policies and harmonization of laws. The times called for a new Constantine, a British Constantine who would renew the faith and direct the reunification of Christendom. The elimination of particularism and extremism so visibly practised in England and Scotland fitted into this Christian imperial vision, as did the issuing of the authorized version of the Bible (1611) which has been the most enduring outcome of the Hampton Court conference. It also meant keeping a watching brief on European religious affairs which ranged from grand designs right down to individual appointments. In his first English parliament of 1604 the would-be emperor mooted the idea of an ecumenical council. Unsurprisingly Pope Clement VIII was cynical. A few years later when Venice fell under papal interdict the English ambassador, Henry Wotton, assisted by his scholarly chaplain William Bedell, future bishop of Kilmore, hoped in vain for a breakthrough in Italy. Again, in 1616, Marco Antonio de Dominis, archbishop of Spoleto, was received into the Church of England with enthusiastic royal backing, amid a flurry of wild hopes for a general realignment in Catholic Christendom away from Rome. Fears of contamination of the doctrine of Protestant Christendom, on the other hand, led to a personal intervention by James against Conrad Vorstius's appointment to a chair of theology at Leiden. In 1618 a great Protestant synod convened at Dort with the king's encouragement to debate articles on grace and salvation put forward by Dutch theologians who followed the teachings of Jacob Arminius (1560–1609). James sent a moderate British delegation. The composition of the delegation and the instructions they were given are worth considering because they had a significance beyond the immediate doctrinal stir. Although dubbed British, the representatives were, in fact, all English with the sole exception of Walter Balcanquhal, a Scot long resident in England. This is an indication of the king's growing infatuation with the Church of England as the one most befitting a monarch. The delegation was given explicitly eirenic instructions. They were careful to steer clear of metaphysical speculation and, by and large, pursued a pastoral rather than coldly doctrinal course and so avoided making too stark, too cold, too pessimistic a statement of predestinarian theology. James wished the delegates to do this, and just as importantly, they wished it too. This desire to remain squarely within the Reformed tradition but also offer a practical, pastoral, divinity was as essential to the Jacobean church as the promotion of preaching. Avoiding speculation which might perturb Christian consciences was a thing imbibed deeply by Prince Charles who was growing up in that same church. At Dort the firm rejection of the Arminian position and the formulation of a set of canons as an epitome of the Reformed position had important consequences for clergy and educated laity who were inclined to think in terms of thesis and antithesis. If these canons were Reformed then they were also, naturally, Protestant; therefore the Remonstrant Arminians were not of the Reformed and so at odds with Protestantism and therefore popish. This equation of 'Arminian' with 'popish' would prove to be important in the next reign.

Enhanced conformity 1625–1637

James VI and I did not die in 1625 trailing crowds of Constantinian glory but rather as he began in 1603 with the religious nerves of his Protestant and Catholic subjects strained and jangled. This was not, in fairness, the fault of his domestic policies but rather the result of the confessional politics of foreign events. The king had always been far happier with the idea of a general council than of a grand crusade. He did not, as previously mentioned, come to the aid of his son-in-law Frederick V of Bohemia in 1619 nor go beyond making sympathetic noises after Protestant forces were routed at the battle of the White Mountain in 1620. There was no prospect of the British Emperor placing himself at the head of a grand Protestant European coalition. In consequence, relations with even the English bishops, the most Erastian of souls, turned chilly. When in 1623, Prince Charles and the duke of Buckingham embarked on their picaresque jaunt to Spain to woo the Infanta, most Protestants prayed for deliverance and most Catholics for happy triumph. For Irish Catholics, at least, the prospect of a match paid off, as Dublin castle was forced to call off a more than usually vigorous and prolonged attempt to enforce the recusancy laws. The last English parliament of the reign, in 1624, was nervous and fretful, urging war on Spain, petitioning for condign measures against Catholics, and looking for guarantees that there would be no future abrogation of the penal laws. This incensed the aged king but Prince Charles did make a formal declaration to the house of lords that if he married a Catholic his wife would have liberty only in her own household and no concomitant benefits would be forthcoming for recusants as a whole.

At James VI and I's funeral in 1625 Archbishop Spottiswoode of St Andrews refused to give precedence to the archbishop of Canterbury and would not wear the proferred English vestments. He stood apart, black-clad, from the English bishops. His dramatic gesture reflected the gap that still lay between two of the king's churches. The clergy of the established churches in all three kingdoms were themselves in something far less than a serene state in the closing years of James Stuart's reign. In August 1622 directions had been issued to preachers in the English ecclesiastical provinces of York and Canterbury forbidding any pulpit discussion of matters of state. These measures were necessary as a result of growing clerical anger at the prospect of the Spanish match. Hints at increasing theological ferment are to be found in the further direction forbidding those below the rank of dean to treat of the deeper points of predestination and election. In the same year a royal commission was issued for investigation of the church and state in Ireland. The findings made plain that the official church had failed to make any serious headway in winning the hearts of the native population. Even the belated publication (in comparison to Welsh) of a Gaelic translation of the Book of Common Prayer (*Leabhar Na nUrnaightheadh gComhchoidchiond*) in 1609 made no apparent impact. In Scotland the synod of St Andrew's 'benorth Forth' reported in October 1622 the absence of 33 of its 100 ministers. Earlier, at Easter, Patrick Galloway of Perth resorted to a bizarre genuflection—one leg bent, the sole of the other foot on the ground while still sitting on the bench—a physical expression of the uneasiness of the kirk after the articles of 1618. Vigorous preaching, the intended antidote to empty formalism and predestinarian despair, and kneeling, the intended antidote to a religion of the ear, contained within themselves seeds of dissension and disruption. Royal supremacy had struck very different roots in each of the three kingdoms but everywhere it required careful pruning, judicious watering, and endless training. James VI and I forgot, quite often, to be a canny gardener but Charles I never knew how to do it to begin with.

In many respects, the pivotal year of Charles I's reign was 1633 when he finally, and seemingly grudgingly, journeyed north to be crowned in Scotland. The father had used the English liturgy during his 1617 visit and so did the son. Charles was quiet and distant where James had been garrulous and familiar. His father's very success at nurturing the supremacy in Scotland proved to be a snare to the son who thought it was time to harvest the fruit before the blossoms were even out. Here, as thirty years earlier, were the king and the bishops gathered in a church. This time the display was very different and very shocking for the subjects of the ancient Stewart kingdom. The abbey kirk of Holyrood boasted, for the occasion, a railed stage, a communion table arranged altarwise with candles and a tapestry decorated with a crucifix. Six Scottish bishops, one of them Spottiswoode, appeared in rochets and golden copes. The king of Scots was crowned in the manner like that of England in 1625 and made a new promise to preserve canonical privilege and defend the bishops and the churches under their government. This new oath made the old Hampton Court quip, 'no bishop, no king', a sworn duty of the monarch.

Assisting on the dais was the dean of the English chapel royal, William Laud. He was, as in 1625, the chief choreographer and two months after the Edinburgh ceremonies he would become archbishop of Canterbury. Since Laud's trial in 1644 many historians have tried to determine who shaped the religious policies of the late 1620s and 1630s. Verdicts range from a kindly and well-meaning archbishop urged on by a cold and imperious king to a monarch dominated by a devious seventeenth-century type of Cardinal Wolsey. This effort to find the 'culprit' as it were and explain the ferment of the 1640s and 1650s has not been very rewarding and has tended to conceal some of the questions asked and sometimes shouted by contemporaries. Was there an attempt to impose a particular vision of the Church of England on the other churches? Was Caroline rule flirting with Rome rule?

Charles had made a special vow to defend the canonical privileges of the clergy. James VI and I had rehabilitated them, endeavoured to finance them and defend them against lay encroachments. Charles would go further and attempt to elevate them, to elevate the clerical estate as a whole, to elevate them in their jurisdiction, in their revenues, in almost everything. Evidence from all three kingdoms indicates that clerical confidence soared, that their claims became more extravagant, gradually creeping forward to threaten lay interests. The church, quite literally, became more and more visible. In Ireland one old diocese, Cloyne (which had been attached to Cork in the fifteenth century), was not only revived but peremptorily re-endowed by pulling ecclesiastical assets out of lay hands. A new diocese of Edinburgh was carved out of St Andrews. In the three capital cities expensive and often burdensome campaigns, of what can best be described as a semi-voluntary nature, were launched to re-edify and beautify the cathedrals of St Paul's, Christchurch, and St Giles. Inside these mother churches an increasingly bumptious episcopate turned auditorium back into sacramental space.

When lay proprieties were irritated by the jostling of clergy for deference and precedence darker worries began to surface. The dissolution of the old monasteries, friaries, and chantries had boosted landed wealth and created a new aristocracy and gentry. There were even those who, especially in Ireland, had remained Catholic yet had benefited from the land bonanza. However, broad acres and treasures were only one side of the wealth of the medieval foundations because through benefactions and other means they had come to control revenues and patronage of parishes outside their walls. The new lay owners were the legal successors of the abbots as heads of houses. For example, in Ireland in the parish of Julianstown in County Meath, Gerald, Viscount Moore of Drogheda, now took the rectorial tithes and employed a vicar or curate to attend to the spiritual needs of the congregation. The fact that the 'impropriator' of the revenues could be a recusant is a nice demonstration of the manner in which these inherited rights to income were considered to be pieces of property. Impropriations, tithes, and ecclesiastical lands made up part of a campaign that ruffled the landed interest on both islands. In Scotland, Charles announced a revocation (a legal device for recovering royal lands granted away during minorities) in July 1625 which, given his age, just inside the legal maximum, was really just a figleaf. The scheme was hastily devised and legally botched but still attempted to recover for the crown all ecclesiastical land secularized since 1540. The similarities with a revocation proposed by the Catholic Holy Roman Emperor Ferdinand II only served to heighten anger and panic in Scotland. Ferdinand, in fact, backed down but Charles I pressed ahead. He did change tack a little by establishing in 1627 a commission for 'surrender and teinds (tithes)' which would offer cash compensations to impropriators returning tithes to the church. This commission and the entire scheme not only backfired but also had the effect of accustoming Scottish society to collusive action, to near disobedience to an absentee crown, and to regarding the bishops as the chief agents of royal arbitrariness and excess.

Efforts to restore the patrimony of the church of Ireland were more successful but only by dint of stretching viceregal powers, manipulating parliament, and making barely concealed threats to landowners. The Irish parliament of 1634–5 brought in statutory restraint of excessive leasing of ecclesiastical lands which mirrored the kind of action Laud and other English bishops were taking voluntarily as leases fell in on their own estates. An Irish scheme for buying in of impropriations was run quite successfully by Bishop Bramhall of Derry but it really depended for its success on the way in which Dublin castle had scarily and swiftly overthrown the title of the earl of Cork to vast swathes of church lands in Munster. In all three kingdoms the temporal claims of the church were mapped out and researched with a new precision through the compilation or updating of special inventories known as terriers. The king took undisguised and very public interest in the outcome of lawsuits, such as that of the London tithes, involving the clergy. This entire approach to clerical revenues and estate was not just based on a simple notion of restitution for sixteenth-century asset stripping. It was shot through with a belief that lay incursions on ecclesiastical endowments amounted to sacrilege. Henry Spelman's *History of Sacrilege* caught the mood nicely by cataloguing, almost lovingly, the terrible misfortunes which befell the unhappy possessors of former monastic estates. In 1635 the very belated revocation of Lindores abbey sparked rumours that all of the old monastic land was going to be restored to the church. This desire to restore the temporal fortunes of the church is best seen not as a meticulously planned campaign but rather as a general outlook or cast of mind which was shared by Charles, Laud, other bishops, clerics, and some lay figures. This is evident from the persistence with which it was pursued from 1625 onwards and by the great array of instruments used in that pursuit, whether prerogative powers, proclamations, statutes, canons, visitations articles, or others. This was no narrow Anglicizing approach either because as it happened the very least could be achieved in England due to common law constraints, as Laud remarked wistfully to Wentworth on one occasion. It permeated both royal and episcopal government. This sense of there being a dominant note or guiding spirit in religious affairs was dangerous for the crown and bishops because once, however reluctantly, it had been identified as threatening or pernicious or subversive of liberty little room was left for political manoeuvre. A clear-cut campaign can be ended or suspended but it is much harder to change style of government. Charles, for his part, never wished to change nor even give a decent impression of wanting to do so.

Episcopacy exalted

Reacquisition of broad acres and rebuilding of churches made up just one part of an overall change of atmosphere. The visibility of clergy in public life began to add to the sense of change in the air. As in so many other things this was no break with the previous reign, because James had brought the bishops back to office and back to the privy council, but it was a perceptible intensification of what had gone before. In 1635 Archbishop Spottiswoode became lord chancellor of Scotland, in 1636 Bishop William Juxon of London lord treasurer of England, and by the winter of 1637 there were strong rumours that Bishop Bramhall would become lord chancellor of Ireland. Laud himself was now chancellor of both Oxford and Dublin universities. Change was not just confined to the highest offices and here Scotland led the way. In 1634 all of the bishops were made justices of the peace, with a role, according to one historian, not entirely dissimilar from the lords lieutenant of the county in England. Ministers were also placed on the commissions of the peace. Ireland and England followed suit. In the localities, then, clergy took their places beside the gentry and at court the bishops beside the aristocracy. Just as with land recovery, there were more than pragmatic considerations at work. As early as 1626 Laud had urged the king to publish papers of the late Bishop Lancelot Andrewes which argued the episcopacy was *iure divino*, of divine sanction. As the reign continued there was a growing sense in which many bishops, not to mention the king, saw their function as being ordained officers of a sacred monarchy rather than as royal *intendants*.

Charles I's reign had also commenced with a theological conference held at York House, the home of the duke of Buckingham, in February 1626. The debate was prompted by the publication of a tract by a cleric, Richard Montagu, entitled a *New Gagg for an Old Goose*, and was organized by prominent laymen who hoped to establish the 'heretical' Arminianism of the author. The conference was also an expression of aristocratic anxiety about the damage which might be caused by corrosive doctrinal dispute. This time it was the king's favourite who was present rather than the king himself. It has been said that Charles was theologically 'dyslexic' but it is probably more accurate to say that he was uninterested. This Stuart much preferred a 'practical' divinity of obedience and rituals of solemn hierarchy in heaven and on earth. Accordingly his June 1626 proclamation for 'establishing the peace and quiet of the Church of England' declared that theological controversy originally intended for refutation of popery had now caused so much dissension that Catholics were actually hopeful of a schism in the established church. The 1622 directions to preachers had muzzled clergy below the rank of dean but now *all* subjects in England *and* in Ireland were commanded to be silent in word and in print on 'any new inventions or opinions concerning religion than such as are clearly warranted by the doctrine of the Church of England heretofore… happily published by authority'. Many observers then, and afterwards, have chosen to view it as an assault on the Reformed tradition in the church and an encouragement to a small but confident Arminian clique among bishops and clergy in England. The 1629 commons' subcommittee for religion sought reassurances that there would be no countenancing of innovation nor any further pernicious spread of Arminianism. Both the 1626 and 1628 English parliaments had tried to force a restatement of the Jacobean consensus by urging joint statutory authority for the Thirty-Nine Articles and the Irish Articles of 1615. The 1629 subcommittee made pointed reference to the canons of the Synod of Dort as an antidote to Arminianism. A lot of this rather high, even in a more theologically literate time, concern with the deep, near impenetrable, mechanisms of salvation and damnation can be usefully viewed as an expression of anxiety about further change. Again the thinking was syllogistic—religious change is hazardous and could lead to popery, Arminianism leads to popery, therefore religious change is Arminian.

The year 1629 brought a series of individually innocuous royal directions which nonetheless added to the sense that there was a significant shift in direction. A proclamation in October ordered the repair of parish churches and chapels. In December instructions were issued to the bishops to take up residence in their sees, protect their temporalities, and maintain conformity, a conformity which was, and there were many who felt it, losing its Jacobean elasticity. Bishops were told to punish preachers who alleged that there had been any recent innovation or change in religion. Conditions began to change in ordinary parishes in England and Scotland. Again this was not a crude effort at Anglicization but instead an attempt to impose the liturgical standards of the chapel royal on, first, the cathedrals and then each parish. Results varied, just as in the case of church lands, across the three kingdoms but again a particular style and atmosphere became apparent. In Scotland, the Perth articles had been reactivated in 1626, though initially binding only new ministers. By 1629 entire emphasis was put on one thing: kneeling at communion. Officers of state, the councillors, and the judges were obliged to receive kneeling once a quarter in the chapel royal where, of course, the English Prayer Book was in use. All Scottish subjects were told that they would have to take communion on their knees once a year in their own parish church. While these things were broadly unenforceable, they do reflect Charles I's belief that his royal supremacy meant direct exercise of his own authority over the Kirk. Kneeling in one's parish church was not just a mark of greater conformity; it was also a mark of obedience to the sovereign. The royal will was against gadding off to more godly ministers in neighbouring parishes. Communion was also at the core of liturgical changes in the other two kingdoms as well but in a different way. Much attention has been paid to the altar policy in England but perhaps the most explicit statement of eucharistic reordering is to be found in Irish canon 94 of 1634 which stipulates that 'a fair table [is]to be placed at the east end of the church or chancel and a cup of silver for the celebration of holy communion. Which table shall stand covered in time of divine service with a carpet of silk or decent stuff.' The change in mood is most marked when this canon is compared with the English canon of 1604 which reserved the east wall of the church for a board inscribed with the ten commandments. The communion table had usually stood in the chancel but in no fixed spot. Return to the old eastward position and a substantial nod in the direction of permanence marked a new concentration on sacramental grace and on decorum or what is often called the 'beauty of holiness'. As far as can be determined, adherence by Irish Protestant clergy to the canon was pretty minimal. In the Canterbury province Laud's metropolitan orders, also of 1634, stipulated railing in of the altar and reception at the new rails. Episcopal responses did vary, though the policy gained momentum as the 1630s wore on. Lancelot Andrewes practised it in his private chapel, the king liked it, and so did Laud, who was yet slightly nervous about it. In one respect, determining the extent to which clergy and people complied by kneeling or reorganizing their parish churches is less important than realizing the extent to which this kind of action narrowed the definition of what conformity was. Compressing conformity also meant, of course, expanding non-conformity—the very antithesis of the strategy of James VI and I. In pure theological terms there was nothing intrinsically Arminian about concentrating on the sacrament but in that moment it was easy for people to attach that label to it and discern a slide towards Rome. In a time when popery was not what it had been, this presented particular problems.

In 1636 William Bedell stepped down as provost of godly Trinity College, Dublin, causing one of the senior fellows to pray God send them a good head and 'no Arminian, no Italianated man'. Such linkage of foreignness with theological unsoundness or popery was part of the mental furniture of most British and Irish Protestants. The old king had, although married to a quiet convert to Catholicism, still identified the pope as Antichrist. The new king shared a bed with a popish foreigner, made no denunciation, and received openly accredited papal emissaries. The arrival of the second of these, George Con, was rapidly followed by the open conversion to Rome of a number of prominent female courtiers. As promised in 1624, Charles gave Henrietta Maria liberty in her household but after the grand opening of a new chapel at Somerset House in 1632, attended by a congregation of 2,000, some questions were bound to be asked even if, for the time being, they were whispered ones. Meanwhile in Ireland the Catholic Church continued to behave like a national church. An attempt by the Church of Ireland archbishop of Dublin, Lancelot Bulkeley, to raid a public mass in a Carmelite friary being held not far from the castle on St Stephen's day 1629 graphically illustrates the limits of the state Reformation. He was attacked in the street and the arrests which followed were not of the stone-throwing crowd but of Catholic aldermen who had failed to come to his aid. War with Spain at the beginning of Charles I's reign gave Old English Catholics an opportunity to demonstrate that loyalty and recusancy were, after all, easily compatible. Irish Protestant opinion held that proper exaction of the recusancy fine would easily meet the cost of war. Charles promised a series of concessions known as the 'graces', while the Church of Ireland bishops thundered against the dangers of 'setting religion to sale', but the reality was that he did not deliver and, if he had, many New English would have benefited from this wide package as well. The St Stephen's day fiasco of 1629, in fact, initiated one of those sporadic government crackdowns on religious dissent, but the arrival of Thomas Wentworth as lord deputy in 1633 saw the wind change quarter again. While, according to his own accounts, cheerfully playing old and new settlers off one another, he tended not to play the religious card at all. Up to the end of the decade considerable energy was devoted to the reconstruction of the Church of Ireland, leaving the Catholics virtually unmolested. So a legally proscribed organization, then, flourished with a resident episcopate setting up courts, novitiates, and generally building on the achievements of the previous reign. Resumption of normal pastoral relations freed up the secular and regular clergy to squabble over their respective rights and even over possession of the old monastic churches and their impropriations. Dublin castle even took a discreet hand in supporting the seculars. From 1619 Irish Franciscans had been sufficiently vital to restore the old Gaelic links by embarking on a series of missions to the highlands and islands of Scotland. There Catholic numbers were tiny but through the considerable interest of the recusant lords, the marquis of Huntly and the earl of Nithsdale, they enjoyed disproportionate political influence. Throughout all the realms, enforcement of penal laws oscillated between severe crackdowns and long calms. Sporadic efforts by the Scottish bishops to harness strong anti-Catholic feeling into sturdy action had limited success partly due to the intervention of recusant privy councillors and partly because the religious tests for public officers included ceremonial kneeling as the baseline for conformity.

The overall tenor of crown policy in relation to Catholicism—circumspect, reactive, gradualist—barely changed between

1603 and 1640. Protestant perceptions of the issue, both lay and clerical, did change by moving in slow degrees from frustration to annoyance to suspicion to simmering anger. This did not happen neatly, or in a clear sequence, nor were all Protestants at the same stage at the same time, but by the latter half of the 1630s there was widespread belief in some form of a 'popish plot' at the heart of political life. Viewed through this prism, activities at the court, in episcopal palaces, in the courts, and even in the universities began to take on a sinister light. At the same time two loosely related phenomena further contributed to thickening of the religious air.

The first of these was what can be called the fall, or rather, displacement of Antichrist. The second was the push for canonical uniformity. Denunciation of the pope as Antichrist had sustained Marian exiles, rallied Elizabethan Protestants in defence of England, and made a bond of amity across the three Jacobean kingdoms. Almost an article of faith, it certainly assisted in preventing more from taking the road of separation. The dominant hierarchical tone of the 1630s was not easily compatible with the apocalyptic stridency which had earlier unmasked the 'whore of Babylon'. Laud and his associates were far more at home with succession than disruption. Rome might well be corrupt, errant, and sinful but it was not inherently Antichristian. So the answer to the Catholic taunt of 'where was your church before Luther?' changed from 'among the godly remnants and persecuted true believers such as the Waldensians, Cathars and Lollards' to 'here, just here, where it always was' or as Bishop Bramhall would say during his bitter exile of the 1640s: 'I make not the least doubt in the world but that the Church of England before the Reformation and the Church of England after the Reformation are as much the same church as a garden before it is weeded and after it is weeded are the same garden.' This cut two ways. First of all it collapsed any meaningful distinction between a 'true church', the saved, and 'the visible church', the institution in which people worship on a Sunday. This fitted quite nicely, of course, with the renewed emphasis on the grace offered through the sacraments. Secondly, it gave the Protestant churches a 'corrupt' ancestry, so bringing down one of the central pillars of the Jacobean consensus. If the British and Irish Protestant churches were simply the disinfected descendants of their medieval forebears, then in what sense could they be 'true' churches? It meant that the recent history of Christendom and wars had not been about light and dark, truth and lies. Robert Shelford's identification of the Grand Turk as the second beast in his *Five Pious and Learned Discourses* (1635) and others like it were published while a veteran historical controversialist like James Ussher was advised to go into print in Latin and from Dublin presses.

Ussher, a Jacobean warhorse, godly bishop, and scholarly refuter of Catholic error, was a living embodiment of the post-Hampton Court consensus. By 1635 he was so vexed with the state of ecclesiastical affairs that mischievous rumours began to circulate that he was going over to Rome. While this was utterly fantastical, the Irish primate had reasons both to be nettled and much perturbed. Being elbowed out of control of the Church of Ireland was no huge penance for this fervent bibliophile but the outcome of the 1634–5 Irish Convocation was deeply displeasing. The Irish Articles of 1615, incorporating the Thirty-Nine and the Lambeth Articles (which Elizabeth I had refused to ratify in 1594), along with the Scottish Confession of 1616 and the Dort canons had provided a kind of overlapping confessional unity for churches on both sides of the Irish Sea. Charles would not accede to parliamentary requests for statutory confirmation of the Irish and English codes. Instead he, assisted by Laud, aspired to a unity built upon the English canons of 1604—a unity founded on discipline rather than doctrine. By the start of 1637 all three kingdoms had a shared core of roughly forty canons. This expansion of ecclesiastical law was, again, not just a matter of the export of English norms. Instead it opened up new vistas of conformity or, more precisely, defined conformity more tightly than ever before.

The Irish Convocation reduced 141 English canons down to a round 100 but not just through neat condensation. This assembly, virtually bullied into its conclusions by Lord Deputy Wentworth, put a stake through the heart of the Reformed confession of 1615 by making the Thirty-Nine Articles the only test of doctrine in the Irish church. The new canons crystallized (as seen in the case of canon 94) the drift of English altar policy. There was even provision for private confession and a new kind of subscription which moved beyond broad assent to the supremacy, Prayer Book, and Articles to regular and repeated affirmation and declaration of the supremacy, to a complete ban on any kind of criticism of the Prayer Book, and instant excommunication for any attack on the church order and hierarchy. Irish clergy were asked to subscribe to the opinion that Reformation was complete and perfect. Despite some successful but minor rearguard actions by Ussher, the new set of canons not only reasserted the English roots and connexion of the Irish church but set a new standard of conformity up to which the Church of England itself might, in time, be asked to shift. The Kirk was a different story. The Scottish Reformation had been achieved in the teeth of the crown but Charles I forgot this. So the Scottish canons of 1636 were not even brought through a General Assembly (there was none between 1618 and 1638); they were simply settled on the Kirk by royal *fiat*. A 'humble supplication' drawn up but not presented to the Coronation Parliament of 1633 had expressed fears of innovation and of episcopally nurtured Arminianism and now the publication in 1636 of this new book seemed to support the view that here was a despotic absentee whose judgement was being clouded by popish or papistically inclined advisers. These canons which kicked off with a rehearsal of the royal supremacy (mostly lifted from the English code) went on to repeat most of the Five Articles of Perth and to refer to bishops as a distinct order. In this view episcopal authority was conferred by consecration and not by the permission of other ministers. The canons also alluded to a new forthcoming public liturgy which only raised hackles. Auricular confession was to be permitted in certain limited circumstances. There was no mention of General Assemblies, presbyteries, or kirk sessions. It was as if Scotland were England or Ireland. Any claims by clergy or by *laity* that the Prayer Book or the ordinal contained unscriptural matter or that royal supremacy or episcopal government were corrupt, unlawful, or unscriptural were to be punished by excommunication. So by decree and without even the facsimile of consultation the king sought to remould entirely the constitution of the Kirk. In England in 1640 the king would permit convocation to sit even after the dissolution of parliament. Here was a monarch who believed his own will was the ultimate source of ecclesiastical law. The outlines of a new standard of uniformity found in the Irish and Scottish codes were in many respects the contours of Charles I's own will, his own soul.

The Covenant

By 1637 the older looser structure of the established churches held together by the valency of similar doctrines had almost given way, on paper at least, to a unitary structure welded together by the royal will expressed in and enforced by canons, courts of High Commission, and convergent liturgies. The Scottish Prayer Book of 1637 should have been one of the last girders to go in place. Instead it became a wrecking ball. From the start the Scottish bishops, who consequently took most of the blame, were fretful. James VI's drafts from the 1620s were all based on indigenous orders of service because he knew, and his bishops knew, that alteration of the worship of the Kirk was, unless unbelievably subtly and sensitively presented, going to be interpreted as an assault on the very identity of the nation itself. The 1637 book, drafted by the king in person, was based on an English prayer book. But it was not drawn from the 1604 prayer book which itself was, with some minor alterations, Edward VI's 1559 second Book of Common Prayer, but on the boy king's first, 1549, authorization. The 1549 liturgy, as Scots were quick to point out, was even closer to the old missal and so more awful than anything Irish and English Protestants had to endure. This was something even worse than a creeping Anglicization—here was a king using his ancestral kingdom as a laboratory. A nation already accustomed to resistance by the revocation scheme was a nation prepared. The public announcement of the new book at St Giles, Edinburgh on 23 July 1637 (many people knew what was coming because offprints had been used as wrapping paper for weeks beforehand) provided the setting for an organized protest that turned into a popular riot.

The Covenant first signed by nobles at Greyfriars kirk on 28 February 1638 was a national bond. To begin with the Covenanters were only concerned with one of the three kingdoms. The cornerstone of the Covenant was the 1581 Negative Confession forswearing Catholicism combined with a repetition of all those Acts of parliament establishing 'true religion' in Scotland. While the Covenant was judiciously silent on bishops and the royal supremacy, it did throw recent changes into relief by making such a beacon of the earlier legislation. The overall message was crystal clear: the king of the Scots must provide godly government. Still support for this new bond was far from universal even though the Covenant had been deliberately couched in language intended to secure broad subscription. Scottish nobles at court, in Scotland itself, and in Ulster did not sign up. But by the time Charles had backed down after the flop of his 'king's covenant' and agreed to permit the first General Assembly in twenty years, to a revocation of the canons and Prayer Book, and to the suspension of High Commission and Five Articles, so much heat had been generated by subscription campaigns and apocalyptic preaching that even a brilliant tactician would have had considerable trouble in regaining the initiative. The Glasgow General Assembly of August 1638 was packed to the doors with armed Covenanters who feared a royal coup. Nervous and angry, this gathering set in motion an ecclesiastical revolution undoing thirty-eight years of Stuart activity by cancelling at once the royal supremacy, bishops, the Five Articles, canons, and new liturgy. A year later the General Assembly ordered compulsory subscription to the Covenant and irrevocably tipped the religious scales by declaring episcopacy to be contrary to the will of God. 'No bishop, no king'—and so now the royal will of James VI and I and Charles I was deemed contrary to that of the Almighty.

Once the Protestants of one kingdom had made it a principle that episcopacy was inherently sinful they could not but export their message. In February 1639 Thomas Wentworth had anticipated this and wrote to Archbishop Laud proposing that an oath abjuring the Covenant be imposed on Ulster Scots. Intended mainly as a propaganda ploy, the 'black oath', as it came to be known, only served to reinforce the impression that king and court considered Scottishness itself suspect and to heighten the sense that the survival of the Scottish nation as an entity was at stake. Covenanter pamphlets began to look outside the kingdom and plead that the very future of Protestant Reformation was now in jeopardy and that popish plotting was no less a threat to England than to her sister realm. Charles I's decision to raise his standard in 1639 linked war, war on his own subjects, with religion. War required money which required a parliament. The 'Short Parliament' lasted only fifteen days in the spring of 1640, after which the king, bruised by protest and recoiling from any real negotiations, dissolved it. His known willingness to use, if necessary, a mainly Catholic Irish army to attack subjects formally bonded together in defence of the Protestant religion only tended to confirm the rumours of a popish plot which were voiced with increased intensity and commanded ever widening belief in the wake of the Short Parliament. The English Convocation of 1640 did draw up canons designed to prevent the further growth of popery but the use of the royal prerogative to bolster the claims of a clerical estate who appeared to have arrived at the belief that they had their own innate, *iure divino*, authority ensured that hierarchy would feature prominently in efforts to ensure godly government. So it was and the 'Root and Branch' petitions of December 1640 not only pressed for the extirpation of the 'government of archbishops and lord bishops, deans and archdeacons' but also sought to control the king's power over the church. In Ireland the arrest and impeachment of Thomas Wentworth was the signal for a bloody-minded dismantling by both Protestants and Catholics of the church settlement of the 1630s. A year later, in October 1641, religious and political tensions in Ireland would erupt into violent sectarian bloodshed.

In the turmoil of trials, petitions, riots, and angry debates that darkened into terrible war as the 1640s went on there would be many who recalled with all the fondness of hindsight the golden days of Elizabeth I and James VI and I.

Figures Listed in this chapter

Titles given in brackets for rulers or if the individual is referred to in the text by that title only

George Abbot	1562–1633
Lancelot Andrews	1555–1626 (bishop of Ely)
Walter Balcanquhal	?1586–1645
Richard Bancroft	1544–1610

William Bedell	1571–1642
Robert Bellarmine	1542–1621
Richard Boyle	1566–1643
John Bramhall	1594–1663
George Buchanan	1506–1582
Lancelot Bulkeley	?1568–1650
Clement VIII	1536–1605 (pope)
Marco Antonio De Dominis	1566–1624
George Downham	d. 1634
Frederick V	1596–1632 (king of Bohemia)
Patrick Galloway	?1551–?1626
George Gledstanes	d. 1615
Gavin Hamilton	?1561–1612 (bishop of Galloway)
William Juxon	1582–1663
Andrew Knox	1559–1633 (bishop of Raphoe)
Andrew Lamb	?1565–1634 (bishop of Brechin)
William Laud	1573–1645
Toby Matthew	1546–1628
Andrew Melville	1545–1622
Richard Montagu	1577–1641
Hugh O'Neill	?1540–1616
Edward Poynings	1449–1521
Henry Spelman	?1564–1641
John Spottiswoode	1565–1639
James Ussher	1581–1656
George Villiers	1592–1628 (duke of Buckingham)
Thomas Wentworth	1593–1641
Thomas Wolsey	?1475–1530 (cardinal)
Henry Wotton	1568–1639

A MAD DESIGNE:
OR,
A Description of the King of Scots marching in his Disguise, after the Rout at *Worcester*, With the Particulers where He was, and what He and his Company did, every day and night after He fled from *WORCESTER*.

Figure 4 A Mad Designe, or A Description of the King of Scots.

3

The Rule of Saints and Soldiers: The Wars of Religion in Britain and Ireland 1638–1660

John Morrill

Introduction

At no point in the history of Britain and Ireland has the whole archipelago experienced such sustained and brutal internal war as in the 1640s and early 1650s. The English people was at war with itself and a king was tried, convicted, and executed, the crown deemed 'unnecessary, burdensome and dangerous to the liberty, safety and public interest' and the house of lords declared to be 'useless and dangerous to the people of England'.[1] Yet in the course of these wars internal to England in the 1640s, perhaps one in four of those serving in arms came from Scotland and Ireland; and perhaps one in five of all adult males bore arms and perhaps one

[1] S. R. Gardiner, *Constitutional Documents of the Puritan Revolution 1625–1660* (3rd edn. Oxford, 1906), 385, 387.

in twenty adult males died in battle or of campaign-related causes. The Scottish people was more spasmodically at war with itself, though a larger proportion served in England and Ireland than in Scotland so that a similar proportion of the adult population served in arms and died. Each of the peoples of Ireland (the Gaels, the Gaelicized descendants of the Anglo-Norman settlers, the un-Gaelicized Anglo-Normans, and the England and Scottish communities who had come over since the Reformation) was at war with itself and with the others, and almost every inhabitant of Ireland was at some point vulnerable to attack by British armies. In addition, at least one in ten adults had died in the conflict and (at least) another one in ten went into exile or was transported during the 1650s. These were wars of religion as much as any wars in early modern Europe were wars of religion—that is to say, they were about many things other than religion, but confessional poles were those around which all kinds of other issues clustered. And they were also wars in which most of the leaders were desperate to redefine the constitutional relationships that bound together the three component polities of England (and Wales), Scotland, and Ireland. Yet separation and independence was an issue for few. The only group with a serious commitment to breaking up rather than reshaping the state system created since 1534 were those who governed England in the years immediately after the establishment of the English (and Irish) Commonwealth who wished to wash their hands of Scotland.

The British billiard ball[2] 1637–1643

By 1637, Charles I's policies in church and state had generated bitterly muttered resentment in all three kingdoms, but impotent resentment for all that. In those politically sophisticated communities where fear of anarchy was far more intense than fear of Charles's controlled and mild tyranny, there was no quick or automatic resort to armed resistance. Aggrieved subjects looked

---

[2] This metaphor was devised by Conrad Russell, 'The British Problem and the English Civil War', *History*, 72 (1987), repr. in P. Gaunt (ed.), *The English Civil War* (Oxford, 2000), 94.

to the courts for protection against the abuse of executive power, but in a number of high-profile cases in each of the kingdoms they had looked in vain. They lobbied the king and his council, but few counsellors were men of ancient riches with deep regional roots; rather they were a group of nouveaux riches *arrivistes* and career bureaucrats. Important strands of opinion were now excluded or marginalized, and local magistrates in England in particular no longer found that partial implementation of conciliar wish-lists was acceptable. They practised passive disobedience and found themselves harried. There was no realistic prospect of a parliament where redress of grievance could be pursued in any of the kingdoms. So there was seething resentment; and some fear. In England, Burton, Bastwicke, and Prynne, a representative preacher, lawyer, and physician, lost their ears for criticizing government policy; but in Scotland (Lord Balmerino) and Ireland (the earl of Cork) it was peers who faced the vindictive partisanship of conciliar yes-men. Furthermore, the king's attempt in both Scotland and Ireland to renegotiate the terms on which former monastic lands had been alienated caused great fury there and raised great anxieties in England. The revision of the Scottish and Irish canons, followed by the introduction of the Scottish Prayer Book which took a form that most firm Protestants would see as *worse* than the English Prayer Book (being based on the 1549 prayer book which showed no 'Calvinist' influence rather than on the 1552/1559 prayer book which showed *some* 'Calvinist' influence) caused alarm throughout Britain. Had it become known that Bishop Bramhall hoped to introduce the 1549 Prayer Book to Ireland, it would have done even more harm. Everywhere Protestant priestcraft was rampant—bishops at the heart of civil government (an episcopal lord treasurer in England, an episcopal lord chancellor in Scotland); and bishops, with the royal supremacy franchised out to them, seeking to reclaim the wealth and jurisdiction of the clerical estate sequestered from them during the Reformation. Very few approved of any of this, but they seethed and muttered. They did not act.

Then in 1638, the Scots rebelled without quite meaning to. There was an honourable tradition in Scotland, where most justice and local administration was devolved upon the nobility, for that nobility to paralyse royal government by a collective refusal to implement royal policy. This is how they had undermined and subverted the Act of Revocation between 1626 and 1633. And the National Covenant in February 1638 was designed to do the same. It was a solemn promise of the people of Scotland under God and to the king that they would not implement royal religious policy. Drawing on the centuries-old tradition of civil bonding and the decades-old tradition of religious oath-taking, this was intended to tell the king of Scotland that his attempt to transform the structures and forms of the kirk would not and therefore could not be implemented. It was *not* a call to arms, and those who subscribed the National Covenant in 1638 were not expecting to have to fight to sustain it. They simply had not considered the possibility that Charles would react as king of a dynastic agglomerate and seek to use the military resources of the archipelago to enforce his policies. In a fairly pure sense, Charles I declared war on his Scottish people. It was this which unleashed violence throughout the archipelago. The Scots were galvanized into military action by the persecution of their more accessible and therefore more vulnerable compatriots in Ireland who had taken the Covenant and by the growing recognition of Charles's intentions to use armies from Ireland and England to impose his will on them. Not the least of Charles's incomprehensions of the difference between England and Scotland was his failure to grasp that the Scots nobility, although they no longer had bands of armed retainers, were capable of rapidly mobilizing an army. A large number of younger sons and brothers serving as mercenaries abroad came back and introduced the Swedish system of military districts and quotas. The Wars of the Three Kingdoms began in Scotland because Charles was weakest there and because the Scots were more able quickly to resort to arms.

Responses to Charles's provocation and to Scottish pre-emptive mobilization were complicated. There were still plenty of Englishmen (many future parliamentarians—the Fairfaxes, for example—amongst them) who disliked the Scots enough to volunteer without demur to fight against them in 1639. And there were others who saw a war with Scotland as a war that would result in the recall of parliament, where the voting of money to defeat the Scots might well be a price worth paying to secure significant long-term reforms of the English state.

Charles's government was in difficulties but not in crisis by the summer of 1638. Ireland was firmly under control and there was no reason to believe that royal power would collapse unless and until the lord deputy launched an aggressive policy of confiscation and plantation. There was no sign of organized resistance in England, although the legal advisers of the peerage and gentry were finding new loopholes in the administrative arrangements for the collection of ship money and there was a growing prospect that the crown would lose the next legal battle to secure that source of revenue on a long-term basis. Even so, the growth of revenue from customs and impositions was sufficient for the crown to be able to look forward to a long period of balanced budgets in peacetime, even without ship money. The enforcement of religious policy was proving a bit too aggressive even for Archbishop Laud, who shared the king's objectives but not his sense of urgency; but again, while resentment was growing, resistance was not. In Scotland, however, Charles had either to accept that he would need to back off from his religious policies or he would have to use the resources of his other kingdoms to enforce his will. If Charles had backed off from his religious policies and sacrificed Scottish policy (we should not forget that his father had done so in the 1590s only to reinstate it again over the following twenty years), then he could have avoided war and resumed his personal rule. The choice was his and he chose unwisely.

In 1639, he planned an assault on lowland Scotland, drawing on the Protestant army in Ireland, a scratch army from England, and such loyalist and opportunistic elements of the Scottish highland nobility as were willing to assist him. Faced by the clear evidence of his intention, the leading 'Covenanters' in the central belt, following a very hallowed custom, wrote to the king of France for help and called on patriotic Scottish officers abroad to return to Scotland to defend kingdom and kirk. Badly coordinated, the king's English army was the first to appear in the field. At the last minute the king, aware of the ragged and unprepared nature of his own army and unaware of the ragged and unprepared nature of the army facing him in the borders, abandoned his plans for the time being. He may have missed a golden opportunity to break the fragile will of the Scots.

Once more the initiative was with Charles. If he had abandoned his Scottish policies, remodelled his Scottish council, and (for the time being) granted Scotland greater autonomy, he could have resumed his personal rule in England. Charles could see that he needed more cash and better credit arrangements in order to mount a really effective campaign against the Scots. There were two ways of securing that cash and credit. One was to call parliament and horse-trade cash and reform in England; the other was to negotiate cash and credit from the Catholic king of Spain and from the papacy in exchange for significant relief for British and Irish Catholics. Charles tried both simultaneously in the spring of 1640. For two weeks the 'Short Parliament' showed itself willing to do business. It did not mount a head-on challenge to the religious policies that were dearest to Charles's heart; and it did raise the prospect of unprecedented financial assistance in return for the cancellation of ship money, coat and conduct money, and a royal promise of further parliamentary sessions. Charles, with impeccable bad judgement, preferred the prospect of Spanish and papal grants and dissolved the parliament. He immediately found that the prospect of Catholic moneys had vanished as the Spanish monarchy was rocked by escalating revolt in Catalonia, Portugal, and Italy.

He was still a free agent. He could still make a much more humiliating surrender to Scottish demands, which would have allowed the Scots effective local self-determination, and sustained his personal rule in England and Ireland, counting on disunity amongst the Scots to give him opportunities in due course to regain some at least of his personal authority. Or he could call another English parliament and make whatever concessions were demanded of him in order to get the money to take on the Scots. Both were unpleasant, but both had more merit than his decision to launch an assault on Scotland without the financial resources to sustain it. This time it was an unequal struggle, and he was humiliated. Worse, the Scots occupied the north-east of England and made it clear that they would not go home until they had parliamentary guarantees of his future conduct and full payment of their war debts.

This was the point—the early autumn of 1640—when Charles I ceased to be in control of events. Now he was required, as a condition of the pacification with the Scots, to call a parliament that would raise money to pay the war costs of the Scots and that would guarantee new constitutional arrangements for Scotland and a new constitutional relationship between the kingdoms. Until such time as these things had been achieved, a Scots army would continue to occupy Newcastle and the north-east of England, behaving in ways that would rekindle ancient distastes and hatreds of the Scots.

There followed a decade of war within and between the three kingdoms, a war of word and sword, a war of pen and printing press, a war of new and competing political and religious structures. We need to take them each in turn.

Paper war(s)

The 1640s saw an unprecedented war of words; and there were no Geneva conventions in the printing houses. In the 1630s about 7,700 titles were published in England and Wales; in the 1640s the total was 18,247. For a few pence, men and women could acquire the first-ever (weekly) newspapers describing the course of the war and commenting on the key military, political, and religious developments. By the later 1640s between ten and fifteen titles were available every week. The parliamentarian newspapers, for all their misrepresentation of events, were grounded in reality; while royalist newspapers took the form of invention or at least of increasingly mendacious commentaries on the events described earlier in 'roundhead' newsbooks. Short on new information, but strong in witty invective, the royalists found a readership even in the heart of London. For a few pence, men and women could also acquire—at least in the early 1640s—copies of what purported to be major speeches by leading members of the two houses. For a few pence they could buy the latest contributions to the formal exchanges between the king and the two houses as each struggled to win a propaganda war. For example, discussion of the king's attempt to seize the town of Hull (in which the magazine from his abortive campaign against the Scots in 1640 was stored) ran into twenty-three items; and the Militia Ordinance in the spring of 1642 generated thirty-three items.[3] By far the largest number of items was that associated with the attack on and defence of the Elizabethan church settlement, above all the Book of Common Prayer and the future form of church government. In the years 1640–3 reforming the Reformation or defending 'the true reformed Protestant religion by law established' (as Charles I himself put it) yielded over 400 pamphlets and broadsheets by clergymen, common lawyers, and laymen.[4] In the years between 1643 and 1647, these debates continued but were overshadowed by the debates within puritan-parliamentarianism between the advocates of a presbyterian system drawing on the experience of Geneva and Scotland, and the advocates of a non-separating Congregationalism drawing on the English tradition of godly conferences and on the recent experience of the New England settlers. In the years after 1647 the centre of gravity shifted again, with heated exchanges between the supporters of compulsory membership of a reformed national church and those demanding religious liberty for men and women who did not wish to be a member of any national church or at any rate not the one the victorious parliament proposed to introduce.

It cost the parliament a few pence a copy to issue every soldier in its armies with a 'pocket bible' (a series of the questions they were most likely to ask themselves and proof texts from scripture to satisfy their minds and consciences) and a 'pocket catechism'. And for a few pence men and women could also acquire copies of the sermons preached at the monthly Fasts held by both houses of parliament, the funeral orations for parliament's fallen heroes, and the letters of the generals on both sides describing their victories in arms (in the case of Cromwell's letters, often expurgated to remove his perorations containing precocious pleas for religious liberty and pluralism). Perhaps most surprising is the fact that at the heart of this most violent of wars, there was an unprecedented burgeoning of the burlesque and scatological in much of the polemical writing. The biting and sophisticated irony of Milton's

[3] Calculated from the sequences in [E. Husbands], *Exact Collection of All Remonstrances, Declarations, Votes, Orders* [etc.] (1643).
[4] Calculated from G. K. Fortescue, *Catalogue of the Pamphlets ... collected by George Thomason, 1640–1661* (2 vols. London, 1908) which arranges them in chronological order and may miss a few.

anti-episcopal tracts of 1641— 'the sour leaven of human traditions, mixed in one putrefied mass with the poisonous dregs of hypocrisy in the hearts of the prelates that lie basking in the sunny warmth of wealth and promotion, is the serpent's egg that will hatch an Antichrist wheresoever, and engender the same monster as big, or little, as the lump is which breeds him'[5]—gave way to the latter's royalist satire of Bruno Ryves or Sir John Berkenhead—as in his description of the tidy and greedy world of the puritans who sat in the Westminster Assembly: 'he divides his text as he did the kingdom, makes one part fight against another; or as (Cornelius) Burges divides the dean of (St) Paul's house, not into parts but into tenements; that is, so it will yield most money'[6]—or the spoof mock dialogues of works like *The Committee Man Curried* (1647). It is rough, bitter humour carried over into the rough woodcuts on title-pages, often with punning intent (as with the satire on Bishop Matthew Wren—*The Wren's Nest Defiled* (1640)—with its appropriately visually punning woodcut).

But the war of words was not confined to the English theatre of war. There were far fewer presses and therefore far fewer titles published in Scotland and Ireland—just over 500 titles in Scotland and 120 titles in Ireland as against 15,627 in London and 17,500 in England. What was published still delivered a strong polemical—and confessional—punch. But perhaps more significant still than the paper wars *within* Scotland and Ireland, were those *between* the kingdoms. In the twelve months between the outbreak of the Irish Rebellion and the Battle of Edgehill, more than one in six of all pamphlets were preoccupied with vivid, inflammatory (and wildly exaggerated) accounts of the massacres in Ireland. The strength of parliamentarianism in the areas alongside the Severn and Dee estuaries and valleys may be directly related to the cumulative weight of this publicity. Similarly the publication in the mid-1640s of Sir John Temple's *The Irish Rebellion* (1646) was to prove distressingly influential in determining the rhetoric of conquest and ethnic cleansing over the next seven years.

[5] John Milton, *Of Reformation* (1641), book ii. See the readily available Everyman version, ed. K.M. Burton, *Milton's Prose Works* (London, 1958).
[6] Cited in P. W. Thomas, *Sir John Berkenhead, 1617–1679: A Royalist Life in Politics and Polemics* (Oxford, 1969), 148.

In a rather different fashion, Scottish commissioners in London were very much in the forefront of putting the case for a rigid *iure divino* presbyterianism and against every manifestation of erastianism, religious pluralism, or liberty for tender consciences. In reworked sermons and pamphlets of all sizes over the years 1641–6, men like Robert Baillie, George Gillespie, Alexander Henderson, and Samuel Rutherford all produced more work directed at an English audience than at a Scottish audience. Their energies were almost entirely counterproductive and they generated strong allergic reactions in some of the most potent and influential parliamentarian polemicists of the decade, including Henry Parker (e.g. *The Trojan Horse of Presbyterian Government Unbowelled*, 1646), John Milton, and (in due course) Marchamont Nedham.

Constitutional war(s)

In the years 1640 and 1641 Charles I lost effective control of all his kingdoms. The Scots compelled him (in a treaty guaranteed by the English parliament) to agree to meet parliament every third year; to agree that all those who made and enforced policy in and for Scotland would be approved by the Scottish parliament or by other representatives of the estates; to accept not only full-blown presbyterianism but a strict separation of church and state. By the autumn of 1641 the Catholic community of Ireland wanted its own version of the Scottish deal: a reformed and regular parliament which would be dominated by Catholics; government of the inhabitants of Ireland by Irish-born men appointed or approved by an autonomous Irish parliament; and a fully independent Irish Catholic Church enjoying, within an (initially at least) pluralistic polity, all the rights the church might expect to enjoy in a Catholic confessional state. Fear that a weak king might be unable to prevent a vindictive English parliament from seeking to create and then to impose a Protestant confessional state led first to a series of major rebellions and then to the creation of just such a Catholic state, which sought to sever all links with *England* but not with *the house of Stuart*.

The English too took the Scottish settlement to heart, securing the passage of a Triennial Act, and insisting with ever-greater urgency on the creation of mechanisms to ensure that the king listen both to the men of 'ancient riches' and those in whom the dominant groups in the two houses could feel confidence. In all the kingdoms the men held responsible for past misgovernment were driven from office and the institutions which were taken to be the most pernicious instruments of their misgovernment (Star Chamber and High Commission in England, Castle Chamber and High Commission in Ireland, and High Commission in Scotland) were abolished. What many Scots and some Irish Catholics sought, however, was not merely a transformation of the institutions of the kingdoms of Scotland and Ireland, but a changed constitutional relationship between the kingdoms. Clause 8 of the Treaty between England and Scotland in 1641, for example, envisaged the creation of a confederal constitution, with simultaneous meetings of Parliament in each kingdom attended by delegates from the other kingdom with a power to veto legislation hostile to the interests of their own people; and the permanent existence of *conservatores pacis*, standing bodies of commissioners from both kingdoms with authority over crucial issues, such as the making of war and peace and the arbitration of disputes between the kingdoms. The Scots also sought joint control of a new ascendancy in Ireland. Believing both Charles I and the Long Parliament had committed themselves to such a confederal constitution, the Scots army returned home in the high summer of 1641 and disbanded. They set up the appropriate bodies and waited—in vain—for the English to respond. The promised changes were reiterated in the Solemn League and Covenant between the Long Parliament and the Scottish parliament in 1643 and the Engagement between the king and the Scottish parliament in 1648. Although it was second in importance in their minds to the introduction of presbyterian uniformity in all three kingdoms, confederalism mattered to the Scots.

But for the Scottish crisis of 1638–40 there would have been no 'Long Parliament' to plan and execute a war in England. There would have been all kinds of political crisis and violence, but the civil war that actually took place would not have happened in anything like the form that it did. But the Scots had returned home by the winter of 1641/2, largely content with what they had achieved. It also took the rebellion in Ireland (without which it is probable that the king would have regained the initiative in England) to cause the collapse into an organized war. Without it, there may well have been nasty, specific regional outbreaks of violence (like those seen in the Stour Valley in the summer of 1642) but they may actually have helped the king further, since this was a society which feared anarchy more than it feared tyranny and a society in which those who really believed that Charles would—intentionally or by default—permit the papal Antichrist to plant his tiara in England remained too few by themselves to be able to make sustained war on him.

The rebellion in Ireland resulted both from the vacuum of power created by the withdrawal (and subsequent execution) of Lord Deputy Strafford and from the all too publicly voiced clamours in the Long Parliament for direct English parliamentary rule in Ireland, for a strict enforcement of (strengthened) anti-Catholic legislation, and for a policy of plantation. As it became clear that constitutional reform through the Irish parliament would be gazumped by direct action from Westminster, a powerful group of Catholic Palesmen plotted a *coup d'état* to secure control of the levers of power. Simultaneously, and semi-autonomously, some of the Catholics dispossessed in the Ulster Plantation a generation earlier, reinforced by the 'Wild Geese' who had fled the country and made their careers as soldiers of fortune in the Habsburg armies, determined to take their revenge for past sufferings. The ensuing bloodbath, in which perhaps 2,000 or more Protestant settlers were killed (although reports put the figure as high as 200,000), many more maimed, and many thousands forced to flee back to Britain, was an outrage that required immediate and massive retaliation. And it raised in an acute fashion the issue of who was to control the army of conquest. If the king could not be trusted to choose his own secretaries of state or lord treasurer, he certainly could not be trusted to choose his own generals. For what would he do with the army once it had dealt with the Irish insurrection? But handing over that power was something no king could contemplate. The Long Parliament was led by men who wanted a godly reformation, to create a puritan commonwealth. That could never by itself have given it the breadth of support to take on the king. But the Irish Rebellion, and the vortex of fear, distrust, and non-negotiable issues it released, created the conditions for a divided nation to take up arms. Huge numbers dithered and sought to avoid making hard choices. But, driven by gales of distrust, the English state barque foundered on the rock of military control.

Parliament had not the will or (yet) the desperate imagination to find tax revenues to pay for the conquest of Ireland. Instead it borrowed one million pounds against the promise of ten million acres of confiscated Irish land. That pledge was to be the first of many pledges of land redistributions—dean and chapter lands, episcopal land, the lands of 'malignant' royalists, the lands of the crown itself—and a promise of all Catholic land in three of the four provinces of Ireland, which were to fund the war and make negotiated peace much harder to achieve.

And so full-scale civil war broke out in England and Ireland, and the Scots found themselves dragged in, first in 1642 into the Irish War, then (from the winter of 1643/4) into the English War, and finally (from the autumn of 1644) into an internal war. In all parties in all countries there were hawks and doves. There were those who believed that peace was achievable from where they found themselves; and those who were determined to press on to complete military victory and to worry about the terms and conditions of a settlement only then.

No one was more of a hawk than the king. Behind the conciliatory rhetoric of some of his advisers, Charles himself was almost certainly determined to settle for nothing less than a full restoration of the powers he had enjoyed at his coronations. He saw the concessions wrung from him (under duress as he saw it) between 1639 and 1641 as signs of his own weakness and as culpable if explicable betrayals of his coronation oaths. He could consider making some additional concessions to the Irish Confederacy in order to restore his authority in his metropolitan kingdom, but there were limits even there. Under these circumstances even defeat in war did not make him negotiate seriously or appropriately.

The English parliament needed the Scottish parliament to be sure of military victory, but there was never a solid majority seeking (or even willing) to honour the terms of the alliance: when the Westminster Assembly of Divines, with its cadre of Scots, produced a new pattern of church government for all three kingdoms, based on the Scottish model, the English parliament first diluted it and above all the role of the clergy within it, and then granted a liberty of tender consciences to fellow puritans unwilling to accept it; although the parliament set up temporary structures to coordinate the Anglo-Scottish war effort (such as the administrative Committee of Both Kingdoms), it made no effort to lay the foundations for an effective long-term confederalism; the English back-pedalled on allowing the Scots a say in Irish affairs; and they failed completely to divert moneys for the pay and supply of the Scottish Army. By 1647 the Covenanters realized that the English parliamentarians were not their true friends. Disastrously they concluded that therefore the king must be, and they entered into a comparable agreement with a man just as willing to double-cross them.

The Scottish Covenanters, comprising most of the nobility, and almost all the clergy and those who sat in the successive Triennial Parliaments, were united about what they wanted: a self-governing Scotland in a confederated and covenanted Britain and Ireland; but they were not united about how best to achieve it. They split in 1643 about whether a military alliance with the English parliament was a politic and prudent road to it; they split again in 1647/8 about whether a military alliance with Charles I was a politic and prudent road to it; and they split again in 1649–51 about whether an *immediate* military alliance with an insincerely covenanted Charles II was a politic and prudent road to it. These divisions led to eventual brutal if reluctant English conquest and absorption into an enlarged English state.

Those Irish Protestants who had settled in Ireland in the previous two generations mostly spent the 1640s hoping that the English parliament would put their plight higher on its agenda and meanwhile maintaining spasmodic and uneasy alliance with the king's Protestant lord lieutenant and his mainly Old English (Protestant and Catholic) allies and with the Scots. In the context of the 1640s, a much closer integration into a state system centred on Westminster seemed to them inevitable, but many still hoped for a Protestant-controlled Dublin administration and parliament. Ormond and his Old English allies wanted to do everything in their power to help the king win his war in England so that he would do everything possible to restore their power in Ireland. The Confederation of Kilkenny was committed to establishing equality of rights and thereby political hegemony for the Catholic communities of Ireland, but was deeply divided about the desirability and efficacy of assisting Charles in Britain. It contained a disruptive hard-line clerical party, marshalled by the papal nuncio, Gianbaptista Rinuccini, who wanted to reverse both previous plantations and the confiscations of church properties.

In these circumstances, during the 1640s, Protestants in Ireland were often fighting other Protestants, and Catholics were fighting or at least obstructing their fellow Catholics; and even more they were disrupting all attempts at a long-term solution based on compromise of any kind.

The interweaving of events and issues in and between the three kingdoms explains the futility at all attempts at a negotiated settlement throughout the 1640s. And hopes of a peaceful resolution were complicated by the functional radicalisms of war itself. The substantial middle ground everywhere collapsed in the face of the violence and disruptions of the fighting. The administrative needs of war produced new governmental structures in all three kingdoms and provided power bases for new men from social groups outside the traditional elites. In England, by the end of the war, plain russet-coated captains who knew what they fought for and loved what they knew[7] ruled the roost in the army; and swarms of minor gentry, provincial merchants, and jobbing attorneys ran the committees that had managed the war effort, as sequestrators of royalist properties, as excisemen, as tax assessors. In Scotland, effective control of much day-to-day government had passed to the committees made up of shire and burgh commissioners set up in and by the Scottish parliament and the district commissioners operating the Swedish-style military administrative areas. In Ireland, the Confederation of Kilkenny established a whole structure of government appropriate to an independent Irish kingdom (or even an Irish free commonwealth). Achieving settlement meant taking account of the increasingly strident demands of the new men. And it meant taking account of the victims of war: those taxed to the hilt, fed up with free quarter, with plunder, with friendly fire, with conscription. In their thousands they demanded

---

[7] To paraphrase Cromwell's famous appeal for the privileging of the spiritual rather than the social elite in a letter to the gentry who ran the county committee: *Letters and Speeches of Oliver Cromwell*, ed. T. Carlyle (rev. S. Lomas, 3 vols. London, 1904), i, letter 16, 11 Sept. 1643.

an end to them all. In England, this 'plague on all your houses' mentality found full articulation in the neutralist Clubmen movements of 1644–6 and in the petitioning, picketing, and pamphleteering campaigns of the Levellers between 1646 and 1649. In Ireland and Scotland the more characteristic response was the rise of banditry—such as the Tories of Ireland and Whiggamores of south-west Scotland.

By the autumn of 1648, chaos reigned in England, where the king was once more defeated but unchastened, the army determined on calling him to some sort of account, and too many MPs were persuaded that only by restoring him more or less unconditionally could the slide into anarchy be avoided. In Scotland, the Covenanters were settling down to humiliate and destroy those who had signed the Engagement. In Ireland, the Catholics prepared for the expected invasion by the New Model Army by new rounds of mutual recrimination.

Military war(s)

The wars of the 1640s were civil wars *within* and *between* the kingdoms. At the height, in the summers of 1643 and 1644 there were perhaps 150,000 men in arms in England, 40,000 in Ireland, and 20,000 in Scotland. There were between 8,000 and 20,000 Scots in England in every year except 1642. But there were between 6,000 and 11,000 Scots in Ireland, up to 12,000 English soldiers in Ireland, perhaps 5,000 Irish Catholic troops in Scotland, and an unknown (but modest) number of them in England.

It has been calculated that there were 645 engagements in England and Wales in which men were killed; perhaps 46 in Scotland and an unknown number (200–300 is a best guess) in Ireland. Certainly there were twenty-five battles on English soil in which more than 5,000 men were engaged, and another fifteen involving 2,000–5,000 men. About half of all those who died of wounds sustained in action died in these battles. Montrose fought eight battles on Scottish soil in the mid-1640s; and there were seven pitched battles in Ireland. The difference was that in most English battles 5 per cent of the combatants were killed and 15 to 20 per cent were taken prisoner, in Scotland and Ireland 20 to 25 per cent were killed and no prisoners were taken.

However, the civil wars in England and Ireland (but not so much in Scotland) were as much wars of sieges as of open fighting. Over 100 of the 180 corporate towns of England endured sieges or storms of some sort. A majority of the English cathedral towns endured sieges of several weeks or months. In Ireland the proportions were almost certainly higher. Cromwell took twenty-eight towns in his nine-month campaign there in 1649–50; and across the 1640s many towns were taken (and sacked) six times or more. The fierce bursts of military activity on Scottish soil in 1644–5, 1648, and 1650–2 were campaigns of rapid movement and skirmishes with few casualties with only one battle (Dunbar) in the top twenty battles in terms of the number of combatants. It was one of Cromwell's greatest victories and it reminds us that the Covenanters proved capable of winning battles outside Scotland but usually of losing them on home soil.

It was a very regionally diverse war. Those living in Kent, or Suffolk or Cambridgeshire or parts of mid and west Wales saw little fighting, although they certainly knew there was a war going on. Wives saw their husbands march away to fight elsewhere, everyone paid relentlessly to sustain the war effort, and lived in constant expectation of 'invasion' from outside. Those who lived in the north-eastern counties saw little fighting but came to curse the war and the day the Scots entered England on the promise of regular pay from the English parliament. In the absence of any serious attempt to meet that obligation, the Scots were left to live ruthlessly and arbitrarily off the land. Those who lived in the valleys of the Severn, the Thames, or the Trent or in the Midlands plain, saw the worst of the fighting, the constant changes of control, the greatest brutality. Seven of the ten greatest battles of the first civil war were fought within fifteen miles of a straight line running from Taunton to Leicester. Similarly in Scotland, almost all the fighting in the years 1644–6 was in the oblong formed by Ayr, Mull, Inverness, and Aberdeen; whereas the fighting during the Cromwellian conquest focused on a similar oblong to the south of it—formed by Dunoon, Dundee, Dunbar and Ayr.

In Ireland, the war was more terrifying and unpredictable in its shape. There were only seven battles, mostly involving fewer than 5,000 men. For much of the time the 40,000 to 60,000 men in arms lay scattered amongst innumerable garrisons, until one of the many generals gathered together a force and swept through a region killing all that came into his path, but then losing their impetus once they settled garrisons in the newly occupied territory. There were concentrations of violence in 1642, 1647, and 1649–52 (the years in which all the battles fell), but much spasmodic killing in the intervals.

It will already be clear that the war was fought according to different rules in each kingdom. There were civilian massacres in England—but almost all in hot blood, as in Rupert's storms of Bolton and Leicester. There were few civilian massacres in cold blood and none involving more than a dozen deaths. Soldiers who surrendered after battles were usually spared and many sieges were concluded by treaties that respected the lives of soldiers and the lives and property of civilians. The worst massacres of soldiers in cold blood in England involved less than twenty men: 'war crimes did not become a policy, atrocities were individual and sporadic and reprisal was precariously maintained'.[8]

By contrast, killing in cold blood became an instrument of policy of all the armies in Ireland from the outset. When Robert Munro encountered his first Catholic rebels on 30 April 1642, he hanged all those whom he took prisoner. When he reached Newry, he reported that he had rounded up all the townsmen and interrogated them: 'the indifferent being severed from the bad whereof 60 with two priests were shot and hanged'.[9] It became the pattern for the years that followed. But then war in Ireland had for centuries been more brutal than war in England, and the massacres of Protestants in previous months only strengthened British resolve and Irish response. Self-righteousness strengthened the sinew. Cromwell's infamous slaughter of the garrisons of Drogheda and Wexford in September and October 1649 shows no more than that when he crossed the Irish Sea he adapted to Irish

[8] B. Donagan, 'Atrocity, War Crime, and Treason in the English Civil War', *American Historical Review*, 99 (1994), 1146.
[9] Cited by David Stevenson, *Scottish Covenanters and Irish Confederates: Scottish–Irish Relations in the Mid Seventeenth-Century* (Belfast, 1991), 106.

conditions. If anything, his failure to kill civilians in cold blood shows a kind of moderation. The war in Scotland fell somewhere between the extremes of England and Ireland, although Argyll routinely killed any prisoners he took to be Irish, and the death rate in Scottish battles was far higher than in England.

The progress of the war(s)

The fact that the 1640s witnessed a whole series of distinct but interlocking wars makes explaining its outcome especially difficult. The king had the better of the war in England to the autumn of 1643, assisted by unity of command and a clearer strategic objective—a squeeze on London from the north, the midlands, and the south. After that, greater depth of resources, and especially of credit, and greater administrative and military efficiency allowed parliament to grind the king and his supporters down. The Scots 'invasion' hastened the turnaround in 1644. But what if the king had won the *English* civil war? How would he have dealt with a hostile and self-righteous Scotland? And how would he have dealt with the Irish Confederates? He would presumably have been trapped into long, costly, and inconclusive spasms of warfare that could only have heightened insecurity in England. In the event Charles viewed all three kingdoms as caught up in one great war and he constantly sought to use the resources of each kingdom to assist him to regain control of all of them. The constant hope that he might persuade the Irish Confederates to send him a substantial Catholic army hobbled Ormond's attempts to reach a stronger military position from which to achieve an intra-Ireland settlement; and the knowledge that he was scheming for such an army cost Charles support in England. In Scotland, the king had to choose in 1644 between two strategies: to use highlanders and the Macdonnell sept (exiled by James VI from the Western Isles to Ireland) to launch what amounted to a clan war; or to appeal to that simple majority of the Scottish peers who had opposed the Solemn League and Covenant and encourage them to seize power from the minority of the nobles and serried ranks of radical lairds, townsmen, and clergy who had pushed it through (that is, the strategy he did adopt in 1648). As usual, he chose unwisely.

In 1643, the king had the better of the war in the north, the west, and the midlands of England, securing his position in all the main contested areas. His lord lieutenant in Ireland secured a truce with the Catholic Confederation of Kilkenny and that in turn allowed the king to bring back the English soldiers sent to Ireland in 1642 following the rebellion there. As the prospects of a royalist victory mounted, and as the Cessation in Ireland which exposed the Scottish army protecting the Scots of Ulster came under increased threat, the Scots entered the English war on the express understanding that there would be uniformity (not integration) in the doctrine, discipline, and forms of worship of the churches of Scotland, England, and Ireland.

In 1644, Charles lost the war in England. Marston Moor (2 July), fought between on one side the king's principal ('marching') army and his Northern Army under the marquis of Newcastle and on the other an allied army made up of the Scots and of Parliament's Northern and Eastern Armies, was a complete victory for the latter; and although the earl of Essex lost half an army when he became entombed in the Cornish peninsula, the news from most other theatres, especially in the midlands, was good. On 1 January 1644, each side occupied a comparable amount of the country. By 1 January 1645 parliament controlled two-thirds of it. Montrose and his Irish allies had won a spectacular series of six engagements against the Campbells and their allies. At his height, Montrose and his allies controlled all the land to the north of the Tay; but neither interest nor inclination would make them break free of the highland line. In Ireland, a sullen peace periodically broke down into skirmishing and atrocity; but with the Confederates in control of four-fifths of the island, nothing much changed.

In 1645, the reorganized parliamentarian army—the New Model—ground its way to victory in the midlands, and across the southern and western counties. By the end of the year the king had effective control only of a tongue of territory along the Thames from Oxford, parts of Wales and the Marches, and a number of strongly held towns (Chester, Newark, etc.) all under tight siege. Montrose's string of victories was abruptly ended by one stunning defeat; and sullen peace persisted in Ireland. By the spring of 1646 the war was over in England, and the attention of the victors began to turn to Ireland. The crushing defeat of the Scots by O'Neill at the battle of Benburb in Tyrone in June focused the mind; the Confederates were at war with one another, but still occupied 80 per cent of the island; the rebellion was unavenged and the adventurers were lobbying for the millions of acres they had been promised if they lent money for the reconquest.

The year 1647 saw political storms in England and Scotland, and the army's refusal to disband without both a general settlement and a particular settlement of its own claims for arrears, a comprehensive and effective indemnity. And the Protestant settlers in Ireland, together with the Scots and a smaller and rather ineffectual army from England, began to resume offensive warfare against the Confederation.

In 1648, Charles tried once more to use the resources of all three kingdoms to have himself restored. There was a series of regional rebellions in England, in which those who had fought in the first war joined with former parliamentarians disillusioned with the political oppression and religious anarchy promoted by the Long Parliament under pressure from the army. These rebellions culminated in battles and skirmishes across eastern and south-eastern England, south Wales, and the midlands and major siege operations at Colchester, Pembroke, and in Yorkshire; and there was an 'invasion' by the 'Engaged' Scots which was decisively defeated at the battle of Preston. In Ireland it was a year of tetchy negotiation, as those who saw their own long-term security only if Charles was restored in England sought to create a rainbow coalition of Old Irish and Old English Catholics and Protestants. But their efforts were hampered by the hard-line demands of the nuncio, who at one point excommunicated most of the Supreme Council of the Confederation. It was a divided and weakened native population which confronted the Protestant God's avenging swordsmen a year later.

Regicide and the foundation of the English and Irish Commonwealth

The execution of Charles I on 30 January 1649 was an English event with archipelagic consequences. There was no pressure for regicide in Scotland and Ireland and the English army officers, with the scattering of civilian supporters they enlisted, showed no interest in notifying—let alone consulting—anyone in Charles's other kingdoms before they put him on trial and decapitated him.

The regicide was driven forward by a conviction that, by restarting the civil war in 1648, the king had committed sacrilege, had sought to overturn the judgment that God had so clearly delivered in the First War of 1642–6. He was a 'Man of Blood'[10] who had spilt the innocent blood of God's people, a man whom God would call to account, and at human hands. But the regicide was not a *republican* act. The documents that built up the case for regicide criticized Charles I and his eldest son, but not the office nor the family; and there is strong evidence that until the very last minute the army leaders hoped to persuade Charles to abdicate in favour of one of his younger sons. It is not that they thought him unworthy of death; rather, they were appalled at the prospect of making regicide stick. They clearly anticipated massive English, archipelagic, and international outrage and envisaged having to face overwhelming military reprisals. And it was to limit the scale of this disaster that the Rump Parliament made a stunning offer to the Scots in the immediate wake of regicide. It abolished monarchy in England and Ireland *but not in Scotland*. The union of the crowns was portrayed as a disaster for both peoples, and the Scots were encouraged to resume their independence as a people and a polity, free to remain as a separate kingdom to the north of the Commonwealth of England and Ireland. It was an offer completely spurned by the entire Scottish political establishment. Parliament proclaimed Charles II as king of Britain and Ireland and they spent much of the next five years trying to restore him to all his kingdoms. They were bound in a Covenant with God that they could not unilaterally abrogate; and the Covenant was a British and Irish and not just a Scottish document, with obligations relating to all of Britain and Ireland.

The pronouncements of those who urged or carried out the regicide and who then carried out the abolition of the monarchy

---

[10] A reference to Numbers 35: 33. See also P. Crawford, 'Charles I, That Man of Blood', *Journal of British Studies*, 16 (1977), 41–61.

after weeks of agonizing are largely free of the language of republicanism. That language would be afterwards used by some of the propagandists for the regime that had replaced Charles, but that is another matter. Whatever the chattering classes thought in the later 1640s, the men of action did not intend or want to replace monarchy as well as Charles I. The establishment of a kingless commonwealth was a bolt out of the blue. The Scots commissioners in London sent a series of briefing documents back to Edinburgh. They were unambiguous that the Rump intended to try Charles I and might execute him. The best they could do for him was play for time, and that they certainly tried to do.

But these same commissioners in their thorough briefings did not warn the Estates to expect the abolition of monarchy. Argyll and his friends were bracing themselves for a decision of even greater difficulty for them: what to do if and when the English parliament broke the hereditary succession and tried to impose one of Charles's younger sons on the throne. They prepared an oath to bind all of Scotland to the prince of Scotland (as they termed Prince Charles). They were anticipating the crisis of 1701–7. Yet the Scots had miscalculated. Because Charles would not abdicate, he had to be executed. And because he was executed he could not be replaced, for the sheer scale of what it would take to meet the anticipated reaction forbade it. The establishment of a free Commonwealth was a poor second best to the replacement of an inflexible adult king with his consent by a pliable child king. And the dream of a monarchical restoration stayed with that clear majority of defeated royalists and demoralized presbyterian-parliamentarians that remained loyal to the House of Stuart, but also amongst that pragmatic minority of defeated royalists, marginalized political presbyterians, and time-serving lawyers, and even elements in the army, who worked in and under every regime of the 1650s, and who sought to restore monarchy in the House of Cromwell.

Republican responses to regicide

But if regicide was a minority English choice with no resonance elsewhere in Charles I's state system, and if regicide came to carry as a consequence what could be called an unsought 'strong republicanism' (i.e. a renunciation of the title and office of king), then it led on to a much wider exploration throughout the polity of what could be called 'weak republicanism'. This is not the same thing as civic republicanism, that admiration of the superior example of just government afforded by a study of the political ideas of antiquity and the Renaissance, but a radical constitutionalism that saw liberty itself as consisting in a body believing itself to be mandated by God to speak for a free people and to decide what powers it was prudent to confer on a king, and who should be permitted to exercise those powers and under what sanctions. These radical constitutionalists who were willing to suspend monarchy until all those conditions were met. In that sense, the islands were full of 'weak republican' noises between 1647 and 1660.[11]

It is of course true that as soon as the Scottish parliament heard that the English had executed their king, they unanimously proclaimed Charles II as 'the righteous air [heir] and Lawfull successor' to the Kingdoms of 'Britain, France and Ireland by the providence of God and by the Lawfull right of undoubted succession and descent'. But in a less quoted passage, they went on to say that

because his Majesty is bound by the law of God and fundamentall lawis of this kingdome to rule in righteousness and equitie … it is heereby declared that before he can be admitted to the exercise of his royall dignitie he shall give satisfactioun to this kingdome in those things that concerne the security of religioun, the union betwix the kingdomes and the good and peace of his [various] kingdomes according to the solemn league and covenant.[12]

And to ram that point home, two days later on 7 February 1649 An Act anent securing of Religion and peace of the kingdom changed the coronation oath and exacted other guarantees that the king would establish both true religion and the constitutional forms of a

[11] For a range of views on this, see David Norbrook, *Writing the English Republic 1627–1660* (Cambridge, 1999); S. Barber, *Regicide and Republicanism 1646–1659* (Edinburgh, 1998); B. Worden, 'English Republicanism', in J. Burns and M. Goldie (eds.), *The Cambridge History of Political Thought, iii. 1450–1700* (Cambridge, 1991), 453–85.

[12] *Acts of the Parliament of Scotland*, ed. T. Thomson and C. Innes (Edinburgh, 1814–75), vi. 363.

confederated monarchy. Until such time as these guarantees were forthcoming he was suspended from the exercise of the authority. By Scottish constitutional theory in 1649 Charles II had a right to a royal title but not a royal office. This position united the Covenanters in 1649, but determining what represented adequate guarantees was to divide them absolutely and irreconcilably over the following fifteen months, leading to the emergence of the Resolutioners who were willing to take Charles II's promises of compliance at face value, and the Remonstrants who were not.

This might be thought a particularly weak kind of weak republicanism. But if we are going to extend the definition beyond a commitment to kinglessness, it is difficult to draw a line short of this. And if we disallow this, then we must disallow almost all that we normally call Leveller or Army republicanism in England. Harder forms of republicanism did emerge in Scotland; but only under the intense pressure of royal betrayal and the military conquest and absorption into a greater England.

And the same is true of Ireland. The Confederates were willing to proclaim their personal loyalty to Charles II and to the House of Stuart and to the Union of Britain and Ireland, but not unconditionally. He was their king, but they would not allow him to exercise any power over them or make any demands for military or financial assistance from them until he had bound himself unconditionally to their vision of an Irish constitutionalism that guaranteed the independence and autonomy of an Irish parliament, what they chose to decide was the ancient and self-contained constitutionalism of the Irish people, and the full civil and religious equality of the Catholic majority with the Protestant majority. The only exceptions were to be found in Ulster. The case of the disloyalty of the Macdonnells in 1649—their willingness to save their own necks and their estates by disowning the Stuarts and making an expedient alliance with the Cromwellians—had nothing to do with any kind of reflective or principled republicanism, strong, weak, or indifferent. It was a means of escaping the consequences of anarchy and ruin. But it is possible that the O'Neills of Ulster drew—just as Cromwell did—on biblical stories and types to reconfigure the constitutional landscape. In the case of the O'Neills it was the story of Judas Maccabeus. The story relates to the second century BC when Judah was a semi-autonomous part of the Syrian Empire but subject to increasing harassment as the Syrians tried to tax it ever more thoroughly, to integrate it into the Seleucid state, and as the heathen king Antiochus sought to 'compel the Jews to forsake the laws of their ancestors and no longer to live the laws of God and to pollute the Temple'. Antiochus was opposed by Judas Maccabeus and his brothers who came to take the role of chief magistrates on the model of the Judges of Israel who had preceded those kings and who were popularly elected by a free people. The application of this case to the circumstances of early modern Ireland did not overtax the bards associated with Owen Roe; and an embryonic case for Maccabean rule was developed. In the event, the English conquest of Ireland and the death of Owen Roe aborted this development.[13]

The regicide was an entirely English event; but the spread of varieties of weak republicanism was pan-archipelagic. And it controlled the events of the next eleven years. It took Oliver Cromwell to Ireland to execute 'the righteous judgement of God upon these barbarous wretches who have imbrued their hands in so much innocent blood'.[14] It took him to Scotland as the reluctant conqueror of a godly nation badly led by those as drunk with self-righteousness, he told them, as other men were with power and he beseeched them 'in the bowels of Christ' to desist their support for a British king.[15] It led him to dissolve the Rump of the Long Parliament in April 1653 for failing to introduce those godly measures that would turn a people freed from the tyranny of king and bishops from the things of the flesh to the things of the spirit; and it led him thereafter reluctantly to take power as Lord Protector (as a 'good constable set to keep the peace of the parish'[16]), an office which came increasingly to resemble that of a constitutional monarchy bound by the restrictions envisaged by the nineteen Propositions of 1642 or the Heads of Proposals, the document Cromwell had urged on Charles I in the army's private treaty with him in 1647. His death dissolved such bonds as held together the fragile coalition of liberal landowners and army grandees. As

---

[13] J. Casway, 'Gaelic Maccabeanism', in J. Ohlmeyer (ed.), *Political Thought in Seventeenth-Century Ireland* (Cambridge, 2000), 176–90.

[14] *Letters and Speeches of Oliver Cromwell*, ed. T. Carlyle (rev. S. Lomas, 3 vols. 1904), i, letter 105.

[15] Ibid. ii, letter 136.   [16] Ibid. iii. 63 (speech XI).

Cromwell's son and designated heir leaned towards the former, the latter staged a coup and restored the Commonwealth. They then fell out fatally with one another and real anarchy ensued until the faction under George Monck, an English soldier who had served with the royalist forces in Ireland in the 1640s and the Cromwellian army of occupation in Scotland in the 1650s, called a halt by calling for 'free elections' that led to the near-unanimous proclamation of Charles II as king of Britain and Ireland.

Regicide did not, then, lead to a stable republic. But it did lead on to very different social consequences in each of the former kingdoms.

Revolutionary consequences

Regicide did not lead to social revolution in England. In February 1649 the house of lords was swept away, and on 19 March an Act of parliament confirmed it. Apart from abolishing the house of lords, however, and such privileges as derived from membership of parliament, it did nothing to challenge the power, authority, or honour of the peerage. Indeed the Act was at pains to confirm that peers who 'demeaned themselves with honour, courage and fidelity' to the Commonwealth should be admitted to the public counsels of the nation—such as membership of the Council of State, and should be eligible for election to parliament.[17]

The peers lost their prominence in national and local affairs, though more through their own reticence than the determination of successive regimes to keep them out of power. There were peers on most commissions of the peace from 1652, and on many militia and assessments committees. A great majority of the nominations to parish livings made by peers were approved by the Triers. Ten per cent of the peers lost more than 20 per cent of their manors by confiscation and sale, but only two became insolvent. And more than a third had incomes in the later 1650s greater than those of the 1630s. Skilful manipulation of the mortgage market and debt management had pulled most of them round.

---

[17] Gardiner, *Constitutional Documents*, 387–8.

The same is almost certainly true of the gentry. Of the 20,000 gentry families 4,000 had estates sequestered because of the royalist activism of their heads. Sixty per cent of them regained their estates on payment of fines equivalent to the provision of a dowry, 20 per cent paid heavier fines, and 20 per cent failed to compound or were forbidden to compound, and had to repurchase their estates through agents. Many of those agents were friends and relations, however, who made no charge for their brokerage and could often purchase the estates on the cheap. A spectacular example of this was Major-General John Lambert, who purchased and acted as a trustee for his relatives (including his Catholic relatives) in Yorkshire. In these circumstances, the total proportion of all noble and gentry land transferred away over the 1640s and 1650s is unlikely to have reached 10 per cent.

The monarchy was abolished but not much else changed administratively. It is true that these are important years in the history of state formation since all the forms of taxation that were to sustain the British state in its great period of external expansion were introduced in these decades—above all the Assessment, a quota land tax, and the Excise. And the visibility of the army—albeit much exaggerated by most historians covering the 1650s—and the development of the navy and of the bureaucratic departments to administer them was greater than ever before and a new and permanent reality. All this transformed the capacity of the English state to realize levels of taxation appropriate for that state to compete as a principal in international war. The sinews of power that historians have suggested developed in the wars of William and Marlborough were in fact a legacy of the 1640s and 1650s. But otherwise things really do look increasingly familiar with every year that passes. The courts may have become a bit more user-friendly, but the structure and substance of the judicial system was unaffected in Westminster Hall and in the localities. Assizes and quarter sessions were fully restored as the great clearing house of local judicial and administrative business. It is also possible that grand juries, representing the body of freeholders and that group of landholders who straddled the yeomanry and parish gentry, may have become more assertive and secured a greater initiative in local affairs. But with the exchequer back in charge of collecting and auditing the revenues of the state, and with the registration and confirmation of all state documents passing through a sequence of seals that owed everything to Thomas Cromwell and nothing to Oliver Cromwell, Interregnum government resembled not a new beast with many heads but the all too lively ghost of the old regime with its head tucked beneath its arm.

As local studies of the Interregnum have proliferated, it has become clearer than ever that it saw not a breaking of the power of the gentry but a shift of power within the gentry. And as the 1650s progressed, there was a drift back since the proscription on convicted royalists from holding office did not extend to their sons. Perhaps 10 per cent of powerless men and women dreamt unheard-of dreams in the 1650s and dozens of them put them on paper. But none of them were realized.

The contrast with Scotland and Ireland is stark. In Scotland there was no house of lords to abolish. Within three years of the regicide, the Scottish parliament itself was abolished, and the Scottish people offered 30 seats in the 460-seat enhanced English parliament. In the time left to it, however, the unicameral Scottish parliament had shown itself as vigorous and radical in its social policies as the Rump was cautious and hesitant. By the Act of Classes, a much greater proportion of the Scottish elite—at least 80 per cent of the nobility and 60–70 per cent of the lairds—was proscribed from public life, reducing the number of nobles attending the parliament to about twelve in a body whose median attendance was around 120. There was a working majority of burgh commissioners, those least open to noble persuasion. Indeed it is quite clear that a large majority of the members of the Scottish Parliament and the Scottish estates in 1649–51 took their instructions from their presbyteries and synods. The moral authority of the ministers over the lay commissioners peaked in 1649, and a series of major moral reformation measures were rushed through, In February 1649 alone, there were Acts anent swearing, drunkenness, scolding and other pious uses, an Act anent clandestine marriages, an Act anent scandalous persons, an Act anent molifications [sic] and dotations [sic] to hospitals, an Act anent the poor, an Act anent worshippers of false gods, and a short terse no-nonsense Act against the crime of blasphemy, which imposed death on anyone who should 'rail upon or curse God or any of the persons of the blessed Trinity [or] who obstinately deny the Trinity'. This is more of a legislative revolution in the reformation of manners than was accomplished in England by all the parliaments of the 1650s put together. But perhaps the most dramatic Act of those early months was the one that abolished lay patronage rights in the church outright and without compensation. This promised to signal the end (at least for a decade) of lay control over kirks and kirk sessions; and it also signalled a decade during which the nobility sank far lower in Scotland than in the rest of Britain.[18] The Protectoral Act of Union completed what populist Covenanting set out to achieve in 1649. That Act was a calculated attempt to create a sturdy prosperous yeomanry in the Scottish countryside that would look to England with gratitude for the past and hope for the future. First, all tenancies were converted by the Act into secure and alienable holdings on fixed and immovable rents, without any additional service over and above that fixed cash rent; and secondly, all 'superiorities, lordships and jurisdictions' were abolished, taken off, discharged. The economic and judicial control of the nobility was broken and commissioners of the peace appointed by and answerable to the English administration in Edinburgh were substituted. Shrievalties, too, were reformed and to be held jointly by a Scottish laird and an English garrison commander. There was more aspiration than achievement in all this; but there was no backtracking on it during the Interregnum, and given a generation to bed itself down, there is every reason to think it would have worked. In Scotland much more than in England, regicide led on to a fundamental refashioning of political institutions at all levels and to significant shifts in the social distribution of wealth and power.[19]

There was a terrifying and unreversed revolution in Ireland. The Cromwellian Conquest, and more especially the events that flowed from it, represent perhaps the greatest exercise in ethnic cleansing in early modern Europe. It was, notoriously, the aim of the Rump and of its Council to dispossess all property-holders in twenty-five of the thirty-two counties of Ireland and to herd them into the west, or into exile and transportation. That proved

---

[18] *Acts of the Parliament of Scotland*, vi. 368–70, 383, 389–90, 399, 408–9, 411–13; J. R Young, *The Scottish Parliament 1603–1707* (Edinburgh, 1996), 216–32; D. Stevenson, *Revolution and Counter-Revolution, 1644–1651* (London, 1977), 234–45.

[19] Gardiner, *Constitutional Documents*, 418–22.

beyond the political will and the administrative competence of the English Commonwealth. Oddly, its sense of a moral obligation to distinguish the handful of sheep from the huge herd of goats was its undoing. In the midst of the fury to avenge the massacres of 1641–2, it was determined to keep up a semblance of the rule of law. Nonetheless the Act of Settlement of August 1652 is a chilling document. It states that 'it is not the intention of the Parliament to extirpate that whole nation, but that mercy and pardon, both as to life and estate, may be extended to all husbandmen, ploughmen, labourers, artificers and others of the inferior sort'. Few able to read this document could take much comfort from that. It then rammed the point home: 'and that others of higher rank and quality may know the Parliament's intention concerning them, according to the *respective demerits* and considerations under which they fall'. It treats all but the New English as 'persons of the Irish nation' thus anticipating the fusion of Gaelic Irish, Old English, and Pale Nicodemians in their own self-perception as 'Irish'. In the ensuing list of those attainted of life and property the 'O's and the 'Macs' are intermingled higgledy-piggledy with the Butlers, the Burkes, and the Fitzes.[20] In the event the first part of the English plan, the systematic destruction of the Catholic elite, was carried out to the extent that about 40 per cent of the land mass of Ireland changed hands from men born in Ireland to Protestants born in England, resulting in a drop in Catholic and Old English Protestant share in the land from 58 per cent to 15 per cent (a figure that returned to 22 per cent by 1664, before falling to 10 per cent by the century's end). Now this was a fundamental shift in the social, cultural, and economic distribution of wealth and power. The new owners were some 12,000 British soldiers who got over 60 per cent of the confiscated land as payment for their act of conquest, and the several hundred adventurers—gentry, lawyers, and merchants who had invested in the army sent during 1642 to Ireland to protect the British settlers and avenge the massacres. Most of the latter became a significant absentee interest.

The 1650s also ushered in a revolution in the constitutional relationships *between* the component parts of the British Isles. It is

[20] Ibid. 394–400.

a paradox that the English who were least interested in changing the patterns of constitutional relationship were the ones who ended up achieving a dramatic and remarkable change. In Ireland as in Scotland, the characteristic institutions of the semi-autonomous Irish kingdom within the Stuart state system were systematically bulldozed by the English conquerors. It led to the most complete integration of Britain and Ireland there has ever been: from 1654–9 one head of state (Oliver Cromwell as Lord Protector), one central executive council with regional administrative councils in Ireland and Scotland, one parliament (which was to meet for a minimum of five months every third year: and which in the event met in 1654/5, 1656/7, 1658, and 1659), a drive towards uniformity of legal process and substantive law, a religious settlement based upon principles of a Calvinist pluralism and equal access to public life and office for almost every Protestant, and a formal proscription of Catholic worship and access to public life for professed papists.

Conclusion

During the mid-seventeenth century, the peoples of Scotland and Ireland experienced a much more fundamental shift in the social and cultural distribution of power than did the people of England and Wales, and a much greater transformation of their civil and ecclesiastical institutions. In the case of England there was never any question of a revolution in the modern sense and at the Restoration a weakened crown found itself unable to do other than reward and rely upon men of the same families and at the apex of the same social order as in the previous century. The mid-century troubles dealt a grievous blow to the prospects for executive tyranny, but did little to impede the growth of legislative tyranny within the British context, while returning control of the legislature to those at the apex of the old social order. The confessional state suffered a grievous wound, but for two more centuries the established church, and those at the apex of the old social order who controlled that church, maintained a stranglehold on public office. In Scotland there was a real prospect of an irreversible shift in wealth and power, but the Restoration came in time to stymie that shift. It took contingencies separate from the concerns of this chapter to undo the old social and ecclesiastical order in Scotland. In Ireland there *was* an irreversible shift in the social and cultural distribution of wealth and power, and the creation of what had not really existed before 1641, a powerful and vocal absentee colonial interest, together with a transformed religious configuration, in which a particular form of Catholicism and Catholic culture—that of the Counter-Reformation—had (not wholly predictably) triumphed over one that owed more to Celtic Christianity, a religious culture shared by the 80 per cent of the population who owned 20 per cent of the land and wealth, and which rubbed against a fractured and antagonistic Protestantism in uneasy relationship with the host forms back in Britain.

Figure 5 Charles I and Charles II.

4

Restoration or Initiation?

Toby Barnard

Three kingdoms, one king

In 1684, John Wilson, lately recorder of the city of Derry in the north of Ireland, published a *Discourse of Monarchy*. Numerous others in an access of loyalty to Charles II wrote on the same topic. Wilson, however, differed from most in treating 'of the imperial crowns of England, Scotland and Ireland'. As an English lawyer, advanced to act as the chief legal adviser in an Irish corporation riven by confessional and ethnic rivalries, he saw the Stuarts' problems from an unusual perspective. The multinational monarchy over which Charles II had presided since 1660 was threatening to break apart. In the Ulster stronghold of Derry over the course of the seventeenth century, Irish Catholics had been replaced systematically with settlers from England and Scotland. The latter, so far from obeying the distant government, defied it. Already, in 1672, the Protestant bishop of Derry, like Wilson an Englishman rewarded for his royalism by this hazardous placement, cantered back to Dublin when confronted with the intransigence of the Presbyterian townspeople of Derry. Later, in 1679, Wilson reported how the local governors had rejoiced at the news of the murder in Scotland by Presbyterian militants of the archbishop of St Andrews. The plantation of Ulster, undertaken to strengthen the Stuart state, had instead nurtured a British sport, resistant alike to the norms of lowland England and the injunctions from Dublin and Edinburgh.

In the remote eyrie of Derry, Recorder Wilson encountered a peculiarly intractable problem. It might seem so unlike and distant from the challenges which Charles II faced in London, Edinburgh, and Dublin as to be an irrelevance. Yet the northern port was integral to the Stuart monarchy. Indeed, the behaviour of Derry's inhabitants within a few years of Charles's death was felt to have helped to decide the fate of the three kingdoms. Accordingly, the success or failure of the restored Stuart regime hinged as much on what was achieved in such outposts as on the responses of metropolitan England. The extent and variety of the Stuarts' realms presented such multifarious problems that no single policy was likely to solve them. Wilson appreciated this. The apparent amity between England, Ireland, Scotland, and Wales since the king's restoration should not deceive as to the inherently awkward and unequal relationships between the several parts. As Wilson reminded, first Scotland and then Ireland had contributed to the outbreak and outcome of the civil wars. Each country was then conquered by and subjugated to England. After these bruising entanglements, Charles II, his ministers, and the incumbent elites in Ireland and Scotland were content to let government in the three kingdoms return to customary and usually separate channels. But between 1678 and 1681, tranquillity was threatened anew. Three English parliaments, convened in swift sequence, had sought to pinion the monarch and to divert the succession away from the heir presumptive, the king's Catholic brother, James, duke of Albany and York. In their campaign, English politicians enlisted Irish and Scottish evidence of past misdeeds, present authoritarianism, and future dangers. Yet the king's opponents, in seeking to limit royal power and perhaps alter the succession, hardly consulted opinion in the other two kingdoms.

In Ireland, indeed, it was reasonable to suppose that the bulk of its people—at least 75 per cent of whom were Roman Catholics—looked forward to the eventual accession of a monarch of their own faith. When this occurred, in 1685, James II was the first ruler since Mary I (1553–8) to share the Catholicism of the Irish. In Scotland, whither James had retreated while the controversy over his rights raged in England, he ingratiated himself with many influential locals. In 1681, James as the king's high commissioner had presided over a meeting of the Scots parliament which had resoundingly endorsed him as monarch in waiting. Moreover, thanks to his sparkling court in a rebuilt Holyroodhouse, he transformed the Scots' long-standing affection for their own dynasty, the Stuarts, into a personal following. As Wilson implied, the Scots, no more than the majority of the Irish, would lightly set aside the legitimate heir to their crown simply to truckle to the English. The ominous possibility that Ireland and/or Scotland might opt for a different ruler from England and Wales had been briefly raised. With the defeat of any scheme to exclude James from his monarchical inheritance, this alarming genie was conjured back into its bottle. Yet it reminded of the variations in political and confessional cultures within and between the component territories of the British Isles and Ireland. Throughout this period, only the person of the monarch was common to all.

In so far as this was the message in John Wilson's treatise, he introduced one theme in the discordant history of 1660 to 1688. In dealing with his three kingdoms, Charles II backed away from the integrative and unitary approach of his father. Even more brusquely, the restored monarchy repudiated the unpopular unionism of the 1640s and 1650s, when Scotland and Ireland had been tacked onto the commonwealth or free state of England and Wales. Only momentarily in 1669–70 did hopes of aiding Scotland's ailing economy put union on an official agenda. Lack of interest quickly killed the project. After 1685, the restless projector, Sir William Petty, enriched as an architect of Ireland's resettlement under Protestant ownership but mortified by his lack of political leverage, badgered an apparently receptive James II with schemes for union. Petty's plan, utopian and impracticable as only the very clever could make it, appealed to no one but himself. Exchanges of peoples between the distinct territories harked back to the enforced transplantations in Ireland earlier in the century. Inappropriate to the time, they were beyond the resources of the state to achieve. Legal union with common institutions, such as a parliament for all three kingdoms, was never seriously contemplated.

Later Stuart administrators discerned the truth that the cases of Ireland and Scotland were not the same. Scotland, in consequence, was left as an independent entity. Locals were identified who undertook to keep the place outwardly placid. Mostly peers—Cassilis,

Crawford, Glencairn, Lauderdale, Middleton, Rothes, and Tweed-dale—all but Middleton, an old soldier, had once sided with the Covenanters against the Stuarts. So long as the Scots stayed quiet, those to whom authority had been devolved were little troubled by English meddlers. They wrestled amongst themselves for local supremacy. By 1663, Lauderdale had insinuated himself so deep into the king's good graces that he could be regarded in practice if not in title as the viceroy of Scotland. Since Lauderdale's pre-eminence depended on his secure base at the English court, he remained vulnerable in Scotland. There he entered into a variety of alliances. His policies were trimmed to the prevailing winds. So he tacked between indulgence and repression. Throughout much of the 1670s the latter predominated. It made Lauderdale hated, but he retained a share of power until 1681.

Ireland, a constitutional dependency of the English crown, was drawn closer to England. In the treatment of Ireland, public interest and private profit had long converged. From the sixteenth century, property and power were transferred from unreliable Catholics to docile Protestants. Many of the latter were imported into Ireland from elsewhere. The pace of these transformations quickened after the Irish were beaten. By 1652, much land and many offices were available for opportunist English, Scots, and Welsh to grab. Ireland as an ample cornucopia from which to glut the hungry in other countries had long beguiled English monarchs, their ministers, and ingenious projectors. It bewitched Charles II. Motley courtiers, sufferers, creditors, and toadies were recompensed from Ireland. Several high in the restored administration—James, duke of York, Sir Henry Bennet, earl of Arlington and secretary of state, and the king's mistress, Barbara Villiers, Lady Castlemaine—acquired stakes in Ireland and with them a reason to interfere in its affairs. Furthermore, it had long been an axiom of English policy that only by staffing government, the judiciary, and the church in Ireland with Protestant immigrants would it be brought to heel. So the deserving, ambitious, and venal were inserted into *ad hoc* commissions in Dublin, the customs, and onto the judicial and episcopal benches. Simultaneously, newcomers colonized the estates confiscated from the rebellious Irish Catholics. By 1670, when the latest stage in this complex process ended, about 7,500 fresh proprietors were registered. This was fewer by far than the

35,000 envisaged by the Cromwellians. Nevertheless, it represented an upheaval in proprietorship without parallel in the Stuarts' other nations. These changes in land ownership were merely the most striking of the measures by which Ireland was subjected ever more rigorously to England. The importance to the English (and Welsh) of Irish offices, manpower, and money led the lords of the Treasury, the War Office, and Admiralty in the early 1680s (as well as the king and his ministers) to tighten their grip on Irish operations. Ireland, more populous and prosperous than Scotland, promised greater dividends.

An interest in annexing the island more firmly to the Stuarts' schemes suggested that by the 1680s there was some grand design into which these separate countries could be fitted. What exactly these ambitions were is far from clear. Some attribute to Charles II and, more strongly, to James II a wish to rule untrammelled by captious parliaments. Opportunities to free themselves from parliamentary fetters beckoned after 1681. It was unlikely, however, that either monarch, whatever his temperamental inclinations, possessed the means, even with the supplement of a loyal Scotland or friendly Ireland, to be absolute rulers. The cosmopolitan Stuarts, after 1681 unconstrained by bigoted MPs, can be portrayed as embarking in earnest on the more conciliatory courses from which Charles had been diverted by his first, intolerant parliament in the 1660s. A consideration of what was afoot in the 1680s brings out the awkwardness of treating all three kingdoms and Wales as a monolith. It suggests, too, that this decade introduced new issues. The chief was the accession of a Catholic to the throne of four dominions and the unexpected birth in 1688 of a legitimate heir likely to perpetuate James's Catholicizing programme. All the Stuarts' realms, other than Ireland, contained only puny Catholic populations and pulsed with fierce anti-Catholic prejudices.

Forgiveness and vengeance

The sequence which culminated in Charles II's jubilant re-entry into London on 20 May 1660 could be traced back to his northern kingdom. George Monck had governed Scotland for Cromwell.

There he had suppressed stirrings on behalf of Charles Stuart. Once Cromwell was dead, Monck watched with misgiving the shifts to preserve order. At length, alarmed by the knots of radicals and soldiers running the three countries, on 1 January 1660 he moved his army south. From the environs of London he threw this formidable weight behind first the return of the parliament dispersed in 1653 and then the election of a Convention, which assembled at Westminster on 25 April 1660. This was the latest incident of a series, in which, since 1647, the army had interposed in politics. Monck had left Scotland behind; his soldiers were mainly English. Yet inevitably he retained agents and contacts there, through whom he could coordinate actions in Edinburgh and London. Earlier in his career, Monck had soldiered in Ireland, and now stayed in touch with what the Irish Protestants were doing.

In each country, there was an overriding need to guarantee the basics of government. Taxes had to be collected and order maintained. Behind these immediate tasks, the knotty question of the future shape of government remained. In Ireland, an elected convention, of between 138 and 158—all Protestants—was to gather in Dublin for 25 February. This initiative, in advance of those in London or Edinburgh, raised English fears that Ireland might reassert its independence or be the first to invite back Charles. In the event, the headstrong in Dublin were persuaded to wait until England led. The cautious feared that any unilateral action by either Ireland or Scotland would jeopardize a peaceful settlement and again invite retribution from a more powerful England. But, in deciding how best to settle the three nations, the Convention at Westminster was disunited. Veterans from the parliament of the 1640s hesitated over the terms on which a king should be recalled. They hankered after the conditions with which they had hoped to hobble the errant Charles I during the 1640s. In contrast, the numerous novices elected to the English Convention remembered little of the unhappy dealings with the previous monarch but much about the exorbitancies of the usurpers in the 1650s. The hesitant were shouldered aside.

Doubts, in any case, had been allayed by the skilful declaration of intent which had been issued in Charles's name at Breda on 4 April. It took time for its implications to be gauged. Only on

11 May, for example, did the Protestant corporation of Dublin effusively thank the king for this promised generosity. On the same day, the southern port of Kinsale had also received copies of the Declaration. By then, events had accelerated so quickly that the newly loyal in Protestant Ireland were in danger of lagging at the rear of the well-wishers. It took time for news to travel from London to Edinburgh or Dublin. Although the interested in Ireland and Scotland had independent means to learn of what was doing in the king's entourage, the propensity was to wait on events in England. On 1 May, the English Convention had voted that government henceforward should be 'by King, Lords and Commons'. On 8 May, Charles was proclaimed king. Scotland kept in step. On the same day, a similar proclamation was read in Edinburgh. Only on 14 May did Dublin echo as Charles was acclaimed. This done, the notables from these provisional governments and the recent Cromwellian order jostled for passages to England and competed for fast mounts to carry them to London. They knew that others, untainted by collaboration with the usurpers, steadfast exiles or earlier converts to the Stuart flag, were better positioned.

The Irish who now turned to Charles were wary of his lord lieutenant from the 1640s, James Butler, marquess of Ormond, who had never been far from the king throughout the 1650s. More threatening still to the interests of those who had worked with the Cromwellians was the presence about the exiled court of members of the families which had been expropriated in the last decade. Daniel O'Neill, Theobald Taaffe, Richard and Peter Talbot not only looked set to prosper under the returning monarchy, but to hoist their kindred and perhaps the entire Irish Catholic political community to prominence. Behind these threats lurked a yet larger one. These intimates might prompt Charles to undo the recent redistributions of power and property. The Interregnum had seen the Catholic share of land dwindle from 59 per cent to 22 per cent. Catholic worship had been banned, and priests and monks exiled when they had not already been killed. Government and office were now monopolized by Protestants. All these policies—and with them the continuance of a Protestant Ireland—seemed vulnerable under a king temperamentally attracted to a more inclusive approach and grateful to the Irish Catholics for their support. Irish Protestants, as they hastened to London, sensed that they would have a protracted fight to hold on to power and property. Others from England, Wales, and Scotland, equally tardy in taking their places in the queue to do homage to Charles, awaited their fates.

Here, at least, Charles adhered to what had been enunciated at Breda. Like Cromwell before him in the 1650s, the king wanted to base his regime as broadly as possible. Also, a witch-hunt against the activists of the Interregnum could only perpetuate animosities and so unsettle. Reconciliation was to be the motto. In so far as he could, Charles set an example. Only thirty-three were excepted from pardon. Eleven of these would be tried and executed. In symbolic retribution, the remains of Cromwell and other close associates were disinterred and strung up at Tyburn. In Scotland, three ringleaders from the Covenanting era, Argyll, Johnston of Wariston, and the Revd James Guthrie, were similarly treated. Drawn from the three groups that had attacked the Stuart monarchy in the later 1630s—the nobility, the covenanting lairds, and the obdurate Presbyterian ministers—the trio made apt sacrifices. These ghoulish rituals vented the hatreds and frustrations which had festered during the 1650s. Unfortunately they did not slake the thirst for retribution. Many among Charles's diehards lacked his lofty disengagement. Expecting recompense for what they had lost and endured during long years of fighting, dispossession, and seclusion, they were disappointed with the often meagre rewards. The aggrieved ignored the king's injunctions. Instead they settled old scores. They carried their vengeful attitudes into the parliaments which were elected in 1661 and (in England and Wales) into their work as lords lieutenant, deputy lieutenants, magistrates, and special commissioners. Empowered by statutes like the Corporation Act (1661), the Militia Acts (1661 and 1662), and those against religious nonconformity (between 1662 and 1670), and by their commissions as justices of the peace, some ultras harassed old adversaries. Charles's and his ministers' aim to rebuild the harmony which, fondly but erroneously, they imagined had existed before the wars, was defeated by the passions still excited by the issues and personalities of the conflict. As the succeeding decades would show, neither Charles nor James could escape dependence on the propertied to implement their policies.

Many of the propertied were partisans. Forced to share seats with the one-time supporters of parliament and Cromwell, whether at the king's council table, on the county magistrates' bench, or in town council chambers, passionate royalists scarcely hid their disdain.

Charles in composing his privy council set the precedent which he wished others to copy. Alongside the exiles of the 1650s, such as Edward Hyde, earl of Clarendon and lord chancellor, Lord Southampton, rewarded with the lord treasurership, and Ormond, were more recent recruits to the king's banner. Conspicuous among the last were Monck, whose importance led to his ennoblement as duke of Albemarle, the Cromwellian general at sea, Edward Montagu, soon earl of Sandwich, and Anthony Ashley Cooper, a Dorset landowner whose ambivalence towards the usurpers led on to his emergence in the 1670s, when earl of Shaftesbury, as an eloquent critic of royal policies and powers. Others associated with the parliamentary opposition of the 1640s, like Arthur Annesley, elevated to the earldom of Anglesey, Northumberland, and Holles, were also included. The very capaciousness of the body, intended as a merit, proved its undoing. Divisions, both personal and principled, soon weakened it, and encouraged the king to consult outside the formal council. Temperamentally inclined to secrecy, Charles confided in few. Behind his superficial openness in manner lay a deviousness which increasingly reminded of his father, and caused comparable political problems. It made sense for the king to play off competitors for power one against the other. However, the resulting factiousness destabilized successive ministries. The ill-assorted quintet ('the Cabal') which dominated the highest offices between 1667 and 1673 or the broad-bottomed council into which he was forced during the tribulations of 1678 to 1679 merely strengthened the king's habit of taking advice elsewhere. The system run on the king's behalf by his lord treasurer, Sir Thomas Osborne, earl of Danby (and in time a duke), between 1674 and 1678, pleased Charles more. Danby caressed MPs through a blatant appeal to Anglican intolerance and individuals' cupidity. Again, from 1680, the king acquired malleable and congenial ministers in the shape of the 'chits': Sidney Godolphin; Clarendon's son, Laurence Hyde, earl of Rochester; and Robert Spencer, earl of Sunderland.

Personalities, policies, and principles

Behind the personalities and ambitions of particular ministers survived a long-standing constitutional conundrum. The monarch's liberty to choose whichever advisers he liked remained intact. All critics could do was to starve ministers of taxes or impeach them through parliament. The second method, redolent of the confrontations of the early century, was proposed in the cases of Clarendon in 1667 and Danby in 1679. Calling ministers to account and reversing unpalatable policies belonged to a longer list of questions which the Restoration settlements failed to answer definitively. Soon novel problems swelled the inherited ones. The seemingly unanimous gratitude of subjects rapidly turned to strident disagreements. As a result, these years are thought by some modern analysts to have originated an adversarial mode of politics. Given the alignments during the baronial struggles of the fifteenth-century Wars of the Roses or the changes in state religion in the sixteenth century, an entirely consensual approach to public questions had probably never existed. The mid-seventeenth-century contestation cast a long and chilling shadow over the rest of the century. After 1660, the well-meaning decried the polarization of their communities, while the nostalgic pleaded for a restoration of an imaginary concord. But partisanship had arrived to stay. Moreover, partisans would soon form themselves into parties. Meetings of parliament early in the reign in all three kingdoms acted as effective incubators of opposition. In addition, the decisions taken by parliament—particularly in the sphere of religion—widened the fissures. The wide spread of religious nonconformity accounted in part for the political mobilization of many outside national and county government. Those of modest means, the middling sort such as craftspeople and traders, had been drawn into the war effort and separatist congregations of the 1640s. No longer would they jump obediently when their superiors shouted. Towns with their dense filigree of official, vocational, and voluntary agencies, their rich religious and cultural lives, and the often high levels of literacy and external contact bred diversity, important alike to the growth of opposition and the effective articulation of the royalist cause in the 1680s. The larger the place, the greater the opportunities for this vibrant activity to flourish. Inevitably then, London, with a population nearing 500,000, was the main centre of popular politics. Taverns, coffee-houses, the halls of livery companies, and private houses resounded to debates. The printing presses, from 1679 released from the control of the Licensing Act, deluged readers and listeners with squibs, ballads, pasquinades, and more measured reflections on current events. Other towns, from Edinburgh, Glasgow, Limerick, Cork, Dublin, and Derry to Norwich, Great Yarmouth, Bristol, and Gloucester, echoed with these discords. Each place, although it followed where the court, parliament, or London led, played local variations on the metropolitan themes.

Almost from the start of his reign, the king's outlook diverged from that of numerous influential subjects. It had looked a masterly piece of legerdemain when Charles left to parliaments in all three of his kingdoms the details of settlement. What peers and MPs then enacted would haunt him and his successor. In 1660, three matters had cried out for urgent attention: money, defence, and religion. For all the euphoria of Charles's return, members of his first parliament (soon nicknamed the Cavalier Parliament), whether accidentally or designedly, stinted in what they gave. The main taxes—customs, excise, and hearth money—were expected to yield an annual £1,200,000. They would pay the usual costs of peacetime government. In the early years of the reign, seldom more than £850,000 was collected. The power of the purse, the traditional way in which parliament had obliged wayward monarchs to summon it periodically, had been retained. Charles was irritated at having regularly to rattle a begging bowl in the faces of MPs. The irksome dependency stimulated his advisers to seek unparliamentary alternatives. French pensions were one. The king was suspected of bartering the interests of an independent and Protestant England to become a remittance man. In the 1670s, he also sanctioned a shady deal which delivered the most lucrative Irish revenues into the control of an Anglo-Irish consortium led by an Irish Protestant peer, Lord Ranelagh, who now lived in London. Charles II's inducement was an annual retainer. These supplements never liberated Charles from his parliamentary pay-masters. Buoyant trade instead floated him free in the 1680s.

In part this boom derived from decisions taken in 1660. Then it had been agreed that the aggressive economic nationalism, enshrined in the Navigation Act of 1651, should be extended. Gradually it turned London into an *entrepôt* whither and whence the goods of the expanding trading world were shipped. Since the growing traffic had to be carried in vessels owned and crewed by English, the merchant marine expanded. By the 1680s, its tonnage surpassed that of the rival Dutch and French. Some of the resultant prosperity was diffused among the ports of the Atlantic seaboard, such as Bristol and Liverpool. Even Dublin, Cork, Kinsale, Sligo, and Derry felt benefits. But in general, Ireland and Scotland were denied the principal advantages of the Acts, so accentuating England's commercial vitality and the continuing backwardness of the other two kingdoms. Further discriminations hit the chief branches of Irish trade. The Westminster parliament bowed to regional lobbies which blamed Irish competitors for the depressed state of agriculture and so of rents. The 1667 Act which banned the export of live cattle from Ireland to England and Wales reminded of the essentials in the troubled relations between the sister kingdoms. The English parliament felt competent to legislate for Ireland, despite the existence of a parliament in Dublin. The king's ministers had failed to stop the discriminatory Act against Irish commerce. A lobby of interested Irish Protestants, several of whom already resided intermittently in London and had places at court, realized—yet again—that what happened in Ireland was usually concluded in Whitehall or Westminster. The Scots also rued the costs of being dragged behind England. In particular, the two naval wars which Charles II waged against the Dutch (between 1664 and 1667 and from 1672 to 1674) disrupted Scotland's most lucrative overseas trade. By the 1680s, the Irish were repairing the economic damage. Access to the colonies and enlarged markets of the later Stuart monarchy stimulated agricultural production. This by-product of the commercial dynamism of the 1680s interested Charles less than the healthy effect on his own revenues. No longer needing extras from parliament, neither Charles II nor James II summoned it when legally, in 1684 and 1688, under the terms of the Triennial Act, they should have done so. By James's reign his annual receipts regularly topped £2,000,000. The funds allowed him dramatically to expand his army.

From its inception, the restored regime protected itself against domestic and foreign foes. Plots, Venner's in London early in 1661 and then in Dublin and the north in 1663, convinced the nervous that republicans were conspiring to topple the monarchy. A war against Spain had been inherited, but was speedily ended. The habit of the Interregnum of the nation asserting itself in Europe was continued, but with fewer victories. A high priority in 1660 was to disband the army, at once a massive expense and a potential source of disaffection. However, the three kingdoms could not be left undefended. Parliament accordingly overcame its repugnance and allowed Charles the nucleus of a standing army of 3,000. In Ireland and Scotland where even worse dangers survived, larger forces—respectively of 1,200 and 7,500—were authorized. Once money was more readily available and as the domestic and international ambitions of Charles and James grew, so too did the standing forces. The growth brought the likelihood of friction with both the amateurish militia and the civil authorities should the soldiery encroach on routine administration. The ease with which regiments could be moved between the separated kingdoms, reinforcements from Ireland coercing the troublesome Scottish Covenanters or protecting an unpopular James II against his restless English subjects in 1688, added to suspicions about the ultimate royal ambitions. In particular, the remarkable increase in James II's forces—by 1685, 20,000—hinted at as yet undeclared domestic objectives. In addition, the appointment of Catholics as officers, most rapid and large-scale in Ireland—as with the opening of other offices to Catholics—angered those displaced and raised the spectre of an Irish Catholic army domineering over England, Wales, or Scotland: an apprehension last felt in the 1640s. The ethos of the regular army, one which James thanks to his early career in exile shared, inculcated an authoritarianism which gave short shrift to constitutional niceties. Most positively, the localism which riddled the militia was being dissolved by the transnational character of the regular army. Yet, notwithstanding this developing loyalty to James, as his authority was challenged, so leading officers deserted. Similarly, disaffection spread in the navy despite the popularity within it of James, a one-time lord high admiral. In the end, the potential of the armed forces to curb localism and aristocratic self-interest and to promote royal authority was hardly realized.

In England and Wales, defensive needs led to the revival of the lord lieutenancy. Thanks to Militia Acts, this office, central to the defence and policing of the shires, was better defined and expanded. The measure embodied both the initial traditionalism of the Cavalier Parliament and (arguably) an aristocratic reaction. All but three of those commissioned as lords lieutenant in 1661 were peers, rewarded usually for staunch royalism. Their appointments suggested that a military function still attached to the nobility. However, the peers' scope for independent action, pursuing vendettas against hereditary foes in their localities and gratifying their own clients, was curtailed. The use of peers exemplified how the restored regime reconstructed alliances with the weighty in the countryside. Even so, the political gains from pleasing grandees may have been at the cost of military efficiency and local concord. Estimates of the attentiveness and achievements of the lords lieutenant varied wildly. Ormond, appointed to oversee Somerset, was too preoccupied with other duties as head of the royal household as lord steward and, from 1661, lord lieutenant of Ireland, to supervise the west country militia. Shortcomings were glaringly exposed in emergencies: first those posed by the Dutch who, during their wars against the English, might invade coastal counties, and then in 1685 the uprising in the west of England on behalf of Monmouth.

The militia, but not the lieutenancy, was also deployed in Ireland and Scotland. There, too, the results hardly impressed. Necessarily the regime, even if it did not constitute lords lieutenant in Irish and Scottish shires, relied on local notables to mobilize their followings. This, too, could be seen as consolidating the positions of those who already wielded great territorial influence. By 1664, the Scottish government, having dismantled the garrisons and forts of the reviled Cromwellian occupiers, was obliged to erect new ones at Braemar, Inverlochy, and Ruthven of Badenoch to overawe the restless highlanders. Lord Atholl, moreover, was empowered to subdue troublemakers with an independent company of his own. By 1671, the traditional expedient of commissions of fire and sword were issued against unruly highlanders. In addition, by 1668, the Scottish militia numbered 20,000 foot and 2,000 horse. As in England and Ireland, the military traditions and experiences of landowners were channelled into an approved outlet. During the 1670s, the perception of who constituted the gravest threat to Scottish stability shifted from the highlanders to the Presbyterian Covenanters restive at the requirement of conformity to the new episcopal order. After 1677, the highlanders had been sufficiently rehabilitated to be deployed against the rebellious presbyterians, especially in the south-west. The use of this highland host prefigured James's enthusiasm for the chiefs of the area. In England and Ireland, the attractions of the militia as an economical expedient through which the enthusiasm of loyalists could be exploited meant that it was kept. Alongside it, however, a more professional and centrally directed force was progressively expanded. Particularly in Ireland, the militia, conceived as an exclusively Protestant force, found itself at loggerheads with the largely Catholic regular army of James.

The churches

So far as the church settlement was concerned, what was imposed in all three kingdoms differed from what Charles and his close associates had wished. Bishops were restored without any of the modifications which might have placated scrupulous presbyterians. A new Book of Common Prayer laid down ceremonies from which precisians dissented. Similarly, the Thirty-Nine Articles, to which subscription was required before any could be instituted into the livings of the state church, defined doctrine and government in ways antipathetic to those who could not accept that episcopacy was the divinely decreed form of ecclesiastical organization. In 1662 the English Act of Uniformity sorted the clergy into conformists and nonconformists: 2,209 ministers, lecturers, and teachers were driven from their places, perhaps 10 per cent of the total. The unexpected revival of episcopacy in Scotland, once acceptance of it was turned into a condition of ministerial institution, forced out 268 pastors, many of them from the south-western synods of Galloway, Dumfries, Ayr, and Glasgow. They represented about a quarter of the total clerical strength. In Ireland, first the actions of the bishops and then of the parliament, in passing its own Act of Uniformity in 1666, outed the unreconciled. These ejections were concentrated in the Ulster districts where Scots and Scots presbyterianism were strong and in the few sizeable towns, notably Dublin itself. The impact of these measures could be, and often was, blunted. Nevertheless, they estranged numerous well-organized and well-connected groups. Since parliaments had invented the handicaps, they must remove them. The dissenters' grievances were inevitably political. Only through politics could they be relieved. With similar disabilities in both Scotland and Ireland, a shared burden sometimes elicited a common response. The ejected in the three kingdoms corresponded constantly. Through networks, especially for education and ordination, they sustained one another. Ministers moved easily between the separate kingdoms, especially across the North Channel between Ireland and Scotland.

Religious dissent on this scale had been a problem that Charles wanted to avert. He had been thwarted by his intolerant subjects. Even before parliaments assembled, a swell of allegedly spontaneous feeling wrested churches from the clerical dictators of the 1650s and restored the liturgy and some of the personnel of the pre-war church. Those clerics, dons, and squires who had adhered to the episcopalian order throughout the hazardous Interregnum probably orchestrated the seeming populism in 1660. In Scotland, the domineering and belligerence of the presbyterian clergy had wearied even former allies among the aristocracy and town dwellers. Yet a lay wish to humble the overmighty ministers did not altogether explain the surprising decision to reintroduce bishops, never a popular feature of the Kirk. Middleton, keen to achieve congruity between Scotland and the other two kingdoms, may have pulled this stroke. Across the British Isles, the appeal of the traditional as a rock to which to cleave when all else was being shaken, rather than massive lay enthusiasm for the ritualism and sacerdotalism of high churchmen, largely accounted for the feeling. It often fused with comparable sentiments which commended monarchy after the inconclusive experiments of the usurpation. But the anticlericalism which had taken revenge on the theocrats of the 1640s and 1650s now limited support for episcopalian triumphalists. The discretionary powers of magistrates and of proprietors with the right to fill church livings softened the lash. Bouts of persecution alternated with forbearance. Dissenters, at the mercy of royal whim or local patrons, could not regard this as a happy situation. They suffered, too, from the misunderstandings between king and parliaments. Parliament reversed royal toleration by imposing the Test Acts of 1673 and 1679. Intended to smoke out Catholics from official employments, conscientious Protestant dissenters also fell victim. The casualties, and their many friends within the political establishment, watched for chances to place indulgence or comprehension on a secure statutory basis. Dissent throughout the two reigns and the three kingdoms (and Wales) remained as much a political as a religious issue.

How Catholics should be treated also had long-reaching political ramifications. As with the handling of Protestant dissent, so with Roman Catholicism, the political elites, whether in parliament or the provinces, frequently parted company from their kings. Just as individual dissenters might be shielded and live amicably with neighbours, so the few Catholics in most English, Scottish, and Welsh communities were rarely objects of fear or targets for attack. In contrast, the abstraction of popery, replete with suspicions of foreigners, arcane rituals, and sinister intentions, provoked instant hostility. So too did the Catholicism of the neighbouring kingdom of Ireland. Irish Catholics, thanks to insidious propaganda about the massacres which they were supposed to have perpetrated in 1641 (and might again), were demonized. Protestant fears were strong enough consistently to block royal schemes to allow civic rights and legal toleration to Roman Catholics.

In England, where as few as 1 per cent of the inhabitants were Catholics, or Scotland and Wales, where the proportions were scarcely greater, the zest of Charles and James to admit this confession to equality looked quixotic. In Ireland, by contrast, a device to please the Catholic majority alone offered to end the rebellions which regularly overwhelmed that kingdom. Ormond, viceroy of Ireland during much of the 1660s, hunted for a formula by which loyal Catholics could be attached more firmly to the Stuart monarchy. It was a policy at once obvious but to many unthinkable. To allow confessional diversity within the state, albeit a composite one, subverted contemporary conceptions of the well-ordered polity. Moreover, recent history taught how the Catholics, notably the Irish and foreign, like cuckoos in the Protestant nest, fouled it. Slumbering fears awoke when, in the 1670s, the king aligned himself behind the secular head of Catholic Europe, Louis XIV of France, and when the duke of York confirmed his Catholicism. In 1678, a supposed popish plot to kill Charles II and replace him with York was uncovered. Panic, in part spontaneous, but much of it contrived, generated sectarian violence. It claimed as sacrifices a decrepit English Catholic peer, Lord Stafford, at least eighteen priests, and the primate of Ireland, Archbishop Oliver Plunkett.

Parliaments

The inability of Charles II and James II to get their way in religious affairs quickly revealed the limits to their power. As early as 1662 the king was tempted to dispense some from the legal requirements of conformity, but the Commons would not agree. So a pattern was set. A Declaration of Indulgence, issued on Charles's authority in 1672, had to be withdrawn and confessional exclusions were substituted by parliament. In 1686, the normally tractable Scottish parliament declined to endorse indulgence. The refusal of seven bishops of the established Church of England to order that James's most recent declaration on the subject be read from all pulpits in 1688 showed how widely these measures were resisted. Irked by hostile reactions, Charles and James sought means to side-step or change them. The quest would tempt them into actions which ruptured traditional compacts and created new ones.

Immediately after Charles's return, noble power was revived and supplemented. Customarily aristocrats were the intimates and counsellors of kings. Charles, no snob, admired talent wherever it was located. His favours were never confined to the scions of the ancient peerage, much to the chagrin of its members. Peers, like other landowners, suffered from the depressed rents of the 1660s and 1670s. Magnates with ample acres were cushioned against this hardship. Office also helped, as Ormond, lord steward and Irish lord lieutenant, or Beaufort, lord president of Wales, discovered. Although saddled with costly duties, these grandees could recompense themselves and their clienteles. Rifts opened up between a favoured few, handsomely endowed and rewarded, and the generality who, if they blamed parliamentary vindictiveness for originating their problems, resented the failure of the returned Stuarts to help. Whereas the crown and the established church recovered most of the lands stripped from them in the 1640s, private landowners were generally left to their own devices to regain what they had sold and mortgaged in the 1640s and 1650s. Usually this meant recourse to costly and often fruitless litigation.

Just as an outward deference was accorded to the sovereign, so too aristocrats and other landed notables were given their dues as they toured their localities. However, these courtesies did not always translate into obedience as the imperious instructed how underlings were to behave. The rivalry between competing magnates, such as Beaufort and Pembroke in south Wales or Lords Townshend and Yarmouth, could enliven electoral and urban politics. During the 1670s, Norwich, Great Yarmouth, and Lowestoft reverberated to the clashes of the latter duo. However, the townspeople were not merely passive receptors. They had their own interests which neighbouring notables ignored at their peril. Thus, if some recent histories of the seventeenth century extend the notion of a strong baronial reaction beyond the wars of the 1640s into the restored monarchy, others push radical, popular, and even party politics back to the 1670s and 1680s. These interpretations are not mutually incompatible, and generally agree that political activity centred on parliament. Indeed, parliament in all three kingdoms benefited from the restoration. It decided much of the detail of how the state was henceforward to be ruled. Yet, in each parliament, disagreements abounded. In Dublin, members jibbed at clauses in the bills of settlement and explanation (1662 and 1665) because, as profiteers of the Cromwellian land transfers, they would be required to share their spoils with returned royalists and uncompromised Catholics. Nor was the insistence on conformity to a re-established episcopal church unanimously applauded. It required a deft helmsman, Lord Orrery (formerly Lord Broghill), trained in Cromwellian parliaments, to steer through the reefs. After 1666, the Dublin parliament was closed down. A fresh meeting was mooted in 1678, in the hope that it would silence unsettling speculations that the land distributions of the 1650s and 1660s might still be modified. However, when the Popish Plot irrupted, any new assembly was abandoned. A Protestant body in Dublin might all too readily import the ploys and projects of its English and Scottish counterparts into an otherwise quiescent Ireland. In any case, Ireland could as well be ruled by proclamation, judicial decree, English statutes and the king's prerogative. As yet, the Irish parliament, although quick to learn procedural and political arts, was occasional and underdeveloped.

The proficiency and confidence gained by the Scottish body as it ran the country throughout the 1640s could not be completely extinguished. The spokesmen of the royal burghs and humbler lairds, who had asserted their distinctive interests against those of their economic and social superiors in a single chamber assembly, were not entirely silenced in the 1660s. Nevertheless, the political reaction against recent developments seemed most complete in Scotland. The Act Recissory of 1661 wiped away all that had been enacted by the Scottish parliament since 1633, despite the fact that some measures had been approved by the king. Scottish society, polarized between a few territorial magnates and the rest, was felt by some to be more susceptible to a thoroughgoing aristocratic reaction than either England or Ireland. Notwithstanding this apparently simple social structure, other groups did exist. As well as lesser landowners, by the 1680s, burghs like Edinburgh, Glasgow, and Aberdeen contained small but growing numbers of professionals and traders, not necessarily averse to the Stuarts, but not all in thrall to the landed magnates. Furthermore, the displaced Presbyterian pastors, forever splitting into belligerent factions, supplied a focus for opposition. The devices through which traditionally the Scottish administration had guided parliament, notably the steering committee of the lords of the articles, were resurrected. Yet not all members were cowed.

Disgruntled aristocrats like Hamilton and Tweeddale, mortified by the local dictatorship of Lauderdale, protested in and out of parliament. Lauderdale was realist enough to appreciate that he must adjust his policies if this opposition was to be contained. He alternated between repressing and humouring opponents. This followed the lurches of the ministry in England and Ireland, but the timing was not always synchronized. As persecution of religious nonconformists (the conventiclers) intensified in Scotland during 1673, the persecuted sailed across the narrow waters to Ireland, where the authorities were laxer. There, since 1672, the Presbyterians had been acknowledged in a popular Protestant front against popery with the grant of modest allowances by the state: the *regium donum*. Lauderdale's adversaries, baulked of their hopes of dislodging him through their campaign in Edinburgh, joined forces with English (and Irish) critics of arbitrary government. Lauderdale's practices in Scotland were plausibly depicted as a variant, if not the original, of the system which Danby ran in England. The potential of the Scottish parliament to irritate, evident in the harrying of Lauderdale, led the Stuarts and their managers to convene it as seldom as was practicable. Between 1673 and 1681 it was not summoned. In the interval, the alternative of a Convention of Estates met to grant money. This arrangement might reduce but did not end the opposition. However, the one attempt to pit traditional magnate power against the regime failed. Argyll, successor to the Covenanter grandee executed in 1661, mobilized his followers in the south-west against James. In 1685, he paid the price for failure and was in his turn executed. Otherwise, those who directly challenged the new order in 1666 and 1679–80 were religious radicals. In contrast to their predecessors of the 1630s, the later rebels lacked noble support.

Like their father, neither Charles nor James objected in principle to parliament. So long as it was biddable, it offered the most convenient method to make policies enforceable. It also associated the nation with the actions approved by its elected representatives. In 1688, James hoped that his ambition permanently to readmit his Catholic co-religionists to full citizenship could be achieved by parliamentary statute. However, in order to do things in a traditional manner, he was obliged to adopt an entirely untraditional approach to the boroughs and counties which would elect the members of parliament. The unlikelihood of securing a pliant assembly forced him to abandon it. In the absence of fresh laws, he fell back on the innate powers of the monarch, notably to suspend in their entirety, or dispense individuals from, penal laws.

Localities: ideals and ideas

An ideal of harmony still dominated visions of the well-ordered state. Parties, synonymous with factions, were condemned for disturbing that harmony. Some blamed the civil wars for dividing hitherto united communities. In 1660, Charles aimed to reunite the divided. It was a forlorn hope. The principles which had split communities in the 1630s and 1640s survived, together with their capacity to splinter. After 1660, these beliefs, manifest in recent allegiances and behaviour, marked out the dangerous. Towns notorious for their past dedication to a rebellious parliament—Coventry, Gloucester, Northampton, and Taunton—had their walls demolished lest they be tempted again to defy their monarch. They were humbled as dramatically as the defiant cities of Limerick and Galway had been a few years earlier. In thirty-six of the largest English corporations, a third of the councillors and office-holders were removed between 1661 and 1663. Among the justices of the peace even more dramatic remodellings occurred. In 1660, in the West Riding of Yorkshire, only fourteen of the seventy-six magistrates were retained from the previous year; in the North Riding, eleven of the fifty-seven; and in the East Riding, a mere eight from fifty-five. Even so, the extent of these changes varied. In the important towns, two-thirds of those who had served under the Interregnum survived. Moreover, it was possible for the excluded to creep back.

Institutions such as the county bench might be swept clean of known collaborators. However, the substitutes were not all of one mind. Provincials, once entrusted with the implementation of measures, frequently ordered priorities very differently from how the ultras in parliament or government expected. In particular, the drive against Protestant dissenters elicited contradictory reactions. Sympathetic peers and gentlemen, already sheltering ejected nonconformist ministers as tutors and schoolmasters—much as the Anglican squirearchy in the 1650s had harboured the unbending episcopalians—held back in their official capacities from persecuting. In southern Ireland, Lord Orrery, as president of the province of Munster, vital to the good order of that large area, installed as the schoolmaster in his newly created academy a dissenter removed from his English living. In a similar way, the Mansells of Margam in Glamorgan employed ejected clergymen to tutor their sons. Behind these isolated but numerous acts of protection could be detected a feeling, which grew rapidly in the 1670s, that the greater danger came from the Catholics, not from the Protestant dissenters. This belief, for example, animated the influential Welsh Trust for promoting Protestantism.

Monarchist diehards, looking back to the 1660s from the vantage point of the 1680s, traced much of the trouble in the intervening period to the mixture of types and beliefs amongst those governing the localities. A more uniform approach and greater ideological consistency in the functionaries were advocated. Accordingly, county and town governments were more systematically remodelled. Thanks to the furore over the Popish Plot, arbitrary government, and Exclusion, which generated rival petitions and addresses, critics and the lukewarm were much more easily spotted. During the first half of 1680 slightly more than 10 per cent of the 2,559 justices of the peace in England and Wales were dropped. In 1681, three lords lieutenant who had backed exclusion—Essex, Manchester, and Suffolk—were removed. Meanwhile, in the boroughs, the half-hearted tinkering of earlier decades gave way to more thorough purges. Through the legal process of *quo warranto*, questioning on what authority corporations acted, existing charters were scrutinized and cancelled. Between 1682 and 1687, 134 new charters replaced the old. Partisans within many boroughs offered themselves as the sole and proper defenders of the Stuart monarchy in the locality. Now their claims were believed, as they were installed in town halls across the land and their opponents dismissed. The duke of York was understandably delighted that at last 'old friends, the Cavalier and Church party' everywhere dominated.

There existed, at least in England and Wales, sufficient of the propertied of proven loyalty to man the local machinery of the state. In Ireland, an exiguous Protestant interest offered a more precarious foundation for the reaction of the 1680s. The viceroy, Ormond, was reproved for keeping on known Cromwellian collaborators and suspected republicans. The continuing exclusion of Catholics from Irish offices reduced dangerously the supply of candidates who had never swerved from the cause of the Stuarts.

The regime prized servants motivated by personal fealty to the monarch or unquestioning in their support for the Stuarts as divinely denominated rulers. The confessional tests, beloved by parliament, no longer seemed the most accurate way to segregate loyal sheep from independent goats. After 1685, James II altered the rules for entry to the governing club.

A Catholic king

In Ireland from 1686, respectable townsmen, professionals, and squires from Catholic society were reinstated by the new Catholic governor, Richard Talbot, soon earl and later duke of Tyrconnell. Thereby the strategy of entrusting authority to the customary local leaders, applied in the other two kingdoms since 1660, was belatedly followed. In Ireland, what its Protestant inhabitants and their worried allies in Scotland and England had prophesied had come to pass. As in England, so in Ireland, boroughs, erected as bastions of English (and since the 1650s of Protestant) industry and values, received new charters. In 105 corporations, Catholics now mingled with dissenters and the compliant Protestant conformists. The shrievalty, commissions of the peace, judiciary, and privy council all proved equally amenable to an infusion of Catholics. These alterations occurred just at the moment when, in England and Wales, tried and tested officials were supplanted by the obscure. Because Ireland was unique among the Stuarts' possessions in its confessional composition, it was an inappropriate laboratory in which to perfect what later might be applied in the other kingdoms. Tyrconnell's actions, nevertheless, generated rumours that church lands alienated and secularized since the Reformation might soon be returned to the Catholic hierarchy. Beyond this rumour was the worry that the Catholic Church might share some emoluments of the established Church of Ireland and in time replace it as the official cult. Already ominous, and carrying implications for the treatment of the other territories, were the speed and thoroughness with which the army of Ireland had been transformed into an Irish Catholic force. By 1688, 90 per cent of its members were Catholic. Cashiered Protestant officers made their way to Holland either to earn their bread or station themselves close to the likeliest saviour, the king's son-in-law, William, prince of Orange. Others joined the refugees who landed along Britain's western seaboard. They soon chilled their hosts with tales of Catholic aggression. The supposed atrocities of 1641 were deliberately recalled and elaborated. These fugitives combined with the influx of French Protestants, expelled by James's persecuting ally, Louis XIV, to warn that throughout western Europe Counter-Reformation Catholicism was on the offensive. Irish Protestants encouraged the belief that, as in the 1640s, they were in the front line as the forces of Antichrist battled against the beleaguered Protestants. This mode of thought continued and deepened the strident rhetoric of the Popish Plot. It played on collective memories and the deeply embedded notion of the English and Scots as chosen peoples. It could excite the normally calm to act. The pervasiveness and persistence of such ideas were important in taking the political and succession crises of 1678 to 1688 beyond the precincts of parliament. Indeed, with parliament sitting at Westminster for only two months between 1681 and 1688 and not at all in Dublin, most political activity necessarily occurred away from the parliamentary chambers. Alarm over which side Charles and James took in the European fight for confessional survival united Protestants scattered throughout all the Stuarts' possessions. Even then, though, it has to be allowed that the nature of the threat posed by Catholics and Catholicizing policies was never uniform. Only in Ireland were the recent overlords comprehensively tumbled. There, too, recent history taught that Catholic troops might overrun the island and align it against Protestant England and Scotland.

The small number of Catholics outside Ireland did not stop James from elevating them wherever he could. Although insignificant as a proportion of the total English, Welsh, and Scottish populations, Catholics were disproportionately represented within the peerage and gentry. Now they came into their own. In 1687, as James and his minions prepared the ground for a possible parliament, likely supporters of Catholic emancipation were cherished. Out went many of the Anglican loyalists advanced in the early 1680s; in came a coalition of Protestant dissenters, Catholics, and pliable Anglicans. Between 1687 and 1688, the lords lieutenant in twenty-one counties were changed. Thirteen Catholics and three—Fairfax, Huntingdon, and Mulgrave—friendly to dissent were appointed. It was objected that many wielded little influence in their counties and therefore were unlikely to be much use in the king's schemes. Two hundred and forty-five justices of the peace were dismissed. Of nearly 500 new names, 64 per cent are thought to have belonged to Catholics. Trusted churchmen, such as the second earl of Clarendon and the earl of Rochester, sons of Lord Chancellor Clarendon, were pushed from the ministry. The lord president of Wales and its marches, the high Tory Beaufort made way for the Catholic marquess (later titular duke) of Powis. Everywhere devoted royalists, such as Sir Thomas Meadowes in Great Yarmouth, were supplanted. James's main ministers in each kingdom were now all Catholics. In Ireland, Tyrconnell, as we have seen, had long headed the political movement to improve the lot of the Catholic Old English. He exploited his long acquaintance in exile and at court with the Stuarts, and had already succeeded in having the allegedly closed question of the land settlement reviewed. Such credentials hardly reassured the Protestants over whom he ruled, or observers on the other shore of the Irish Sea. Agile converts, in Scotland, the Drummond brothers, earls and eventually dukes of Perth and Melfort, and in England, the earl of Sunderland, served the king's turn. They had cut the path which, it was feared, other fair-weather Protestants might soon tread. More immediately, with the government of Ireland largely entrusted to Catholics, and so many of the traditional governors of England, Scotland, and Wales dethroned, it seemed—as in the 1650s—a topsy-turvy world. That improbable alliance—of Catholics and Presbyterian republicans—on which sensationalists had blamed the overthrow and execution of Charles I, and which royalists accused the exclusionists of reconstructing in 1679, by 1688 had been knowingly recreated by his younger son. Its consequences were almost as disastrous for James as they had been for his father.

Kingship: representations and realities

With bewildering rapidity, after the bright morning of 1660, the storm clouds had rolled in. The inherent instability of the arrangements through which confessionally disparate realms were to be governed was glaringly exposed. The kings themselves, the sole element common to all, for a time skilfully balanced their several needs. Charles made a virtue of his pliancy. His mastery of subterfuge in the end may have confused supporters. If fixity of purpose and application to business were foreign to Charles, his political suppleness served him admirably. Often he seemed a blank screen onto which contrary images of kingship could be projected. As king by divine right, he was protected by conventional notions of hierarchy, patriarchy, and obedience. Inventive royalist impresarios wished to swaddle him in the trappings of majesty. Charles was tempted, having encountered some of the ceremonial during his continental exile and hearing more of what Louis XIV was doing at Versailles. Nevertheless, attempts to enfold the king in baroque splendour were ruined by his penury and his informality. After the restoration, Charles accepted the utility of an artfully propagated cult of Stuart kingship. The sacerdotal and magical properties of monarchy were advertised as he touched many who flocked into his presence to be cured of the scorbutic disorder known as 'the king's evil'. Charles travelled confidently about England (but not Ireland or—after 1651—Scotland) even when plotters threatened to kill him. His pleasures, notably of the turf and venery, were not to be cramped by republican incendiaries. He could use his presence to intimidate. He attended the house of lords regularly. In the critical session of 1680–1, he was present for fifty-one of the fifty-nine sittings. Seated by the fireside, he overawed all but the boldest. The larger than expected margin, of thirty-three votes, by which the lords rejected the bill to debar James from the succession probably owed much to this personal lead from the king. Similarly, at his council board, especially as he guided the faint-hearted through the crisis of 1679–81, he silenced the garrulous and troublesome.

Charles's boredom threshold was low. He craved the company of wits, women, and womanizers. The smart hobby of experimentation amused him, and he helped to institutionalize the Royal Society. In other respects, however, he looked backwards. Chivalry, sometimes of a markedly archaic type, was fostered. A project to band together the cavalier heroes of the civil wars in a Royal Order of the Oak, taking as its emblem the tree in which Charles had hidden after the battle of Worcester in 1651, foundered. However, Charles did involve himself in the rituals of the long-established Order of the Garter. He halted on his triumphal progress back to London in May 1660 to preside over installations of knights in Canterbury cathedral. Later he sponsored both an exhaustive history of the coterie and impressive rooms for its ceremonies at its Windsor headquarters. He regarded the select group of knights as his boon companions. In Scotland, James VII and II, equally attached to tradition, regulated the knights of the thistle. Ireland, in contrast, would not acquire its own order of chivalry, the knights of St Patrick, until 1783. Occasionally, the favoured from Ireland and Scotland, such as Ormond, his son, Ossory, and Lauderdale, were given the garter. It was too sparingly bestowed to assist in any larger process of integrating the elites of the separate kingdoms. This was in keeping with the indifference which both Charles and James exhibited to the non-English elements in their inheritance. Other than for what the Scots and Irish might supply, these subjects were little valued. Charles had been turned against Covenanting imperiousness during the brief interlude in 1650 when he was crowned king of the Scots and swore the Covenant. Enjoyment of the badinage of personable Irishmen, both Catholic and Protestant, produced kind intentions but no coherent policy for Ireland. James's Scottish sojourn, and the favour directed towards the highlanders, alarmed and divided, as did his more concrete help for Irish Catholics. In the minds of the last, if not of the Scottish *dévots*, James remained too much the Englishman to satisfy their ultimate aspirations. This showed most gallingly in his reluctance to dispossess the propertied Protestants in Ireland.

Sycophants certainly credited the two sovereigns with holding together the fragile conglomerate. Charles and James were awarded lineages which reached back into the mythic pasts of each of their peoples. Welsh bards celebrated their monarch as the descendant of Brutus, supposed founder of Britain. In the revamped Edinburgh palace of Holyroodhouse, panels specially commissioned in 1684 portrayed the 111 kings who linked the present incumbent with King Fergus. From the west of Ireland, an antiquary of Old Irish pedigree congratulated James on antecedents among the Milesian kings of ancient Ireland. Yet more fulsomely, an Irish Catholic eulogized the Stuarts in 1686 as the line 'in which all the several rights and titles of the Irish, Scotch, Pictish, Norman, Saxon and British kings are so miraculously concentrated'. Such claims singled out the monarch's relationship with one component territory rather than as head of a United Britain and Ireland.

Iconography, shows, and appearances conventionally assisted rulers. Projects to house Charles II more fittingly revived schemes dear to his father. Throughout the 1660s lack of spare cash stopped the conversion of the sprawling congeries of Whitehall, royal residence and government offices, into a purpose-built classical complex. When modest amounts of money appeared during the 1670s, the king preferred to adorn Windsor. The choice was significant; so too were the decorative programmes. Already Charles, weary with life close to a critical parliament and unruly city, dreamt of moving the royal capital to a more congenial location. In this he may have imitated Louis who had forsaken Paris for Versailles. Windsor, as well as incorporating ceremonial spaces for the Garter knights, received a sequence of imposing rooms. Painted ceilings gloated over the restorations of the monarchy and episcopacy. The ensemble was to be completed with a domed mausoleum, reminiscent of the funeral chapel of the Bourbons at St Denis. There the martyr of the dynasty, Charles I, already interred in Windsor, would be venerated. This expensive plan was a casualty of the political crisis of 1678. As Charles emerged strengthened from the ordeal, his distaste for London had also grown. Now awash with money, he decided to move his court to a new site: Winchester. There Christopher Wren could erect a sumptuous palace. Unencumbered with any recent political associations, the city was nevertheless redolent of a mythic past which royalists cherished. Capital of Wessex and Saxon Britain, it housed the round table around which King Arthur and his knights had congregated: the model for Charles and his companions of the Garter. Only the king's death stopped this impressive centre of Stuart power coming into use.

James, although well enough supplied with money, differed in his priorities. His buildings would trumpet his confession. James concentrated again on the traditional power house of Whitehall. The best craftsmen made over the buildings to provide magnificent chapels in which the Roman rites could be performed. This public assertion of Catholicism against a dazzling backdrop of marble, gilding, painted wood, and canvas startled even loyal courtiers. Catholicism had long been fashionable at the Stuart court. Since 1603, each monarch had been married to a Catholic. Understandably, the consorts had turned their courts into Catholic enclaves. Also, sometimes bombastically, at other moments more discreetly, ambassadors practised the cult in their own chapels. Periodically these offered targets for popular anger. From 1686, however, the king himself publicly worshipped according to Catholic ceremonies. He had spent heavily, but for the glory of his God not of himself.

This architecture had practical as well as symbolic significance. The powerlessness of the later Stuarts to impose their preferences on their subjects seemed to be aptly summed up by the main monuments of their reigns. Instead of a durable royal palace, St Paul's cathedral, the mother church of the Anglican communion, and over fifty churches soared above the calcined city. Parliament and parishioners willingly financed these works. Winchester, in contrast, stood only as an incomplete shell. Grinling Gibbons's elegant baldacchino and statuary from James II's Whitehall were quickly crated up, and reused in less controversial settings. In Scotland, the ancient palace of Holyroodhouse was modernized while James bided his time there, but much of the stylistic innovation came from landowners who prospered under their absentee rulers. Ireland's low place in the Stuarts' thinking was shown again by their repeated refusals to devote much money to the improvement of the viceregal pad in Dublin. Hopes raised by the pre-war viceroy, Wentworth, that the grandeur of the office might be reflected in an opulent country seat slumbered after 1660. This was in keeping with the economical government of the kingdom. The idea that a member of his own family might deputize for the sovereign in Ireland was aired in the later 1670s. The popular royal bastard, Monmouth, was named as a possibility. It came to nothing. Unlike the Habsburgs of Spain, the Stuarts were not abundantly furnished with princes—or princesses—of the blood royal who might be promoted to this position. Furthermore, there were fears that a successful incumbent could build up an Irish base from which to launch a bid for more power. Already, Monmouth's victory over Scottish insurgents during 1679 warned of how he might increase his claims as a Protestant alternative to the Catholic James.

Here, indeed, was an element in the ominous problem of the later stages of Charles's reign. Notwithstanding his legendary virility, he had failed to father a legitimate heir. A succession crisis loomed. Those willing to think of options other than the accession of a known Catholic in the person of the next in line, James, contemplated either Monmouth or the king's nephew, William, prince of Orange. Since 1677, William was also the husband of James's elder daughter, Princess Mary. Even without the risk that by appointing any one of these to the Irish government their chances of succeeding to the crowns of all three kingdoms would be improved, the Stuarts habitually valued Ireland less than the kings of Spain esteemed the Spanish Netherlands. Thus Dublin never became the site of a vibrant court presided over by royalty after the fashion of Brussels or even of Edinburgh during James's short stay. Thereby a chance to speed the Anglicization of at least the Protestant elites was lost. In keeping with this approach, it was not any official residence for the governor but a hospital for military pensioners at Kilmainham which constituted the most impressive addition to the Dublin sky-line in these years. Moreover, Kilmainham Hospital, modelled closely on Les Invalides in Paris, was Ormond's rather than Charles II's enduring memorial.

The king through his distribution of favours could bind those from the outlying areas to him. But such sweeteners were given too haphazardly and were in any case too sparse to create more than individual obligations. After 1660, few Scots chose to locate themselves permanently in England and fewer than formerly were tied to the royal court. The Welsh through the royalist grandee Worcester (advanced in 1682 to the dukedom of Beaufort) and later through successive secretaries of state, Sir Leoline Jenkins and Francis Gwynn, enjoyed useful access to the court and its perquisites. More of the places once enjoyed by the Scots were taken by the English of Ireland. Ormond and his family were the principal winners. Others who found comfortable berths close to the king included Anglesey, Conway, Ranelagh, Sir Robert Southwell, and Sir William Temple, while the restless Orrery aspired to a place. Irish Catholics who had amused and helped Charles in exile were also welcomed. Their presence helped obtrude Irish questions. They also ensured that Irish evidence was included in the attempted indictments of arbitrary government at the end of the 1670s and, again even more centrally, during James's and Tyrconnell's rule.

Images of the monarch familiarized subjects with their obligations. Coins in the pocket, coats of arms hung in churches, statues erected in public places or frequently reproduced canvases reminded of the persons and order under which all lived. Reactions to these served as something of an index of attitudes towards the Stuarts. Reports from Dublin in 1667 that pictures of the king and queen had been trampled and torn warned of the growing disenchantment among both disappointed Catholics and alarmed Protestants. The decision of 1684 of the senior trading company in Dublin, the Merchants' Guild, to purchase a portrait of Charles II might seem rather belated. This group had nevertheless been caught up in a wave of loyalist sentiment, part spontaneous but also engineered, which had engulfed all three nations. In Edinburgh, the placing of a posthumous equestrian statue of the king in a prominent square elicited jaundiced comments. Apart from the extravagant cost, some thought it wrongly placed, with the tail pointing towards the figure of justice on the door of the Parliament House. Others were puzzled that Charles should be personified as a Roman emperor, although it was not an uncommon image. 'The vulgar people' were simply amazed. Some compared it to the brazen image of Nebuchadnezzar before which all should fall down and worship. Another identification was with the pale horse ridden by death in the Book of Revelation. Fanciful as these reactions might be, they warn that the imagery consecrated to the service of the dynasty could be variously interpreted. Under a veneer of deference to the ageing roués on the throne between 1660 and 1688, there survived tenacious traditions of independence and criticism. These coalesced with new grievances. By the end of 1688, James VII and II had estranged more than he had enchanted.

Figure 6 The Tichborne Dole, 1671, by Gillis van Tilborgh (1625–78).

5

The Economic and Social Context

J. A. Sharpe

Writing the social and economic history of the British Isles over the seventeenth century presents the historian with the formidable task of controlling and disciplining a mass of material which encompasses a sometimes bewilderingly diverse repertoire of experiences. This was, in the social and economic spheres, a century of change, and sometimes of very marked change, for the British Isles. Yet this process of socio-economic transition would have looked very different from the viewpoint of a Norfolk yeoman farmer, a Bristol merchant, an Edinburgh lawyer, a highland crofter, a Manx fisherman, or a Connacht cottar, while the womenfolk and children of such men would also have brought their distinctive perspectives to bear. That such a transition occurred is incontrovertible: by 1700 the British Isles contained what was one of the most advanced commercial sectors in Europe, which enjoyed trading links with most of the known world and, in particular, with a burgeoning empire on the eastern seaboard of North America. But this tale of commercial progress must be modified by the awareness that most of the population of the British Isles lived in small rural settlements, were involved primarily in sometimes very traditional forms of agriculture, and constructed their social horizons primarily in terms of the region, or perhaps even the community, where they lived. The difficulties of achieving a correct balance between continuity and change are especially acute when attempting an overview of the experiences of the numerous regional societies and economies which existed in the British Isles in the century after 1600.

Population and subsistence

We must, therefore, acknowledge and accept diversity. This is obvious, to take a logical starting point, in the very topography of the British Isles, and in the restrictions and opportunities which topography offered that fundamental economic activity, agriculture. Agrarian historians have variously identified ten or forty farming regions in Tudor and Stuart England, although perhaps the most simple distinction is that between a highland and a lowland zone, the dividing line running from the mouth of the Trent to the mouth of the Severn. In Scotland, more familiarly, historians, whether social, economic, cultural, or political, have long regarded the divide between highlands and lowlands as crucial, although both elements in this dichotomy contained a number of sub-regions. In Ireland, where the relatively wet climate favoured pastoral rather than arable farming, areas of high ground and bog both contributed to a diversity of agricultural regions. Turning to smaller geographical units, we find that individual counties usually contained a number of distinct agricultural zones: thus in Glamorgan the barren pastureland of the Blaenau, where peasant farmers raised cattle, contrasted with the fertile plains of the Bro, characterized by commercial arable farming and a stratum of increasingly wealthy gentry living off the profits of agriculture. Even in the Isle of Man, whose land surface of 220 square miles made it smaller than most counties, it is possible to differentiate between an upland region with the worst climate and the poorest soils, a number of plateaux surrounding that region, and a lowland zone where arable farming was possible.

The populations supported by this topographical diversity varied enormously. As will be appreciated, calculating populations in this pre-census era is an inexact science, and differing estimates have been produced. Broadly speaking, the population of England roughly doubled over the century before the 1630s, reaching five or five and a half million by that point. It then stabilized, staying at about that level or slightly below it for the remainder of the century. The populations of Wales and Scotland followed a similar trajectory. In Wales, there were perhaps 400,000 people, perhaps slightly less, in 1630, a figure which may be contrasted with estimates of 278,000 in 1536 and 489,000 in 1750. In Scotland, where documentation is even less helpful than for England and Wales, there was a population of perhaps 700,000–800,000 in the late sixteenth century, and probably a million by 1700. In all three countries the demographic expansion which had been such a feature of European life since 1500 or so halted just before the middle of the seventeenth century. Similarly, in all three countries population density increased more in some areas than others. In England, it was the south which gained proportionately most from population increase. In Scotland, even though the population remained much more evenly spread between lowlands and highlands than it was to become in later periods, the greatest population growth was in the central lowlands.

The population history of Ireland for this period is more problematic, constituting a variation from the European norm. Here the population seems to have lacked the dynamism which characterized much of Europe over the sixteenth century, but expanded throughout the seventeenth, in contrast to other parts of the British Isles and much of continental Europe. Ireland's population (and it must be stressed that these figures are estimates) stood at perhaps 1.4 million in 1600, 2.1 million in 1641, 2.2 million in 1687, and 2.8 million in 1712. This increase is all the more remarkable given the demographic disaster that the warfare which set in from 1641 constituted for Ireland. This conflict was, in the words of one Irish poet, *an codadh do chriochnaigh Eire*, 'the war that finished Ireland'. Not only was traditional Celtic society shattered by the war and the subsequent settlement, but between 15 and 20 per cent of Ireland's population died. The subsequent recovery must owe much to Ireland's underdeveloped, indeed colonial, status. The economy in the second half of the seventeenth century, despite brief episodes of volatile instability, was expanding, while the agrarian base in particular had sufficient potential for growth to be able to absorb population increase. Fortunately, renewed warfare after 1689 lacked both the intensity and the longevity to inflict serious demographic damage. Ireland also, in consequence of its political subjugation to Britain, experienced a massive inflow of settlers, most notably the Scots who planted Ulster. There were maybe 100,000 British settlers in Ireland by 1641, a presence augmented by the Cromwellian soldiers who settled in the 1650s (many of these married Irish women and, to the despair of the authorities, went native) and the Scots who came to Ireland in the aftermath of famine in Scotland in the 1690s. This influx, to return to the theme of varied regional experiences, meant that Ulster, in the early seventeenth century a backward and underpopulated region which had been wrecked by warfare, was by 1700 the most heavily populated part of Ireland, and enjoyed a relatively advanced economy.

Demographic developments were of great significance for early modern societies, not least because the population fluctuations were one of the most important influences on the economy. An increase in population was, generally speaking, the most important cause of increased demand for both agricultural and manufactured goods. Over most of Europe, in the late sixteenth and early seventeenth centuries, this increased demand was met by a relatively inelastic supply: in many areas, to put it simply, economic expansion did not keep pace with demographic increase. There was not enough work to go round, so people who were dependent on wages found that they had greater difficulty in obtaining work, and that the real value of their wages declined. To take one index, it has been calculated that for building workers in southern England a day's pay in the 1610s would buy only about a third of the food which a day's wages would have bought in 1500, and that the value of their real wages did not regain their late medieval levels until well into the nineteenth century. More dramatically, the precarious relationship between agricultural production and population meant that in times of harvest failure a large proportion of the population would face hunger, and possibly death through starvation or those famine-induced diseases which malnutrition or the eating of contaminated food might bring on.

This assertion raises the problem of what people actually ate. Evidence for the upper classes, and especially the nobility and gentry, is plentiful. To take one of many such examples, the account books for 1671 of the Scottish nobleman Robert, Lord Carnegie, reveal that he and his household consumed soup and broth, meat twice a day, other protein foods such as birds and fish, bread, a considerable amount of alcohol, very little milk, a few eggs, and a fair amount of vegetables. This was probably typical of the nobility, although on special occasions greater quantities of sometimes more ornate food might be eaten. In general, as a result of this high protein diet, members of the elite were on average fitter, longer lived, and taller than the peasantry. Conversely, overindulgence in food and alcohol could bring its own problems, and some of the comfortably off were, if nothing else, certainly fatter than most of the common folk. Thus the Montgomery gentleman Arthur Williams (if we may borrow an example from the early eighteenth century) was so overweight when he died in 1723 that he had to be buried quickly, 'he being so corpulent he could not be kept'.[1]

Exploration of lower class diets is as yet barely begun. Substantial farmers and the better off tradesmen doubtlessly ate well, with meat regularly on their tables. The poor, so the current level of knowledge suggests, ate badly. The admittedly impressionistic evidence suggests that those at the bottom of society lived on a diet from which meat, except perhaps in the form of bacon, was largely absent, and which was marked by its dependence on cereals and its monotony. On the Isle of Man the poor ate milk, butter, cheese, barley bread, and oatcakes, although they also consumed herring and other fish. Much the same situation obtained in Wales. In Cardigan, for example, an agricultural labourer would live on oatmeal bread, cheese, butter, a little meat, leeks, cabbage, onions, peas, beans, and eggs. In Scotland, the basis of the diet was oatmeal, eaten as bannocks or gruel (the first unequivocal reference to porridge comes from an English traveller, Richard James, in 1615), supplemented with milk, butter, cheese, and kail. In Ireland the poor ate griddle-baked oatcakes (one observer spoke of large brown oatcakes a foot and a half broad), barley bread, peas, dairy produce, and cattle blood mixed with oatmeal to form a primitive black pudding. By the end of the seventeenth century the diet of the Irish poor had extended to include potatoes, a crop which was also becoming known in northern England and Scotland.

---

[1] Cited in Geraint H. Jenkins, *The Foundations of Modern Wales: Wales 1642–1780* (Oxford, 1987), 99.

The diet of the poor depended heavily on cereals. The consequences of a failure in the cereal crop were therefore very serious. All parts of the British Isles had suffered from a run of bad harvests in the 1590s, and the spectre of famine was to return again in the early 1620s. In that decade bad harvests led to starvation in Scotland, with 1623 being an especially bad year, a crisis in Ireland was averted when the authorities banned grain exports, while parish registers in northern England record numerous deaths from famine. Consider, for example, the registers of Greystoke, in Cumberland. These noted in 1623 the death of 'a poor fellow destitute of succour' who was brought to the house of a parish constable, where he died; of Dorothy Patterson, 'a poor hungerstarved beggar child'; of James Irwin, 'a poor beggar stripling born upon the borders of England. He died in Johnby in great misery'; of Thomas, 'child of Richard Bell, a poor man, which child died for very want of food and maintenance to live'; of Jane, 'wife of Anthony Cowlman, of Johnby, late deceased, which woman died in Edward Dawson's barn of Greystoke for want of maintenance'.[2] As these grim entries suggest, it was the marginal elements in society, the young, the very old, and the poor who were generally most prone to die when the harvest failed and bread prices went up. It was, perhaps, a sign of the increasing sophistication of English agriculture that this was the last dearth which saw mass mortality. The prospect of bad harvests remained a constant cause of concern in England, and there were series of harvest failures in the middle years of the century, and in the 1690s. Many went hungry, and doubtlessly not a few died from malnutrition or diseases to which their resistance had been weakened by hunger. Crimes against property went up (from the 1590s an infallible indicator of economic dislocation in England), and there were grain riots. But mass starvation was a thing of the past.

North of the border things were very different. As we have noted, Scotland had already suffered badly in 1623, with Dumfries losing a fifth of its population in that year, and Dunfermline at least that proportion. In the 1690s, it has been estimated, between 5 and 15 per cent of Scotland's population either died through

---

[2] *The Registers of the Parish of Greystoke in the County of Cumberland, 1559–1757*, ed. A. M. Maclean (Kendall, 1911).

famine or emigrated, mainly to Ireland, to escape such a death. In some areas the population loss was more than a third. The situation was graphically described by an observer of 1699:

For want some die in the wayside, some drop down in the streets, the poor sucking babe starving for want of milk, which the empty breasts of their mothers cannot furnish them. Everyone may see death in the face of the poor that abound everywhere; the thinness of their visage, their ghostly looks, their feebleness, their agues and their fluxes threaten them with sudden death if care be not taken of them. And it is not only common wandering beggars that are in this case, but many householders who lived well by their labour and their industry are now by want forced to abandon their dwellings. And they and their little ones must beg, and in their necessity they take what they can get, spoiled victual, yea, some eat these beasts which have died of some disease which may occasion a plague among them.[3]

Anybody wishing to romanticize the pre-industrial past would do well to ponder such passages.

They would also do well to consider another fact of seventeenth-century life, virtual helplessness in the face of disease. Diaries from the period are full of references to minor ailments, and to the discomfort which might accompany attempts to have more serious ones treated by contemporary doctors. At least the most feared pestilence of this and previous centuries, the bubonic plague, left the British Isles in the late seventeenth century, famously celebrating its departure from England by killing 70,000 or more Londoners in 1665. But there were other killing diseases: smallpox, typhoid, typhus, and the distinctive childhood diseases of diphtheria, measles (which often led to pneumonia), and scarlet fever. Some indication of their collective impact is provided by the consensus among historians that the end of population growth in the 1630s and the subsequent stagnation of population owed much to the presence of more virulent strains of existing diseases.

Infant mortality was especially high, with something like a half of children dying before their first birthday. Even so, the high birth rate in an age which was largely innocent of contraception meant that the population was a young one, with perhaps 40 per

---

[3] Sir Robert Sibbald, *Provision for the Poor in Time of Dearth and Scarcity* (Edinburgh, 1699), 3.

cent or more of the populace being aged under 21. And, for those who survived to 21, the chances of living to a reasonable age were not too bad. The average life expectancy in the early eighteenth century was perhaps 35 in England, and 30 in Scotland. But in both countries, as in all of Europe, such averages were consistently kept low by high infant mortality.

Social structure

The early modern British Isles therefore possessed a distinctive age structure. They also possessed a range of distinctive social structures. In England, the key socio-economic configuration was that which prevailed in the south-east, East Anglia, and the east midlands: an agricultural system which was marked by nucleated villages and commercial farming at whose hub lay substantial farmers ('yeomen' in contemporary parlance) who worked large, compact farms which they rented from gentry landlords, and who employed landless or near landless agricultural labourers to work the land for them. The social structure was not, of course, as simple as this (there were still many 'husbandmen', or middling tenant farmers, for example); but the logic of the steady rise of commercial farming in England was the emergence of that tripartite division into tenant farmers, landlords, and labourers which was taken to be characteristic of English agriculture by about 1800. Behind this division there lay a history of changing tenurial arrangements and changing forms of agricultural organization. Traditional tenures, and any vestiges of the communal influence on farming through manorial institutions, were gradually eroded. The emphasis now shifted towards individual holdings, leasehold tenures, and the maximization of profit.

The situation was very different in other parts of the British Isles, although in many areas the logic of capitalism was challenging traditional social and tenurial arrangements. Developments in lowland Scotland remain under-researched, yet were clearly complex. Outside of the Lothians, which had been settled in the early Middle Ages by Anglian incomers, there was little by way of nucleated settlement, and agriculture had traditionally been practised through farms held in joint tenancy, frequently worked by kin groups, and always depending upon cooperation and agreement over common crops, common rotations, and common dates for sowing and reaping. But from about 1660 lowland agriculture was increasingly involved in providing wool, beef, mutton, skins, and cereals for the urban sector in Scotland and northern England, and agriculture accordingly became more commercial. Thus on the Panmure estates in the Forfarshire lowlands, one of the few areas where intensive research has been carried out, by the late seventeenth century over 67 per cent of farms were held in single tenancy, a sophisticated system of debt and credit was emerging, and differentiation in size of holdings indicates the evolution of a social structure marked by successful, commercially minded tenant farmers on the one hand and poor cottars on the other. These cottars would own little more than a hovel to live in, a kailyard, the right to grow a little grain on common arable land ('intack'), and the right to graze a few animals on the moor.

In the highlands, traditional social structures survived longer. Here the key lay in clan organization. But as many Scottish historians have commented, although the clan undoubtedly existed (and, of course, the institution is central to popular conceptions of Scottish history) its exact nature and functions remain elusive. Its origins lay in kinship (the term is derived from the Gaelic *A'Chlann*, literally the children), and a notion of blood-ties remained central to clan ideology. Yet from an early date clan networks incorporated individuals or groupings connected to the clan by fictive kinship, and others who owed service to the clan chief through what was basically a feudal set of arrangements. Highland agriculture was predominantly pastoral, with arable farming being organized through various communal arrangements, most famously runrig, a system analogous to English strip farming, which generally depended on joint tenures, and, in some areas at least, involved periodic redistributions of land. Throughout the seventeenth century central authority in Edinburgh and London was anxious to incorporate clan elites more closely into the Scottish, and indeed British, political systems, and in this they were in large measure successful. There are also indications that the market economy penetrated highland farming. Certainly by the late seventeenth century cattle were being sent from the highlands into lowland Scotland and England, and it is perhaps indicative of the degree of integration with the wider world of capitalism which the highland elite had already achieved that those controlling and hence profiting from this trade were clan chiefs, lairds, or those leading clan tenants known as tacksmen.

It was Ireland which was to experience the most cataclysmic change in landholding arrangements. In 1600 there was something like English manorial organization, frequently involving farms let on twenty-one-year leases and sharecropping, in the Pale and other Anglicized areas. But over most of Ireland farming was carried out by kin groupings, and there seems to have been little notion of private property in land or of large-scale commercial farming. As in highland Scotland the most important element in agriculture was raising cattle, and there were rhythmic seasonal movements of herds in a practice known as hooleying. These traditional arrangements were first challenged by the plantation of Ulster, and were shattered definitively by the settlement which followed the mid-century warfare. In 1642 the English Parliament, having apparently already decided that all the Irish were guilty of complicity in the 1641 Rebellion, passed the Adventurers Act which allocated 2.5 million square miles of Irish land in return for £1,000,000. The Cromwellian army's victory was followed by the implementation of English land law over all of Ireland, and the expropriation of Ireland's Catholic landholding elite, most of whom were relocated in the poorest area of Ireland, Connacht. The effects of these changes on that elite, and on traditional Irish tenurial arrangements, were massive. But if Irish landlords went, most of the Irish tenantry remained: even in Ulster, they continued to farm the uplands while the more fertile lowland areas were settled by the Scots. Irish agriculture remained largely pastoral and relatively uncommercial, while even in Ulster rural settlement was characterized by scattered farms and hamlets rather than nucleated villages.

The urban sector

As in much of early modern Europe, the most important elements in the economy and society of the British Isles were agriculture and rural social structures. But there as elsewhere in Europe one of the signs of economic advance was the presence of an urban sector. There was a variety of reasons why towns expanded in this period. Perhaps the most obvious was trade, whether the global trade which was to motor the growth of London in the post-Restoration period, or the purely local trade which helped foster the growth of dozens of urban centres throughout the British Isles. But towns also supplied services, notably those offered by lawyers, doctors, and educational institutions. Many of them were also centres of government, either national or regional, their mercantile elite being complemented by administrators, army officers, and senior churchmen. These factors helped make towns more attractive to elites as lifestyles changed among the aristocracy and gentry: the norms of genteel or polite society, which were becoming so important by 1700, flourished more happily in an urban environment which could offer a concentration of people of taste and fashion, and of the cultural facilities upon which such people depended.

For England, and gradually for the British Isles more generally, the crucial factor in urban history was the growth of London. In the Middle Ages 'London' meant the City, the walled area, and perhaps the immediately adjacent suburbs. But certainly by 1700 'London' is a shorthand for something which is perhaps better described as greater London, a metropolitan area which encompassed the City of London, the City of Westminster, an increasingly urbanized area of Middlesex which was spreading into what was later to become known as the East End, and, south of the Thames over London Bridge, the important borough of Southwark. In round terms the population of this megapolis stood at 200,000 in 1600, 375,000 in 1650, and close on 500,000 in 1700, by which stage London was the biggest city in Europe outside Constantinople, with perhaps one in ten of the population of England and Wales living there. London dwarfed other cities in the British Isles in importance as well as size. The court was there, the leading legal institutions for England and Wales were there, the financial institutions which supported a burgeoning world-wide commerce were there, and it was there that matters of taste and fashion were decided. London's needs also acted as a stimulus to internal trade, with grain production in East Anglia, coal production on Tyneside, and cattle raising in northern England and lowland Scotland all locked into the London market.

Although London was by far the largest city in the British Isles, there were a number of other urban success stories. Perhaps the most significant was that of Dublin, whose population reached 60,000 by 1700, making it the second biggest city in the British Isles. Dublin's fortunes were linked firmly to the British ascendancy, but by the late seventeenth century it was clearly an important and sophisticated city, boasting a theatre, a philosophical society, two cathedrals, a university, a college of physicians, and a flourishing book trade. Cork, the only other Irish city of any size, had a population of 20,000, Limerick and Galway about 5,000 apiece. In Scotland the most important city was Edinburgh, which, with Leith, its satellite port, had a population of 40,000 by the end of the century. Edinburgh, like Dublin, had a metropolitan feel to it, even after the royal presence was removed in 1603, with a substantial number of lawyers, town houses owned by noblemen (these probably increasing in number and importance as the century progressed), a population which included wigmakers, doctors, and coachmakers, and flourishing cultural and intellectual life. This intellectual and cultural life was underpinned by Edinburgh's university, which began to function in 1583, and the Advocates Library. The latter, established in 1689, from 1709 enjoyed the status of a copyright library, entitled to a copy of every book published in Britain, and, of course, was destined to be transformed into the National Library of Scotland in 1925. Yet if Edinburgh was Scotland's largest city, the one which experienced the most marked proportionate growth over the seventeenth century was Glasgow, which became the second largest Scottish city, with a population of 14,000, by 1700. Norwich, with 30,000 inhabitants, was then England's second largest city, but was being challenged by Bristol, with its population of 20,000. Newcastle, whose elite was growing rich on the profits of the coal trade, had 16,000 inhabitants.

Despite the existence of these centres, urban life remained undeveloped over much of the British Isles. In the Isle of Man, the main towns of Douglas, Peel, Castletown, and Ramsey were little more than substantial villages. One of the major deficiencies in the economy of lowland Scotland was the absence of those small towns of 3,000 or so inhabitants which could be so important to the local economy. In Wales a number of urban settlements experienced a marked proportionate population increase in the late sixteenth and seventeenth centuries, but the absolute size of their respective populations remained low. Wrexham, with 3,225 inhabitants in 1670, was then the largest town in Wales, with Swansea having just under 1,200. Economically, many Welsh were linked by trading networks associated with English towns: Bristol for south Wales, Shrewsbury, an important outlet for Welsh wool producers, for central Wales, and Chester for north Wales. The urban experience was therefore a mixed one, with some towns experiencing declining economic fortunes. But by the late seventeenth century many English towns were enjoying something of a renaissance as they shifted their functions from industry to providing services and leisure facilities for the local gentry. The process became more marked in the early eighteenth century, and is perhaps neatly symbolized by Beau Nash's arrival as master of ceremonies at Bath in 1705. But by that date York, Preston, Norwich, and a number of other county towns were making the transition towards being centres of entertainment and services for the county elite and other visitors.

The fact that most towns were small (there were probably less than ten in the whole of the British Isles with a population of more than 10,000 by 1700) meant that in many ways the experience of urban life was not that dissimilar from a rural existence. A large proportion of any urban population was composed of recent immigrants from the rural areas, while even in London the sights, sounds, and perhaps above all smells, of city life were very similar to those of the countryside. Nevertheless, urban social structures showed some distinctive characteristics. Most towns of any size were dominated, socially, economically, and politically, by an elite of merchants who controlled or sought to control the local economy and who, via borough or similar institutions, controlled local government. Edinburgh, for example, was dominated by the burgesses, the merchant elite into whose ranks entry was eased for those who had been apprenticed to a burgess or were married to a burgess's daughter. In London, too, holders of high civic office were recruited from a very small group, and the trend towards urban oligarchy can be traced in such diverse towns as booming Newcastle upon Tyne, industrially stagnant York, small towns like Maidstone, and that emergent manufacturing centre, Sheffield. As well as the traditional merchant oligarchs, towns contained other groupings of important people. Edinburgh, as we have noted, possessed a thriving community of lawyers, in ecclesiastical centres like York the clergy played an important part in urban life, while in most provincial towns a handful of doctors and lawyers would ply their trades and develop a middle-class lifestyle.

Urban dwellers beneath these substantial merchants and professionals are usually badly documented and have been comparatively little studied. The ballast of urban society was provided by craftsmen, the men of middling fortune, some at least of whom, through a mixture of diligence, business sense, and luck were doing well out of the economic changes of the period. Medieval guild structures had lost much of their power, but in many of the larger towns, not least London, craft organizations survived and were still of some importance. It was a sign of the growing economic sophistication of the period that opportunities for tradesmen were there, and were taken advantage of. Thus the urban vitality of Edinburgh, Glasgow, and Dublin was demonstrated by a thriving and ever more complex body of tradesmen and craftsmen, and even such small centres as Castletown and Peel in the Isle of Man could, by the end of the century, boast slaters, glaziers, coopers, carpenters and joiners, tailors and blacksmiths. The less wealthy craftsmen and tradesmen, however, would shade imperceptibly into the ranks of the urban poor. Most of these would be casual or unskilled workers, labourers, porters, charwomen, and so on, while, in the larger urban centres at least, there was also a stratum of petty criminals, beggars, and prostitutes. The urban poor, many of them recent immigrants into the towns where they lived, remain a shadowy group, most frequently entering the historical record when they got into trouble or requested poor relief. Condemned to live in the worst housing, more vulnerable than the richer townsfolk to disease, ill fed even at the best of times, and with uncertain employment prospects, their lot was a hard one.

Trade and manufacture

Towns meant trade, and over the seventeenth century the commerce of the British Isles was affected fundamentally by the emergence of the Atlantic economy, and the primacy of London, and to a lesser extent Bristol, within that economy. In 1550 London's trade, like that of England generally, had been overwhelmingly with Europe; by 1700 it was global. Cloth, still going mainly to Europe, remained England's main export, its value rising from a maximum of £3,000,000 in 1640 to £4,500,000 in 1700. By that date, however, the quays of London and Bristol were stacked with other goods, many of them virtually unknown at the beginning of the seventeenth century. In 1619, for example, Virginia had sent 20,000lb of tobacco to England, where it was a luxury, selling at £1–£2 per lb. In 1700 some 22,000,000lb of tobacco were exported from the colonies to England. Three-quarters of this were re-exported to Europe, but the remainder was consumed at home, enjoyed by all classes at 1s per lb. Yet England's commercial revolution included one element which precludes any simple celebration of mercantile success. The late seventeenth century saw the arrival of the slave trade, which developed rapidly after the Navigation Acts of 1660 and the formation of the Royal Africa Company in 1672. The company was extremely successful, exchanging calicoes and assorted manufactured goods for slaves on the West African coast, perhaps 5,000 a year by the late seventeenth century, shipping them for sale to the West Indies and the American colonies, the company's ships then returning to England filled with colonial goods. After 1700 Bristol and Liverpool merchants joined their London counterparts in this lucrative but shameful trade.

Recognition of this major upsurge in long-distance commerce must not obscure the continuing importance of short-range trade along well established routes. Scotland had long enjoyed trading links with Scandinavia, the Baltic, the Low Countries, and France, and despite the growing importance of commercial links with England after 1603, trade between Scottish ports and these areas continued. South Wales and Ireland exported to France and the

Iberian Peninsula, while the Isle of Man also enjoyed limited trading links with France. Generally, all of these areas exported primary goods: meat, dairy produce, wool, corn, cattle, hides, and timber (from Ireland), and in return imported fruit, wine, tar, pitch, timber (into Scotland from Scandinavia), and a variety of luxury and exotic goods. There were also, of course, seaborne trading zones within the British Isles. The Newcastle coal trade depended primarily on sending coal by ship to London. In the twelve months following Christmas 1684, 616,016 tons of coal were shipped from Newcastle to the capital, and by 1703 some 600 ships, most of them built in the north-east, were involved in the trade. A more cosmopolitan trading zone seems to have centred on Bristol, involving other ports in the English south-west, south Wales, and ports on Ireland's eastern and southern seaboards. Tragic testimony of patterns of seaborne trade within this zone comes in 1652. In that year the small Welsh port of Haverfordwest, barely recovered from devastation caused by the civil war, was ravaged by a visitation of the plague. The pestilence had arrived in Galway, brought by a Spanish ship, in 1650, had then followed the trade routes to Limerick, Waterford, and Dublin (where 1,000 people died in one week in September 1650), and went from there to Bristol, where it was firmly established in 1651. It then spread into south Wales, and was brought to Haverfordwest, according to local tradition, by two sailors from Milford Haven who visited the town's Saturday market. But usually the ships calling at the various ports in the area brought more welcome cargoes than the plague, and helped, via Bristol, to integrate Wales and Ireland into the Atlantic economy.

Seaborne trade, much of it carried in very small craft, was therefore of considerable importance. It was made more so because of the difficulties of inland trade. Throughout most of the British Isles the state of the roads created major complications for the transit of goods by land: it was, for example, cheaper to import timber to lowland Scotland from Denmark than it was to bring it down from forests in the highlands. Yet despite the problems of road transport (and one is perhaps a little too dependent on the impressionistic accounts of travellers here) internal trade, with goods carried by pack pony, cart, or on the backs of pedlars, developed steadily over the seventeenth century. The wills of people of even moderate property demonstrate the spread of small manufactured items and luxury or semi-luxury goods, of pots and pans, clothing made of cloth from distant regions, of clocks and books.

Many of these wills, indeed, attest to the development of industry or, as the age would have put it, manufactures. The British Isles were still a long way from real industrialization: factories were unknown, and manufacturing was mostly carried out in the household, often as a secondary occupation for men, or as a way in which women or children could supplement the family income. The most important product was textiles: there were important areas of textile production in England, notably in East Anglia, Wiltshire, Somerset and Devon, and West Yorkshire, but most other areas produced at least some wool or cloth, much of it admittedly of an inferior nature. Metallurgy was underdeveloped, although there was considerable iron production. Shipbuilding, for the coastal trade, for long-range commerce, and for the Royal Navy, was a major enterprise, while the rebuilding and urban expansion of the period made work for quarrymen, brickmakers, and building workers. Coal mining, too, was growing in importance. The most dramatic development here was the massive expansion of the Tyneside coal industry. In the accounting year 1597–8 some 162,552 tons of coal were shipped from Newcastle, a figure which rose, as noted, to 616,016 tons by 1683–4. By the end of the century the Tyneside pits employed a large and diversified workforce, and also enjoyed fairly sophisticated mining technology. The Tyneside coal industry was the most advanced in the British Isles, but mining was well established elsewhere. There was coal mining in Yorkshire and Lancashire, in lowland Scotland, and in the hinterland of Swansea, where an important expanding coal industry, highly capitalized and using relatively advanced technology and skilled workers brought in from Germany and other parts of Britain, had been established by 1700.

Commerce and manufacture made a few merchants rich. Isolated success stories might include Sir William Dick, the provost of Edinburgh, the richest merchant in Scotland, who was ruined when he lost his fortune after lending it to the Scots Covenanting army in the 1640s, Sir Humphrey Mackworth, who made a fortune out of coal mining and lead and copper smelting in south Wales, and

David Murray, a Manx merchant who made most of his money from re-exporting tobacco, and was worth £3,657 when he died in 1704. Yet throughout the seventeenth century, and long beyond its end, the wealthiest and most influential social group was the upper reaches of the landed nobility.

Changing elite lifestyles

Despite the wealth of some of their most prosperous members, the landed orders were a variegated group comprehending individuals and families of very varied fortunes. In England and Wales the problem of analysing the landed orders has been compounded by a historiographical tradition which has regarded the peers (that is, landholders with titles who sat in the house of lords) as a social group separate from, and at times in conflict with, lesser landholders, the gentry. A more productive approach would seem to be to regard the peers and the gentry as strata within one landholding elite: certainly, some of the richer gentry, who might themselves expect eventually to receive titles, were as wealthy as the peers, and were culturally and educationally on a par with them. The gentry, however, included not only these very rich and polished adornments of the *nobilitas minor*, but also uncouth and impoverished landholders hanging on to the merest rags of gentility, in many ways indistinguishable from the more prosperous yeoman farmers among whom they lived. Not only the upper gentry, but the titled aristocracy stood in contrast to these 'mere' gentry. In 1559 an English peer's average income was some £2,000, a figure which had risen to £5,000 by 1640. As always, averages mask variation: throughout the seventeenth century some peers were extremely wealthy and also wielded considerable power. They were, however, now less likely to express their power through the mobilization of armed men, but rather maintained their ascendancy and gained their political ends through local patronage networks and the control of parliament.

In Scotland, by about 1600 the nobility were becoming affected by those shifts in noble lifestyles and in the power relationship between nobility and monarchical authority which was one of the great themes of early modern European history, and which had already created some marked changes in England. Scotland in the late fifteenth and sixteenth centuries had been unlucky in suffering from a run of monarchs whose premature deaths had resulted in a series of royal minorities. James VI was determined to redress the consequent dilution of monarchical power, and set about establishing a relatively effective state which, as in other parts of Europe, was effective because it incorporated the nobility. What is striking is that, once royal power had been asserted and spectacular terminations to the careers of a few especially wayward aristocrats had been engineered, the nobles, in the lowlands at least, seemed happy to be incorporated. As with England, there existed in Scotland both a *nobilitas major*, composed of peers, and a *nobilitas minor*, the lairds. Like the English gentry, the lairds were a very mixed group, ranging from men of wealth, education, and political power to the 'bonnet lairds', some of them indistinguishable for all practical purposes from wealthier tenant farmers. But the Scottish nobility, like their equivalents elsewhere in Europe, were gradually becoming more cultured, and were being sucked into royal government. James VI, like most effective early modern monarchs, ruled *through* rather than *against* his elites. Although an attempt to introduce English-style justices of the peace foundered, local landholders became more involved in government, some of them became royal bureaucrats at Edinburgh, and yet others sent their younger sons to university to become lawyers. James's accession to the English crown in 1603 extended the opportunities for the richer and more enterprising of the Scots nobility, and from that date the Scotsman on the make became a recurrent feature of English society.

Incorporating the highland nobility proved a more difficult and more lengthy task, compounded as it was by the political troubles which afflicted Scotland from 1637 and which were not really brought to an end until 1745. Yet even the highland chieftains were gradually incorporated into the Scottish and British political and economic networks. In the later seventeenth century the traditional way of life of Scots Gaeldom was undermined by the Edinburgh government, and perhaps even more markedly by the commercial managerial strategies of noblemen like the dukes of Argyll. These steadily moved clansmen to a system where traditional tenures were replaced with short leases, rents were raised, traditions of hospitality and patronage diluted, and in which petty clan gentry, tacksmen, were given a closely monitored role as local estate managers.

But it was the Irish landholding classes who were to suffer the most dramatic, and least desired, changes in their fortune. In the early seventeenth century, whatever the hierarchical divisions within them, Irish landholders were divided into two groups, the Gaelic ('Old Irish') and the Anglo-Irish (or 'Old English'). The Tudor conquest had left both of these groups, however unhappy they may have been with being recast as English-style landowners, in possession of their lands: the Tudors had been more anxious to assert sovereignty than expropriate. But the 'flight of the earls' in 1607, and the unsuccessful revolt of Sir Cahir O'Doherty of Inishowen, left the way open for the expropriation of Ulster's landowning elite and its replacement with English and Scottish 'undertakers'. Both 'Old Irish' and 'Old English' landholders remained in other parts of Ireland, but with the latter group in an especially ambivalent position, given that it claimed to be loyal to the crown despite the Catholicism of many of its members. Yet the Dublin government, like nearly every government in Europe, had to rule through established landed elites, and both the Old English and the Old Irish might well have maintained their social and economic ascendancy had it not been for the Irish Rising of 1641 and its terrible aftermath. The English reconquest of Ireland in 1650 was followed by the expropriation of Catholic landholders, Old English and Old Irish alike, the transplantation of those that survived to Connacht, and a massive influx of English and Scottish landowners and settlers. There was some readjustment after the Restoration, but from the late seventeenth century the dominant gentry and peers in Ireland were of English or Scottish extraction, were Protestant, and looked primarily to England for their cultural models.

Peers and upper gentry, whether English, Irish, Scots, or Welsh, enjoyed wealth, prestige and power. Individual families might crash at any time, due to bad luck, political miscalculation, or economic mismanagement, while the later seventeenth century seems to have been a generally difficult period for the landed orders, with a proportion of the lesser gentry going under economically and being forced to give up their lands. Those landholders who weathered such adversities have left us lasting symbols of their well being in the form of their houses. The late Tudor and early Stuart periods were the time of the 'great rebuilding' in England, when peers and gentry celebrated the buoyancy of their rent rolls by building new country houses. An outstanding example was Hatfield House, built between 1607 and 1611 on the site of an old royal palace by Robert Cecil, earl of Salisbury, James VI and I's first minister in England. This tendency for the very great to build large houses was continued (if we may extend our argument into the early eighteenth century) by Blenheim Palace and Castle Howard. But there were also many smaller country houses built in England in the seventeenth century, notably Wilton House near Salisbury, and Stoke Bruerne in Northamptonsire, both constructed in the 1630s and both showing early vestiges of the Palladian style which was to become so dominant two generations later.

The urge among nobles and gentry to build grand houses was less marked in other parts of the British Isles, but certainly in both Scotland and Ireland the generally pacific conditions at the end of the century encouraged a demilitarization of the housing of the landed orders. In Scotland in 1632 Sir Robert Kerr, writing to his son about renovations to the family's fortified tower house, suggested that the inconvenient old windows, designed for defence, should not be replaced, on the grounds that the existing peaceful conditions in Scotland might be replaced by a return to the old habits of feuding. A generation later Patrick Lyon, earl of Strathmore, obviously very much at ease with what he perceived as a new era of tranquillity, commented that 'there is no man more against the old fashion of towers and castles than I am, for who can delight to live in his house as a prison?' He continued that such houses were 'quite out of fashion, as feuds are, which is a great happiness, the country being generally more civilized than it was'.[4] Strathmore was, however, responsible for the major renovation of an old fortress, Glamis castle, which was almost as ruinous as were his family fortunes when he took possession of his estate in 1660. Between 1670 and his death in 1695 the earl lived in Glamis: thus, despite the extensive

---

[4] Cited in T. C. Smout, *A History of the Scottish People 1560–1830* (London, 1969), 117.

refurbishments he made, contrary to the observations just quoted, Strathmore inhabited what was the grandest example of old Scottish baronial. Yet the sentiments he voiced are instructive: all over the British Isles, noblemen were celebrating the virtues of civility, and were willing to express it through both the exterior design and the interior decoration and furnishing of their houses.

Most people lived in rather less magnificent structures. Many prosperous English yeomen had shared in the 'great rebuilding' of the decades around 1600, while the survival of substantial late seventeenth-century farmhouses in many parts of Wales and lowland Scotland testifies to a growing profitability in agriculture in those areas. The poor, conversely, for the most part lived in dismal dwellings. An observer in Scotland in 1679 described the poor living in 'such miserable huts as never eye beheld; men, women and children pig together in a poor mousehole of mud, heath and some like matter; in some parts where turf is plentiful they build up little cabins thereof with arched roofs of turf without a stick of timber in it'.[5] Such dwellings were temporary: 'when their house is dry enough to burn, it serves them for fuel and they remove to another'. A similar note was struck by a report of the housing of the poor at Welwyn's castle in Pembrokeshire, mud-walled hovels, built from 'a sort of extempore erection of dirt and clay called *clom*',[6] while other accounts from Wales describe houses walled with clay or turf, roofed with rushes, windowless, with an open hearth and no chimneys, one-roomed hovels in effect. Sir William Petty, the great 'political arithmetician', provides us with statistics for late seventeenth-century Ireland. He estimated that there were 100,000 houses there worth less than 10 shillings rent annually, and a further 60,000 which, although of a higher rentable value, had no chimneys, but rather an open hearth and a hole in the roof. The first of these categories of dwellings, wrote Petty, running together what he evidently regarded as the main symptoms of backwardness, were places where the inhabitants 'live upon milk, potatoes and weeds, and in which no English is spoken—all Catholics'.[7]

---

[5] P. Hume Brown, *Early Travellers in Scotland* (Edinburgh, 1881), 260.

[6] Cited in Jenkins, *Wales 1642–1780*, 105.

[7] *The Petty Papers: Some Unpublished Writings of Sir William Petty*, ed. Henry William Edmund Petty Fitz Maurice (2 vols. London, 1927), ii. 58.

Social problems and disorder

The presence of a vast body of poor, the outcome of that great demographic expansion of the late sixteenth and early seventeenth centuries, was an accepted fact of life. Legislation passed in 1598 and 1601 for England and Wales had probably gone further than anywhere else in Europe to establish a nationally applicable system to deal with them. At the core of the system lay the regular rating of more substantial householders, for whom payment of the poor rate probably became the most familiar form of taxation. The money thus collected was kept in the custody of the overseers of the poor, parochially appointed officials who were also responsible for disbursing poor relief and providing the parish with an annual account of what they had collected and disbursed. Scotland, too, passed a series of poor laws in the late sixteenth century, although the system of compulsory rating was not introduced there. Obviously, money collected and disbursed through the poor law could do little more than partially remedy the poverty which was endemic at the best of times and which could reach terrifying proportions in periods of harvest failure or economic dislocation. Even so, a number of individuals, notably widows, received regular payments of a few pence, temporary relief would be given to unusually large families, or ones where the breadwinner was ill or out of work through no fault of his own, while individuals might receive a small dole when they were down on their luck. The poor law, along with a continuing tradition of private charity, could only ameliorate the harsh lot of the poor temporarily and partially: but the fact that at least some effort was being made speaks to the credit of the poor's more prosperous neighbours.

Concern over poverty was linked to the threat of disorder. Old-style feuding was waning, but crime in something like its modern sense was emerging as a problem. Gaps in the records and the geographically patchy nature of research make it difficult to speak for the whole of the British Isles, but for England at least the pattern is clear enough. The assizes, centrally directed courts presided over by trained and usually very experienced judges, tried serious crimes, among them homicide, robbery, theft, burglary, rape, and arson. Such samples of assize or equivalent records as have been studied show that theft, burglary, and homicide were the most frequently tried serious offences (felonies). Unexpectedly, however, indictments for felony and the executions of those convicted of it were running at a much higher level in the early than in the later seventeenth century, while it was property offences which were most commonly prosecuted and most likely to lead to execution. Levels of property offences and executions were high following the bad harvests in the late 1590s, and reached a new peak in the 1620s, that troubled decade which saw bad harvests, plague, dislocation of trade, and the disruption caused by troop movements. Provisional figures for the county of Cheshire, the records of whose court of great sessions enjoy almost perfect survival, suggest that there were 337 death sentences passed between 1580 and 1619, 274 between 1620 and 1659, and 85 between 1660 and 1709. Within these three periods 294, 210, and 47 of these sentences respectively were passed against persons convicted of property offences, mainly theft and burglary. By the later seventeenth century, the courts were trying far fewer cases of serious crime, and many of the accused were escaping with lesser punishments than death, evidence of some measure of flexibility in the workings of the courts and the attitudes of judges and juries.

Although the evidence is as yet far from totally conclusive, it seems probable that it was during the seventeenth century that the public execution acquired the central importance in English culture which it so clearly enjoyed in the eighteenth. Felons were now expected to make a speech from the gallows, in which, customarily, they admitted their guilt, confessed to an earlier life of sin and delinquency, and accepted that not only the monarch's laws but also God's justified their death. It was this religious input, underpinned by the role of the clergy in preparing the unfortunate criminal for death, which seems to be the strongest feature of these seventeenth-century execution speeches. One of the major concerns of the officiating clergy, and of the execution pamphlets upon which our views on these executions are founded, was to demonstrate how even a felon about to be executed could be reintegrated into the moral community: the lost sheep had to be brought back to the flock, even if he or she was about to be converted into mutton.

Concern for order was reflected not only in the prosecution of serious offences at the assizes, but also in the control of local communities. Once more we confront an infinity of local experiences, but over much of England at least there seems to have been a pattern whereby the more marked social stratification, and in particular the greater cleavage between rich and poor, which followed the demographic changes of the period was reflected in a more energetic attitude to law and order problems. Village elites of petty gentry, substantial farmers, and craftsmen, who filled the local offices of constable, churchwarden, overseer of the poor, and manorial juror, made increasing use of the courts in hopes of disciplining what was perceived as a growing body of disorderly poor. The work of the Scottish kirk sessions would probably reveal a similar picture, while high levels of litigation in the Isle of Man suggests another local variation on this theme. Throughout the British Isles, town governments sought to control crime, and urban elites everywhere were concerned with the problem of order.

But in an age which feared social breakdown, one major form of disorder at least had passed. The old habits of noble feuding had gone. In England and Wales they had been very weak in the sixteenth century, while in Ireland they were smashed along with other vestiges of traditional Gaelic culture. In Scotland they persisted into the seventeenth century, but even there the combination of an ever more intrusive state and cultural changes among the nobility led to that situation where the earl of Strathmore was able to comment that feuds had quite gone out of fashion. But the ending of noble feuds overlapped with the arrival of a new threat to order, the riot. The history of popular disturbances in the British Isles is a lengthy one, but the late sixteenth and seventeenth centuries witnessed the arrival of a new phenomenon, rioting carried out by the lower orders, what eighteenth-century observers were to describe as the mob. For the seventeenth century most of our evidence comes from England, where a more advanced economy had already created something like a class hierarchy. Certainly from the years of dearth in the 1590s the lower orders in England became accustomed to riot over the price of grain and its export away from their localities, while in many of the larger towns workforces would riot in defence of their pay and conditions. But these riots, many of which were essentially what modern terminology would describe as demonstrations, were less threatening to order than many contemporary observers and some later popular historians have made them out to be. Rioting frequently displayed a striking order within disorder, with rioters rarely causing injury to persons, frequently showing respect to property, and often willing to back down if the local authorities showed a willingness to conciliate, which the local authorities, as aware of the rules of the game as the rioters, were frequently willing to do.

The seventeenth century continued to accept the reality of another distinctive form of disruption, that offered by the witch. Most evidence for witch prosecutions in this period comes from England and Scotland. Doubtlessly the Catholic population of Ireland feared witchcraft, but it was little prosecuted among them, such cases as are known being restricted to accusations made among English or Scottish settlers. Similarly, levels of prosecution in Wales were low, while in the Isle of Man witchcraft was, for the most part, regarded as a problem for the church courts, who obviously regarded witch beliefs as a symptom of peasant superstition and a source of community disruption rather than as evidence of demonic influence. But in England between the passing of the 1563 Witchcraft Act and the last known execution in 1685 perhaps 500 people were hanged for witchcraft, while in Scotland upwards of a thousand alleged witches were executed, usually by strangulation followed by their bodies being burnt at the stake. Most of those who suffered were women, about 85 per cent in Scotland, perhaps a little more in England, and most of them were poor. And in both countries, despite the emphasis that demonologists and other theological writers placed on the pact supposedly made between the witch and the devil, it was peasant fear of *maleficium*, the doing of harm by witchcraft, which underlay at least the initial stages of most prosecutions.

Despite these similarities, the history of witch persecution in England and Scotland followed distinct patterns. In southern England at least it seems that prosecution of witches before the assize courts was declining by 1600, and that by the 1630s witchcraft was not being taken very seriously in high governmental circles. The civil wars, which brought both social and intellectual disruption and the unleashing of a more virulent strand of puritanism, changed that. The mass trials in eastern England of 1645–7 led to over 250 accusations and over 100 executions, there were smaller local panics, and witchcraft was revived as a matter of intellectual debate. Yet throughout the century most accusations were made between neighbours, involved individual witches or small groups of them, and were generally treated with circumspection by assize judges. Scotland experienced several waves of persecution, in 1590–1, 1597, 1627–8, 1649, and 1661–2. The context in Scotland was provided by a less secure state, a tendency to devolve the trial of witches down to local lairds, clergymen, and lawyers, and the presence of the aggressive Protestantism of the Kirk: it is notable that most Scottish accusations were restricted to the lowlands, where the Kirk's influence was strong, and that by the mid-seventeenth century Scottish witches, obviously schooled by their clergy in Satan's ways, were confessing to making a pact with the devil, and having (usually not very satisfactory) sexual intercourse with him. Both the English and Scottish Witchcraft Acts were repealed in 1736, although trials were almost unknown by that date. In England growing scepticism among assize judges led to a very low conviction rate, while in Scotland the influence of that apologist for Stuart absolutism, Sir George Mackenzie, helped dampen legal accusations from the 1660s. More generally, growing ideas of gentility among elites helped marginalize witchcraft beliefs as something held only by the peasantry and backward country clergymen: among the educated, the end of belief in witchcraft probably owed more to snobbery than the spread of new philosophical or scientific ideas. As the odd act of violence against the witch and the continued recourse to good witches demonstrated, belief in witchcraft and sorcery persisted among the lower orders well beyond 1736.

The quality of life

Consideration of the concept of witchcraft, so distant to most modern readers, leads to a more general contemplation of the overall quality of life of our early modern forebears. It is all too easy either to romanticize the early modern period, or conversely to portray it as an age of backwardness, barbarity, and discomfort.

The reality of the experience of life in the British Isles during the seventeenth century fell somewhere between the two extremes indicated here. Life in this period (as in any other) was, of course, in some measure determined by one's place in the social hierarchy, while, as I stressed at the beginning of this chapter, the inhabitants of the British Isles lived in a myriad of regional contexts. Without doubt, hardship and suffering were there. The rich and comfortably off did well, but for most of the population, even those of middling rank, the economic realities meant that life was an unending struggle to make ends meet. For the labouring poor, the experience of work was usually a harsh one. Industrial and agricultural workers alike sustained long hours of toil, the latter in particular having to work in all weathers. Some groups of workers experienced declining fortunes, perhaps the most extreme example here being lowland Scottish coal miners who had a form of virtual serfdom imposed on them and their children. All social groups experienced helplessness or near helplessness in the face of disease, and had to undergo the realities of medical treatment and surgery in an age which was innocent of anaesthetics and antibiotics, which had only an elementary idea of hygiene, and which regarded vomiting, purging, and bleeding as suitable treatments for many ailments. And then there were those accidents which, since the age was also innocent of insurance, might also bring disaster even to the comfortably off: the fires which could bring destruction and ruin, most famously to London, but also to many other towns and isolated farmhouses and gentry residences; the risks inherent in the contemporary structures of debt and credit; and the impact of warfare, which came most harshly to Ireland and highland Scotland in the 1640s and 1650s, but which affected all parts of the British Isles in those decades.

There is, then, much to encourage a pessimistic view of the life experience of our seventeenth-century ancestors: certainly, extravagant claims have been made for the unpleasantness of both community life and family relationships in this period. Conversely, closer research on such matters has suggested that, even among the poor, human and familial relationships were frequently, despite the harshness of life, warm and caring. The local communities in which most people lived could be limited in their horizons and sometimes repressive places, where deviants or social nonconformists could be the butt of gossip, ridicule, even ritualized expressions of communal disapproval. But these communities incorporated most of the informal social networks and formal agencies which could bring relief in times of distress: traditional patterns of good neighbourliness, mutual obligation, and hospitality were nowhere completely absent. Similarly, there were a number of factors which might lead to low levels of affectiveness in family life: high infant mortality rates, adult mortality rates which meant that roughly the same proportion of marriages were ended by the death of a spouse as are currently ended by divorce, patriarchal values which, for at least some men, sanctioned wife-beating, and those economic realities which entailed that when choosing a wife or husband any notions of romantic love had to be tempered by a consideration of the future partner's earning capacity. Yet scattered evidence points to the existence of real affection within even the families of the poor. Evan ap Henry of Llanfihangel Genan'r-glyn was a man of very small property. When he made his will early in the seventeenth century he left a pot, a pan, a coffer, 2 shillings worth of tools, some clothes, the total value of his estate being 18 shillings. The clothes went to his youngest son, William, the rest to his daughter Margaret 'as well for the natural love I bear unto Margaret verch Evan my eldest daughter and also for her filial, obedient & tender care of me her father old and bedridden, being languishing after the death of her mother'.[8]

This image of Margaret verch Evan nursing her dying father reintroduces a point made in my first paragraph: that the experience of women in this period was in many ways distinct from that of men. Women's history for the seventeenth century is still a relatively undeveloped field of research, while such research as has been completed has focused more on women in England than in other parts of the British Isles. Once again, we need to confront the difficulties created by region and social hierarchy. And again, it is all too easy to write this history as a simple tale of brutality: women were generally legally disadvantaged, subjected to the constraints of a patriarchal and male-dominated social system, the richer of them mixing with men who for the most part regarded

---

[8] Cited in Gerald Morgan, 'Dowers for Daughters in West Wales, 1500–1700', *Welsh History Review*, 17 (1994–5), 547.

the intellectual and moral inferiority of women as axiomatic, the poorer among them in waged labour receiving only about half the pay which a man would earn for equivalent work. But here too historians are slowly piecing together a better informed and more complex picture, in which the female experience of the past is being reconstructed. The problem is that this female experience was an essentially varied one, as affected by considerations of class and geographical location as any other aspect of the human experience of the period. This makes it impossible to argue that the position of women was either worsening or improving over the seventeenth century: such evidence as we have is simply too contradictory to support an argument in either direction. What is striking, however, is that, despite the assumptions of the period, in practice many men loved and respected their wives, and valued what they contributed to marriage, for many couples a more overtly economic enterprise than at present. Thus we find men in their wills happy to make their wives executors, and anxious to ensure that other members of the family should care for them after the husband's death. Similarly, wills suggest that many men, within the narrow limitations of their culture, tried to do their best for their daughters. And, as in other periods, it is possible to find women (and especially widows) pursuing various trades and running business enterprises in towns. One feels that the situation for women was not as bleak as a superficial reading of the more patriarchal and misogynistic texts of the period would suggest.

Mention of women, that half of the human race who are so often written out of the history books, constitutes an attractive point at which to conclude this chapter. Just as it is the male experience which has so often been privileged by the writers of history, so it is the centralizing 'core' perspective which has pervaded so much of the historiography of the British Isles. Over the eighteenth century, as Britain was invented and the British state and the British Empire flourished, London and the south-east of England became Britain's dominant political and cultural zone, while, given the assumptions about the importance of the Atlantic economy and of the advanced farming techniques of lowland England, it is all too tempting to write the economic and social history of the British Isles in terms of the progressiveness of that area. Yet the perspective may have seemed very different from the point of view of those living in other parts of the British Isles, and in the seventeenth century many were disadvantaged by the changes which were taking place. Somebody normally has to pay the price of progress, and many of those living in Ireland, in the Scottish highlands, even agricultural labourers in south-eastern England, would have been less convinced than some later economic historians about the virtues of the commercial revolution and the quickening pace of agrarian capitalism. And, of course, after 1660 English domination meant that Irish and, before the Act of Union in 1707, Scottish commerce were placed under severe disadvantages by statutes from Westminster.

But it is impossible to deny either the commercial progress, the economic integration which had taken place between the component parts of the British Isles, or the fact that these developments offered opportunities for a broad range of people, a range so broad as to include Dublin craftsmen, tenant farmers in the Scottish lowlands, and those who wrote for the growing market of tracts published in Welsh. Yet awareness of this range brings us back to the overwhelmingly local context in which people lived their lives, and earned their living. In a chapter of this length, there has barely been space to describe national experiences, still less those local ones which were perhaps the most important for the bulk of the population. Perhaps I might best conclude by acknowledging this diversity again, and by recognizing what underlay that diversity: that in trying to grasp the social and economic context in which the inhabitants of the British Isles lived in the seventeenth century, the historian faces tremendous problems in balancing continuity and change, in illuminating the interaction between traditionalist, static elements in both society and economy, and those innovative and dynamic ones which have been so celebrated in the textbooks.

Parliament of VVomen.

With the merrie Lawes by them newly
Enacted. To live in more Eafe, Pompe, Pride,
and wantonneffe : but efpecially that they might have fu-
periority and domineere over their husbands : with a new way
found out by them to cure any old or new Cuckolds, and
how both parties may recover their credit
and hozesty againe

London, Printed for W. Wilfon and are to be fold by him in
Will-yard in Little Saint Bartholomewes. 1645.

Aug: 14 London 1646

Figure 7 Parliament of Women. © British Library Board. All Rights
Reserved. E1150(5).

6

'What ish my Nation?': The Cultures of the Seventeenth-Century British Isles

Clare McManus

Alexander Seton, a man of high culture and urbanity, has laid out and ornamented this villa and gardens near the city, for his own pleasure and the pleasure of his noble descendants, and of everyone else of culture and urbanity. This is no place of warfare, designed to repel enemies. Instead, there is a welcoming and kindly fountain of pure water, a grove, a pool, and other amenities—everything that could afford decent pleasures of heart and spirit.[1]

Written on the wall of a Renaissance knot-garden in 1613 at Pinkie, the Musselburgh house of Alexander Seton, Scottish chancellor of

Thanks go to Kate Chedgzoy, Peter Davidson, James Knowles, and Ceri Sullivan for their comments and thoughts on this chapter. All errors are, of course, my own.

[1] Inscription, Pinkie House, Musselburgh (1613).

James VI and I, this inscription is an appropriate place to begin a discussion of the seventeenth-century cultures of the British Isles. I do not want to suggest that this house and motto somehow encapsulate these cultures, partly because it would not be possible to find one representative in miniature of such an exuberant and problematic period. But decoding the assumptions which the motto communicates can illuminate some central concerns of this diverse and vibrant period of cultural expression.

One of the main ideas communicated in this motto is the image of Seton himself. Pinkie House and its motto are reflections of the virtues and qualities of the man who commissioned and built it; the house is a display of its owner's good taste, 'culture and urbanity'. In its careful, welcoming richness, which seems open and beneficial to all, the house and motto work together to communicate a sense of Seton's rank, wealth, and hospitality. Of course, the problem is that we cannot be sure that this is an accurate picture of Seton himself, an unmediated glimpse into his nature, since it is first and foremost an act of representation. And, equally, as this chapter will explore, the concept of identity is a complex one, made up of several factors such as class, gender, nationality, race, age, religious affiliation, education, political allegiance, or occupation.

Built in the early years of the century and very much a product of its time, Pinkie and its inscription can be used as a point from which to compare the century which followed and in particular the social upheaval which would be its keynote. In its invocation of noble descendants, the motto conveys a profound sense of security in the future; Seton's confidence that his descendants will be able to take his place, and that they would want to, speaks volumes to those lucky enough to indulge in hindsight. Pinkie's garden motto gives a strong sense of the future made stable and unchanging, a future in which government will continue, and in which descendants will inherit their predecessor's wealth, ideals, privileges, and responsibilities. However, as we know and Seton did not, neither this stability nor form of rule were to survive the century intact. Instead, the events which followed would make Seton's confident assertion of the virtues of European humanism look ironically optimistic. In fact, these later events, such as the response of the Scots to Charles I's attempts to impose Laudian religious reform, Charles's own eventual execution at the hands of his subjects, and the republican government of Oliver Cromwell would alter perceptions of the monarchy to such an extent that in 1688 rebellion was a conceivable alternative to the rule of the Catholic King James II. Indeed, Seton's own career as the Catholic chancellor of a Protestant government who was involved in the post-1603 union negotiations, and who built Pinkie at the height of his power, points to some of the complexities of early modern 'Britain'. Seton's confidence in the security of future generations, the investment of his society in patriarchy and patrilineage, give some idea of what it meant to be an elite man close to the centre of government in the early seventeenth century.

Another way of decoding Seton's motto is to consider the apparently simply word 'man' itself. What, in fact, did it mean to be a man in the seventeenth century? An important part of this seems to be the need for descendants, for children. The Pinkie text focuses on the idea of inheritance, of passing property on to one's descendants and in this society this usually carried the assumption that one's descendants would be male, since women often—although not always—did not inherit. So, through the codes of kinship and inheritance, the eldest son was intended to inherit name, social standing and title, territory, and wealth from the patriarchal father. Seton's motto depicts himself as the fertile source of a future society and, for the noble and non-elite alike, one aspect of masculinity was indeed the need to secure the future through marriage and the procreation of heirs.

Interestingly, the women necessary for the securing of future generations are absent from the motto text, and this is symptomatic of the often silent status of women in a social order which privileged men. However, it would be simplistic to suggest that women were only oppressed by this social structure. In fact, the seventeenth century was one in which ideas of femininity shifted and altered and its cultures were deeply involved with changing ideas of the nature and role of women. For instance, despite the fact that this century was to be dominated by kings, it had also to negotiate the legacy of female rule left from the sixteenth century by Mary Stuart, Mary Tudor, and Elizabeth I. One generalization that can safely be made here is that the status of women shifts dramatically throughout the century: for example, the early years of the seventeenth century saw female theatrical roles played by cross-dressed boys; the military upheaval of the mid-century was also a period of female political and religious involvement with many female prophets and writers emerging; and the century concluded with professional Restoration actresses playing the sexualized representative of the witty and educated woman on the public stage. Such concerns with the nature of manhood and womanhood in this period have also increasingly preoccupied readers and critics at the end of the twentieth century and beyond, and their investigations into women's political, social, and cultural roles have provided some of the most significant critical works of recent times.

To return to Alexander Seton, another important aspect of his manhood is his elite status. After all, Seton was by no means an everyday man; the nobility which the motto boasts of separated him from the majority of those in his society, as did his wealth and education. The motto is, like the house, welcoming; setting itself up in opposition to a martial idiom, it speaks of the access it grants to all those who deserve it. But does this mean access to all, or only to all of those like the wealthy, influential, and privileged owner? And what of those excluded from the nobility; what of those who worked on Seton's own estate, or those who laboured elsewhere? Would they have been seen to possess the 'decency' necessary to grant them access to the improving 'pleasures of heart and spirit' which the gardens and house offered? If the walled garden proclaimed openness only for those akin to its owner, how open, then, was seventeenth-century society?

The civilizing pleasures, those 'decent pleasures of heart and spirit' which both complement the virtuous man and improve others, came from a concept of classical civilization central to the Renaissance. The rediscovery of classical texts and arts speaks to the influence of other cultures and civilizations upon those of the composite kingdoms of Britain. Indeed the very idea of the idealized suburban villa as a political and social location derives from the Italian Renaissance, the site of several such rediscoveries and the powerhouse of the movement known as the 'Renaissance'. Such influences on a Scottish aristocratic house point up the difficulties involved in classifying what belongs solely to one culture—these cultures are affected by cross-currents from the continent and from within what for ease of expression I am calling 'Britain'. In a chapter examining the workings of 'British' culture, it is important to note that, although it came late to the Renaissance, in its 'high' cultural form at least, Britain consciously based its self-expression upon an idea of learning and a value system from beyond its own borders.

The Pinkie wall motto, then, can raise many questions about the cultures of the seventeenth century and about the man who commissioned its text. One significant question remains, however, and will be a central concern of what follows. Through all of this, how did ideas of nationality contribute to identity? Should we look to the seventeenth century for an idea of 'British' identity, and how do the distinct yet related discourses of English, Irish, Scottish, and Welsh identities connect or conflict? What can be said is that Pinkie itself was a meeting point of cultures and this chapter will look at other examples of this phenomenon in an attempt to suggest some ways of answering my earlier questions. Such meeting points were legion. In a society ruled by a Scottish king based in England, whose power extended over Wales and Ireland, the notion of cross-border exchange can tell us much about the cultures which meet across these boundaries. Journeys such as these will be my central focus—the journeys of royalty, poets, players, playwrights, and architects, and the extent to which these travellers took their cultures with them and its alteration under new circumstances. The cultural texts examined here will be both the products of these nations and external representations; we can learn much about English culture from the way in which it perceives and depicts 'Irishness', 'Scottishness', or 'Welshness', and vice versa. Although we may not be able to find straight forward answers for these questions, simply raising them can lead us to a deeper understanding of the cultural interaction of the four nations of the British Isles.

Before moving forward, it is appropriate to spend a brief moment on the title of this chapter. The title quotation is taken from Shakespeare's *Henry V* and I will look in more detail at the motivation behind the question that it asks later. Invoking Shakespeare in this way raises certain questions, however, which are perhaps summed up by the deliberately odd juxtaposition of a famous Shakespearean quotation, in which an English playwright (and in the early seventeenth century at least, an English actor) ventriloquized the voice of an Irish soldier, and a far less well-known motto from the garden of a Scottish aristocratic house.

This encapsulates the relationship between literature and the more diverse field of cultural expression which present-day critics now often take into consideration and which sets literature on an equal footing with the material and the popular. Following this lead, this chapter will look at architecture, painted ceilings, portraiture, poetry, plays, court masques, sermons, executions, secular and religious printed texts, broadsides and newspapers, treatises of statescraft, and the forces of education and cultural influence which mould such expressions. In doing so, I hope to be able to build a picture of the British Isles which does not simply focus on one kind of cultural expression, or one social grouping.

In addition to the idea of 'culture' rather than 'high' or 'low culture', it is now quite common for critics to point out that Shakespeare has, in the twentieth century at least, been read as the marker of either Englishness or Britishness, depending on the point of view of the reader, audience, or interpreter. For those living outside the British Isles, Shakespeare often seems the sign of Britishness; while for those living within Britain, both his work and the iconic image of the writer himself can often seem peculiarly English. Shakespeare, it seems, comes with baggage. I am consciously choosing to focus elsewhere, to look at the diverse and vibrant culture of a century of which his drama formed only a part. After all, to look only at Shakespeare is to ignore a century of vital cultural production, involving men and women of diverse faiths, nationalities, sexualities, and social classes and is, in the end, to impoverish our understanding of a fast-changing, turbulent, and exciting century.

The early seventeenth century: the cultures of the Stuart archipelago

The improving pleasures of Pinkie raise the issue of education, on which this chapter will partly focus. Closely tied to the shifting identities of both men and women during this period, education—the training of the mind and body in a specific cultural model—gives an insight into the kinds of identities which I want to examine and can help us to assess the cultures of the British

Isles from the English accession of James VI and I to the Glorious Revolution. I will begin with education, literacy, and print culture at the start of the seventeenth century, taking the example of the king as one means of reading Jacobean society. James VI was an educated man, tutored by the Scottish humanist George Buchanan. The Scots king was the author of two political treatises, *The Trewe Lawe of Free Monarchies* (1598) and *Basilikon Doron* (1599), the print history of which reveals much about the status of the vernacular languages of seventeenth-century Britain. James initially wrote *Basilikon Doron* in Middle Scots, which, as Jenny Wormald has pointed out, does not fit with the pattern of Anglicization found in contemporary Scottish writings.[2] For example, the playwright Sir William Alexander prefaced his *Monarchicke Tragedies* (1603–7) with the declaration that Scottish readers 'may not justly finde fault with me, if for the more parte I use the English phrase, as worthie to be preferred before our owne for the elegance and perfection thereof'. When *Basilikon Doron* was first printed in a restricted run of seven copies, however, it too was Anglicized. James's treatise went onto the London market in March 1603 in English, a statement of the political beliefs of the incoming king written in the language of his new subjects.

The treatment of James's writings after his accession is also revealing. In 1604, Robert Holland's Welsh translation of *Basilikon Doron* was published in part in London; its dedication to the king asks for the same opportunities for the Welsh to interact with the monarch's writings in the vernacular as were available to the English and Scots. At the same time, of course, the translation disseminated James's politics. In a consistent feature of early modern Welsh culture, the title-page claims Welsh as the 'British' tongue. The Welsh perceived themselves as the original 'Britons', the former rulers of the entire archipelago who were descended from Brutus. Describing the Welsh as 'the very remnant of the ancient Bryttaines', Holland calls them 'A nation of great antiquity, ... contynuing their language so long a tyme inuiolate without change or mixture. For *Brutus* landed heere 2711. yeres

---

[2] Jenny Wormald, 'James VI and I, *Basilikon Doron* and *The Trew Law of Free Monarchies*: The Scottish Context and the English Translation', in Linda Levy Peck (ed.), *The Mental World of the Jacobean Court* (Cambridge, 1991), 36–54.

agoe.'[3] Historians of Welsh culture such as Philip Jenkins have suggested that this myth of Britishness, prominent in the aftermath of the earlier Tudor union with England, in fact facilitated Welsh loyalty to the union and so served the purposes of James I and his predecessors. In fact, Holland claims Welsh ancestry for James, reinstating Wales within the mutual dependency which it had previously shared with the former rulers of the Tudor dynasty.

Holland's dedication set out a sense of Britishness which supported linguistic difference and formed part of an independent vernacular tradition of publication. John McCafferty's chapter in this volume shows the extent of religious influence on seventeenth-century culture, and vernacular printing served the Protestant cause in Wales. In one sense this imposed an Anglocentric religious and cultural model, but it also simultaneously allowed Welsh culture to resist Anglicization through a vernacular tradition of publication which began in the mid-sixteenth century. Philip Jenkins's *History of Modern Wales, 1536–1990* discusses the tradition of vernacular publication, and points out that the first publication in Welsh, *Yn y llyvyr hwn* ... (1547) translated the commandments, creed, and the Lord's Prayer. The translation of scripture continued with the publication of the Welsh Bible, sponsored by the English parliament. By 1567 William Salesbury and Bishop Davies of St David's had translated the New Testament, and the complete Welsh Bible was printed in 1588. These sixteenth-century Welsh-language printings had an ongoing influence. Welsh clerics were increasingly involved in such ventures, publishing a new translation of the Bible and Prayer Book in the 1620s and a popular edition of the Bible in 1630. Clerics entered into the controversy over bardic traditions and the new Protestant learning; the archbishop of Merioneth, Edmund Prys, was involved in this, translating the Psalms into Welsh. The Welsh verses explaining Christianity for the unlearned written by Rhys Prichard, vicar of Llandovery, circulated in manuscript for several decades before being published in the 1660s as *Canwyll y Cymry* (The Welshman's Candle). Their enduring popularity is an indication of the

---

[3] Philip Holland, *Basilikon Doron: Fragments of a Welsh Translation by Robert Holland (1604)* (Cardiff, 1931).

strength of the vernacular in both propagating the Reformation and fostering a sense of national identity.

Similar attempts were made to advance English Protestantism in Ireland by the printing of vernacular religious texts. Marc Caball points out that, with the exception of the Pale, early modern Ireland had a coherent Gaelic culture and so such an attempt was vital to the success of the Reformed faith. Elizabeth I encouraged the printing of the Irish Bible as early as the 1560s, but its publication in 1603 and that of Archbishop Daniel's translation of the Protestant Prayer Book (1604) were pre-empted by William Ussher's vernacular catechism (1571). The Catholic Counter-Reformation movement's first Irish printing was a catechism by the bard Giolla Brighde Ó hEódhusa (1611), printed by the exiled Franciscan community in Louvain. At the same time, Gaelic bardic poetry also took on polemical attributes as Gaelic identity shifted in response to the English Reformation. One Jacobean bardic poem, *Iomdha éagnach ag Éirinn* (Ireland has Many Sorrows), figures Ireland as a debauched woman, open to the sexual advances of English, Scots, and Welsh. Caball identifies this as an early seventeenth-century politicized reworking of the traditional personification of Ireland as 'sovereignty's embodiment', representing an Ireland unified in the face of religious and political colonization. The situation in the rest of the British Isles also shows evidence of religious literary endeavour. For instance, in 1610, John Philips, bishop of Sodor and Man, translated the Book of Common Prayer into Manx, of which no trace now remains. However, in Scotland, a nation never annexed by England, a different picture emerges. In 1567 John Carswell, superintendent of Argyll, translated the Book of Common Order into Gaelic. But beyond Murdoch Nisbet's Scots translation of Wycliffe's New Testament, and the Gaelic publication of some Psalms (1659), Scotland had no vernacular Bible. Indeed, although a Scottish translation had been mooted at the General Assembly at Burntisland, James VI and I's actual involvement with the Bible took the form of the English Authorized Version of 1611, though he did himself translate some of the Psalms.

Like their king, the Jacobean court in Scotland and England held learning in high regard. The English courtier Francis Bacon published the educational treatise *The Advancement of Learning* (1605), and the influence of Bacon's writings culminated in the experimental approach to knowledge adopted by the Royal Society after the Restoration. This investment in scholarship was influenced by Scottish educational traditions; during the Reformation, efforts had been made to establish a school in every parish in Scotland. Although this goal proved impossible, education, driven by the Kirk, tried to guarantee religious conformity. The effect of such a policy was the broadest educational base in Britain and a strong emphasis upon the importance of education throughout society. However, education was also used as a means of social control against specific Scottish communities. In the late sixteenth and early seventeenth centuries, the Gaelic populations of Scotland and Ireland were undergoing a gradual separation as each continued to develop a specifically national sense of Gaelic identity. Within Scotland, however, the Scots Gael was perceived to be separated from 'the Scot' by the highland/lowland divide. In 1616 the privy council imposed an Act which, although never carried out, attempted to instil the Gaelic population of the Islands with loyalty to the crown's lowland power base. The Act decreed that the Hebridean aristocracy should educate their children in lowland or inland schools, imposing the English vernacular and lowland culture. Compared with Scotland, education in seventeenth-century Wales was not widespread. The mid-sixteenth-century foundations of William Barlow and Thomas Lloyd in Carmarthen and Brecon remained influential in the seventeenth century, but the poverty of Welsh sees made the establishment of parish schools difficult.

One area in which all nations were recalcitrant, however, was female education. Although elite women received varying degrees of training, and their citizen counterparts were skilled in household management and business, girls were not allowed to be schooled past a certain age, level of achievement, or outside a certain class. For example, the 1594 records of the mixed-sex Banbury grammar school specified that no girl could attend 'above the age of nine nor longer than they may learn to read English'. James I himself was keen to discourage the kind of humanist training which aristocratic Tudor women had received, requiring women to read only in English rather than the classical languages in which female courtiers and nobility had been fluent during the sixteenth century. And yet, although the Jacobean court did not foster female education, it was a place of opportunity for women. The only documented school dedicated specifically to the education of women in early seventeenth-century England, the Ladies Hall in Deptford, is recorded in the unique manuscript copy of *Cupid's Banishment*, a masque danced for Anna of Denmark (wife of James I) at Greenwich Palace in May 1617. The masquers were girls from the school, and their education and non-courtly status points to the way in which female education—in England at least—would become increasingly available throughout society as the century progressed.

In the universities of Britain, education was also seen as the training of religious conformity and social obedience. Jesus College, founded in Oxford in 1571, was the first Welsh university college; a substantial proportion of the Welsh elite were trained there and many went on to the inns of court in London, which were seen as a suitable place for the sons of the landed aristocracy to hone their accomplishments. The education offered by the college seems to have involved the acquisition of English cultural models alongside the preservation and development of Welsh ones, assimilating England within Welsh culture. Oxbridge itself was buoyant in the early seventeenth century, reaching a peak for admissions in the 1630s, with over half of its population in this period consisting of non-elite students. In Scotland, although the sixteenth-century universities of St Andrews, Glasgow, and Aberdeen had slumped somewhat, Edinburgh University was founded in 1583. Trinity College Dublin was founded in 1592 by Cambridge Puritans—its first five provosts were educated at Cambridge—to further the Reformation in Ireland and stabilize the Tudor colonial administration, educating Dubliners in English 'civility' and Protestant piety. Some recourse for teaching in Irish was made, and the first Gaelic scriptural translations were made under Trinity's auspices.

Theorizations of government were intensely debated throughout this period. James I's own political models form a central part of that debate and inspire many later philosophical developments. I now want to use James's political philosophy to discuss what may at first seem an unrelated aspect of seventeenth-century culture—the theatre. *Basilikon Doron* uses a theatrical model of authority, based upon the monarch's performance 'vpon a publike stage', an idea which would have enormous currency for much of the century.[4] In the same way as politics were considered theatrical, so theatre was political. Spectacle, ritual, and the relationship of theatre to society shifted through the century, but the theatrical interface between the nations of Britain is clear. In 1593–4, James VI granted patents to travelling theatre companies and in 1599 he supported an English acting troupe against kirk protests. English acting troupes also performed Corpus Christi plays in sixteenth-century Dublin. The limited number of conventional plays authored by Scots—Lindsay's *Ane Satyre of the Thrie Estatis* (1540), the anonymous *Philotas* (1603), and Alexander's *Monarchicke Tragedies*—means that Scottish theatre has been neglected by many critics. However, plays were staged in grammar schools and universities, and popular entertainments included 'monsters', rope dancers, and mountebanks. Progress entertainments flourished and provide important evidence of a wider base of female performance than that in England; women of all classes performed for royal entertainments, a notable early precedent having been set in James IV's *Tournament of the Black Lady* (1507 and 1508) in which the title role was played by a black woman who was a slave at the Stewart court. However, when the Stewart court left it took the king's protection with it, leaving a court-dependent theatre vulnerable; as a result of this, Scottish-authored plays were not performed again in Scotland until after the Restoration.

In 1603 one of the most significant of the journeys I am concerned with, and certainly the most high-profile, took place: James VI acceded to the English throne and travelled south. His journey through Scotland and England was marked with spectacle, entertainments, and the occasional bizarre occurrence; for instance, as he passed by Stamford a hundred men on stilts approached to lodge a petition. A performer as well as a spectator, the monarch created power through display. James's entrance into London in 1604 passed through triumphal arches designed by Ben Jonson and Thomas Middleton, which fashioned London itself as a theatre and which demonstrated the extent to which performance underpinned Stuart society. Indeed, the new king was soon to find himself in an uneasy but necessary relationship with the relatively

---

[4] James I, *Basilikon Doron*, in *James I: The Workes* (1616), 137–89.

new and flourishing city theatres. In the early years of James's reign, the city stages played political satires which attacked the new monarch's cultural differences, criticizing the appearance, habits, and accent of the king and his Scottish nobles and performing the reaction of English metropolitan culture to the arrival of the Scots.

One of the most famous dramatic texts of the time, Shakespeare's *Henry V*, provides a context for the representation of Britain in the London theatres, and here we return to the quotation in my title. Staged in 1599 before James took up the English throne, the play is set during Henry V's fifteenth-century French wars of conquest and against the actual background of late Elizabethan colonial expansion as the earl of Essex prepared for war in Ireland. The argument in Act 3, Scene 3, between Fluellen, MacMorris, and Jamy, stereotypical representatives of 'British' nationalities, reveals the tensions between them. At one point the offended MacMorris demands violently of those around him, 'What ish my nation? Who talks of my nation?'[5] This loaded question, represented in Shakespeare's faulty version of an Irish accent, marks the problematic status of Ireland itself on the English stage and in English culture. MacMorris's challenge—is he Irish or British, does he belong to Ireland or to the English monarch for whom he fights, and who (in 1599 at least) was about to fight against the Irish—interrogates the status of the Irish within English colonial activities. In the play, however, this argument is interrupted by the war; the characters must forget their divisions to fight the French and so the tensions between the three nations are subordinate to the cause of Henry V, an English king fighting for French territory.

The most significant of the anti-Scots theatrical satires, *Eastward Ho!*, written by George Chapman, John Marston, and Ben Jonson (1605), and John Day's *The Isle of Gulls* (1606), were performed by the Children of the Queen's Revels (the controversial boys' company), at the Blackfriars theatre. In contrast with open-air public theatres such as the Globe (which was rebuilt as a working theatre and tourist attraction on the south bank of the Thames in the last years of the twentieth century), the Blackfriars was an elite

---

[5] Shakespeare, *Henry V*, 3. 3. 61. ed. Katharine Eisaman Maus, in Stephen Greenblatt *et al.* (eds.), *The Norton Shakespeare* (New York and London, 1997).

indoor arena inside the city wall, charging sixpence instead of the penny needed to stand in the Globe. Known as the 'private theatre', its clientele consisted of lawyers, inns of court students, citizens, and the younger sons of the gentry. Aristocrats and courtiers were also part of an audience which mingled court and citizenry. Another kind of mingling also took place; the induction of *The Isle of Gulls* begins with three 'gallants' demanding stools to sit on the stage. The Jacobean theatre and its Restoration successor did not place barriers between audience and performance in the ways that later theatres would, instead the performers and audience together contested the meaning of theatrical space.

Staging city comedy and court satire, the Blackfriars reported to the city about the court and reflected the city back to itself. London audiences demanded satirical plays and made them profitable; Blackfriars plays were self-consciously about life in London, and it is not altogether surprising that comments against the Scottish newcomers are found there. Day's play, which satirized the Scots in an adaptation of Sidney's *Arcadia*, was the subject of state intervention. *Eastward Ho!*, however, attracted even greater controversy; its anti-union satire is clear in Seagull's parodic Arcadian description of the American colonies in Virginia:

you shall live freely there, without sergeants, or courtiers, or lawyers, or intelligencers; only a few industrious Scots, perhaps, who indeed are dispersed over the face of the whole earth. But as for them, there are no greater friends to Englishmen and England, when they are out on't, in the world, than they are. And for my part, I would a hundred thousand of 'em were there; for we are all one countrymen now, ye know; and we should find ten times more comfort of them there than we do here.[6]

Famously, the ridiculous Sir Petronel Flash, washed up on the Isle of Dogs on his way to Virginia, is described by a passing gentleman with an impersonation of James's accent and a critique of his sale of knighthoods; 'I ken the man weel: he's one of my thirty-pound knights'.[7] Remarks like this point to the way in which a conservative play represents the perceived threat of James's policies to the English status quo.

---

[6] George Chapman, Ben Jonson, John Marston, *Eastward Ho!*, ed. R. W. Van Fossen (Manchester, 1979), 3. 3. 42–52.

[7] Ibid. 4. 1. 197–8.

The parody of James I's Scottish accent is a marker of a kind of cultural exclusion which resurfaced a decade later in Ben Jonson's *Irish Masque at Court* (1613–14). Here, James was privileged spectator to a representation of Ireland scripted by an English playwright and danced by Scottish and English courtiers and actors from the King's Men. Performed for the marriage of James's Scottish favourite, Robert Carr, earl of Somerset, and Frances Howard, *The Irish Masque* is a distanced representation of Irish aristocratic loyalty to the king in celebration of an Anglo-Scottish marriage.

The Jacobean court masque was a display of conspicuous consumption, performed by courtiers and professional actors. A synthesis of arts, the masque is a social, non-dramatic performance, in which silent courtiers do not act, but dance their own identities before their watching peers. A ritual of sovereign power which offered the court confirmation of its ideal nature, the masque could advise and criticize. The masquing stage differed importantly from those of the city theatres; for example, in contrast with the bare city stages, the masque used innovative shifting perspective scenery designed by Inigo Jones. By 1619 the court was dancing masques in the third Whitehall Banqueting House, which is still open to visitors today. This purpose-built space was designed by Inigo Jones; its Italianate classicism shares its source with Pinkie, and it was the beginning of an impulse of classical city-building which carried through the civil wars and into the post-Restoration work of Christopher Wren.

The court masque is particularly important as the only legitimate arena for seventeenth-century English female performance before the appearance of the Restoration female actor. The English embargo on female performance means that perceptions of gender were at the forefront of the performances of all-male theatre companies, or the boy companies of *The Isle of Gulls* and *Eastward Ho!* The female roles in early seventeenth-century theatre were played by cross-dressed boys, drawing attack from anti-theatrical puritan divines such as Philip Stubbes. For these critics, the sight of a male player courting or kissing a transvestite boy was tantamount to sodomy and a temptation towards sin for those watching. Ben Jonson was only one of several playwrights whose work played with these convictions; in *Epicene* (1609), the cross-dressing convention is manipulated and satirized in the marriage of a transvestite boy (Epicene) to the aptly named anti-theatricalist Morose. Playful impulses of this kind had earlier led Stubbes to exclaim.

mark the flocking and running to theaters and curtains ... to see plays and interludes, where such wanton gestures, such bawdy speeches, such laughing and fleering, such kissing and bussing, such clipping and culling, such winking and glancing of wanton eyes and the like is used, as is wonderful to behold. Then the godly pageants being done, ... every one brings another homeward of their way very friendly, and in their secret conclaves (covertly) they play the Sodomites, or worse.[8]

The reasons why women were banned from the English stage are complex, but in simplified terms this embargo is rooted in contemporary perceptions of femininity and again related to Stubbes's sense that the theatre was a sexualized space. Renaissance England was invested in a feminine ideal of chastity, silence, and domesticity. These ideas were inseparable: a talkative or public woman was a promiscuous woman, and promiscuity, the prime fear and fantasy of English Renaissance patriarchy, carried with it the threat of bastardry which would upset the stable succession in which Alexander Seton, for one, was so invested. This suggests why the public status of the actor was unavailable for early seventeenth-century women, while the non-gender-specific silence of the court masque's communal performance offered greater opportunity.

The Irish Masque, however, is interesting for the way it represented perceived Irishness to the Stuart court. As David Lindley points out, *The Irish Masque* represents its ideal in the lords' transformation from the 'barbarity' of Irish cloaks into the 'civility' of costly English masquing costumes. The lords, who have travelled from Ireland to pay homage to James, are introduced by servants, stock representations of what was thought of as Irishness, whose presence during the lords' dance destabilizes the masque's harmony. One remark in particular resonates disturbingly. As the servants watch the dances, Dermock leans forward and whispers, as Lindley puts it, 'conspiratorially' to the king, 'How like tow tish, YAMISH?'[9] English actors, performing an Anglicized version

---

[8] Philip Stubbes, *The Anatomy of Abuses* (London, 1583).

[9] Ben Jonson, *The Irish Masque at Court*, in *Ben Jonson: The Complete Masques*, ed. Stephen Orgel (London, 1975), 211, l. 129.

of Irish culture, identify their Scottish king as an outsider to the English court; in this moment Scotland and Ireland are connected through their shared difference from the English language. The attempted union of Scottish and English culture in the dance of the courtiers is undermined by the overfamiliar question of the English actor who performs the non-courtly 'Irish' other.

James I did not remain in England during the whole of his reign. However, his return to Edinburgh in 1617 caused religious controversy and strained the finances of both crown and burgh. The preparations made for the king's visit reveal both Scotland's need to demonstrate its cultural prosperity to its absent monarch, and the primacy of Anglicized culture. For example, Edinburgh commissioned Flemish tapestries which were made to look like well-worn possessions. Simultaneously, Anglicization took place as the traditional Scottish painted ceiling, adorned with mottoes and iconography and exemplified by those at Pinkie, was superseded by fashionable English plaster ceilings installed by English crafts-men, most notably in Edinburgh castle. From his base in London, Inigo Jones supervised the refurbishments of the chapel royal at Holyroodhouse, employing London craftsmen and English styles. These instances of Edinburgh's apparent self-doubt can, however, be balanced by such confident actions as the construction of the Parliament Building off Edinburgh High Street in the 1630s. In addition, the English perception of the Scottish intellectual also shows positive signs. Ben Jonson travelled to Scotland in 1618–19 to gather information for *Discovery*, a poem about Scotland for James I, and there stayed with William Drummond of Hawthorn-den, one of the last early modern poets to work significantly in the sonnet form. Jonson's visit suggests that the exchange between England and Scotland can be read, to some extent, as a two-way process rather than a rush to the southern 'centre'.

The Jacobean reign ended in 1625 with the death of James VI and I. He was succeeded by Charles I, who presided over a very different court to that of his father. After the apparent excesses of the Jacobean reign and the perceived negative influence of Scottish manners, the Caroline court was seen, at least by its more puritan members like the writer Lucy Hutchinson, to have a reformed sensibility. With his French consort, Henrietta Maria, Charles I led the reformation of his court's behaviour, accompanied by a return to a form of Englishness strongly influenced by the continent. Despite these differences, however, the culture through which Charles expressed his authority was remarkably consistent with that of James.

When the Scottish-born Charles returned to Edinburgh to be crowned in 1633, his visit prompted a further influx of English architecture in the refurbishments of Holyroodhouse. Significantly though, Scottish scientific developments were also incorporated; John Napier's 1614 discovery of logarithms made possible the polyhedral sundial, ornamented with Scottish thistles and English roses, which adorned the Holyrood garden. In the changing religious climate, however, Charles's Scottish coronation was mishandled. The Scots reacted against Charles's Laudian reforms and the Anglicized coronation services—in particular the woven crucifix in the altar tapestry—caused great offence.

The Caroline court, like the Jacobean court before it, was a place of theatre and theatricals. Interest in the Caroline masque has naturally focused on its final performance, William Davenant's *Salmacida Spolia* (1640), danced by Charles I and Queen Henrietta Maria. Critical opinion is divided between those who consider this masque the high-point of the court's escapism and those who see it as an attempt to affect political reality through the creation of consensus. However, *Salmacida Spolia* should be read in the context of a coherent Caroline cultural programme which represented sovereign rule through visual, literary, and theatrical texts. Prominent in this programme was Rubens's painting of the apotheosis of James VI and I on the ceiling of the Whitehall Banqueting House. Completed for Charles in 1635, the ceiling is a political text which shows James being taken up to heaven and so expresses the divine foundations of Stuart power. This text of political deification was so important that when the smoke from the candles which lit the Banqueting House began to damage the ceiling there was no thought of removing the pictures; rather a new masquing house was built instead. Rubens's ceiling also represents James's cherished British project; the dead king is shown linking the crowns of England and Scotland. Displayed in the imperial classicism of Inigo Jones's Banqueting House, both painted text and architecture put forward a vision of absolute rule. The architectural expression of power recurs in the unrealized project for an immense Whitehall Palace which John Webb (Inigo Jones's pupil) designed for Charles I. An attempt to order the chaotic buildings of Whitehall, and expressive of Charles's personal rule, Webb's design was based upon the Spanish Escorial, an allusion to continental Catholicism which did not find favour with the king's critics.

In 1649, the Banqueting House and its painted ceiling formed the backdrop for a defining theatrical and political moment. After being led past Rubens's ceiling, Charles I was executed in front of the hall in which he had fashioned an ideal vision of court and nation. The king was memorialized by the parliamentarian poet and politician Andrew Marvell in his *Horatian Ode Upon Cromwell's Return from Ireland* as a 'royal actor' on the 'tragic scaffold'.[10] The influential twentieth-century French theorist Michel Foucault has identified early modern punishment as spectacular, as controlling the minds of its audience through the theatrical display of sovereign power over the criminal body. Charles's execution, therefore, was remarkable in that the tools of sovereign punishment were employed against the monarch himself. The impact of this reversal is clear in Philip Henry's description of the moment of Charles's death, which was accompanied by 'a Grone by the Thousands then present, as I never heard before'.[11] Although deadly, this stage allowed Charles to perform the role of martyr and leave his son a lasting legacy to which to tie his bid for the crown—a final performance which indicates the theatricality permeating Stuart sensibility.

Charles's execution was the impetus for the further expression of political ideology. *Eikon Basilike*, the royalist text memorializing these events and prepared by the day of Charles's execution, became the focus of royalist support. To seventeenth-century readers skilled in reading the codes of such visual texts, the frontispiece presented the symbolism of the palm tree and the annunciation imagery of shafts of light showed Charles as a divine martyr. Together, Rubens's ceiling and *Eikon Basilike* were the

---

[10] Andrew Marvell, *An Horatian Ode upon Cromwell's Return from Ireland* (1650).

[11] Philip Henry, *Diaries and Letters of Philip Henry*, ed. Matthew Henry Lee (London, 1882), 12.

culmination of the Caroline court's cultural programme and the legible legacy of Charles's scaffold performance.

The city which watched Charles's execution was itself a place of theatre. The work of Ben Jonson, whose writing for the London stage continued until 1633, demonstrates the continuity between the Jacobean and Caroline reigns. Jonson's Caroline contemporary, James Shirley, was another prominent Catholic London playwright and masque-writer. Shirley's career in pre-Restoration London and Dublin demonstrates the dissemination of Anglicized cultural models within the British Isles and the powerful role which theatre played in this process.

Following the closure of the London theatres during the plague, Shirley travelled to Dublin, solicited by John Ogilby. Around 1636 Ogilby, a Scot who worked as a dancing master in London, came under the patronage of Thomas Wentworth, first earl of Strafford, the controversial English lord lieutenant of Ireland and head of an English coterie at Dublin castle. Strafford's trial and subsequent execution are well-known; however his servant Ogilby went on to help found the professional theatre in Dublin and later to script Charles II's 1661 London coronation. Ireland, both Gaelic- and English-speaking, had a tradition of theatrical performance; Alan Fletcher's work has revealed a wealth of performers, be they singers, storytellers, jugglers, harpers, or poets, men or women. In addition to this vibrant and widespread performance culture more conventional theatre was also common; miracle and Corpus Christi plays were performed, English playing companies visited the towns of Youghal and Kilkenny, and there were itinerant players in Dublin when the professional playhouse in Werburgh Street opened at some point between 1635 and 1637, under the patronage of the English lord lieutenant.

The Anglicized theatrical model apparent in Shirley's *St Patrick for Ireland*, which was written for the Werburgh Street theatre and staged there in 1639–40, normalized English rule over Ireland. However, the importation of this model did not mean that it was acceptable to those who were to be its audience. Although the coterie performances at Dublin castle were popular, the Werburgh Street theatre depended upon a paying city audience. Here the imposition of an English theatrical model began to run into commercial difficulties. Shirley's increasingly bitter prologues document this struggle. The prologue to *St Patrick* begins with a complaint: 'We know not what will take; your pallats are / Various, and many of them sick I feare'.[12] The problem, it seems, is one of aesthetics. Shirley rails against those who do not share what he feels should be the universal standards of English taste: 'For your owne sakes we wish all here to day, / Knew but the art and labour of a Play'. Colonial culture is defeated by the commercial power of the city which it seeks to influence: 'sophisticated' English theatre is at the mercy of Dublin's real commercial capital.

Shirley wrote for the Dublin stage until 1640, and *St Patrick* (1640) most clearly demonstrates the interface of English and Irish preoccupations. Shirley's play was an attempt to entice an Irish or Anglo-Irish audience into Werburgh Street, drawing on the founding narrative of Irish Catholic nationalism which the epilogue tells the audience is 'your story, native knowne'. Given the realities of Irish colonization and the presence of an English and Anglo-Irish audience, this claim is controversial, although it does perhaps point to the unity created between the previously divided sectors of the Irish community by the influx of New English colonists. *St Patrick* is a ritual of political persuasion, a theatrical statement of the power of English culture. Although it has been described derogatively as 'spectacular', *St Patrick* transports the London stage's visual capabilities to Dublin, with such sophisticated effects as Archimagus's disappearance into the earth, and masque elements such as the descent of the guardian angel Victor. Shirley educates his audience in the scenic conventions of English metropolitan theatre; political content takes aesthetic form in a synthesis of borrowed Irish national narrative and English theatrical technique.

Although often read as a simple narrative of the beginnings of Irish Catholicism, the play also contains parallels with the English colonization of Ireland. While Shirley is careful to distance Patrick's faith from Rome, reducing it to a generic Christianity, this only increases the parallels between this original act of colonization and the march of English 'civility' and the Protestant faith. Shirley's representation of Ireland's pagan religion before

[12] James Shirley, *St Patrick for Ireland*, in *A Critical Edition of James Shirley's St Patrick for Ireland*, ed. John P. Turner (New York and London, 1979).

the arrival of Patrick calls on Protestant objections to Catholicism. Archimagus, the druid high priest, declares, 'this Kingdome / Shall still be ours, and flourish; every Altar / Breathe incense to our gods, and shine with flames'.[13] This stress upon idolatry—a common charge in anti-Catholic polemic—recurs when Patrick warns against 'A blind devotion of... painted gods' in the first scene.[14] Perhaps most significant, given the representation of Ireland in English colonial literature, is the echo of Spenser's *Faerie Queene*. Archimagus's name mirrors that of Archimago, the disguised Catholic mage who attempts to entrap Spenser's Red-crosse Knight, the representative of militant Protestantism. This may not seem important until we realize that in using this name, Shirley echoes the negative representation of Catholicism of the 'British' epic of one of the most influential writers on Ireland. Spenser's *A View of the Present State of Ireland*, an apology for colonial government written in 1596, was in fact only published in 1633. Conversely, Patrick's references to the energetic new faith prophesied to sweep through Ireland, reforming a debased creed, correspond to Protestantism's own official self-representation. In this way, Shirley uses the original influx of Christianity to discuss the later appearance of Protestantism and the introduction into Ireland of English rule and 'civility'. Patrick's claim that 'we are of Britaine' and the identification of his priests as a 'chorus advenarum' (a chorus of foreigners) furthers the identification between the ancient influx of Christianity and the current one of the 'civilizing' English. The political ramifications of *St Patrick* become further apparent when, anticipating the handover of power from King Leogarius to his converted son, Patrick declares,

> You are, Sir, reserv'd
> To bless this Kingdome with your pious government,
> Your Crowne shall flourish, and your bloud possesse
> The Throne you shall leave glorious[15]

Such flattery is clearly aimed at the watching Strafford. Patrick, the British missionary who represents a utopian unity between England, Scotland, and Wales, brings a new system of faith and

---

[13] James Shirley, 1. 1. 6–8. [14] Ibid. 1. 1. 175. [15] Ibid. 5. 3. 11–14.

government, aligned to the English colonizers. Rather than just evoking the founding myth of Irish Catholic nationalism, *St Patrick* also depicts the colonization of Ireland by the English.

Shirley returned to England in 1640. The Irish Rebellion of 1641 closed the Werburgh Street theatre, and it was, John Aubrey states in *Brief Lives* (1692), turned into a 'cow house'.[16] Shirley continued to write for the London theatres before their closure in 1642. The idea that these theatres were entirely closed down at that point is, however, inaccurate, since the Cromwellian regime which emerged from the conflict was, as we shall see, not overtly hostile to theatre or the arts.

War and its aftermath: culture and identity 1642–1660

Seven years before the execution of Charles I, his son embarked on another journey between the British nations. In 1642, the young Charles, Prince of Wales, travelled to Wales to seek support for his father. Sir Hugh Vaughan's pamphlet, *A Loving and Loyall Speech Spoken unto … Prince Charles* (1642), documents Charles's visit to Raglan castle in Monmouthshire, the home of the earl of Worcester. Welcomed by a speech which Philip Jenkins describes as the redirection of nationalistic rhetoric towards loyalty to the English crown, Charles heard a Welsh perception of the relationship with England: 'it is the glory of the Britaines, that we are the two [sic] remaining and only one people of this Land, … In what the true and ancient Britaines may serve you, you may command us to our utmost strength.'[17] This speech demonstrates the founding of the Welsh relationship to the English throne on a myth of national precedence, drawing on the status of the prince of Wales himself.

Welsh unionist allegiance can again be seen in the entertainments Prince Charles enjoyed. Vaughan's account states that the

---

[16] John Aubrey, *Brief Lives* (1692), ed. Oliver Lawson Dick (London, 1960), 221.
[17] Sir Hugh Vaughan, *A Loving and Loyall Speech Spoken unto … Prince Charles* (London, 1642), 3–4.

rooms 'were richly hung with cloth of Arras, full of lively figures and ancient British Stories' and that a rich banquet was served. These wall-hangings are the backdrop to the ritual of hospitality, informing the moment through the narrative of the founding of Britain and of loyalty to the crown; an inescapable mutual dependency is established between the governors and the governed. However, it is significant that the account was published in London and in English; part of the value of Welsh loyalty, it seems, was its impact on an English readership.

Jenkins suggests that 'Bardic poetry and Welsh prophecy undoubtedly formed part of the entertainment, as both were especially cultivated in the Somerset household'. While the account only mentions the 'British' tapestries, this possibility leads to speculation about the status of Welsh culture during this period. Welsh bards served a lengthy apprenticeship, mastering twenty-four poetic metres and the bardic canon before attaining the rank of *pencerdd* which allowed them to move between great houses. Jenkins cites an earlier version of a standard *cywydd mawl* in praise of an Elizabethan squire, William Griffith of Pembrokeshire:

> Y pur Cymro, pêr gynnydd,
> Pen stôr, post o aur rhudd,
> Pingal wyt, pan glyw'r iaith,
> Pêr frau iôn, pur Fryttaniaeth.
>
> (Thou pure Welshman, of fair increase,
> Of the greatest wealth, a pillar of real gold,
> But thou art a pinnacle when the nation hears
> The pure British language, sweet, tender lord.)

The political elites whose patronage maintained vernacular poetry were well-placed to manipulate it to a unionist agenda. Bardic poetry was intended for public declamation, and there has been speculation that it may have suffered from the introduction of vernacular publication. While the structure of apprenticeship fell out of favour in the 1640s, bards were supported by elite families until the 1680s, after which their decline was gradual. The popular tradition of *anterliwt* or interludes had a longer lifespan, surviving well into the eighteenth century.

Although the civil wars have been famously represented as 'the world turned upside down', not all was disruption between 1642 and 1660. The intake of the English universities fell but they were relatively intact, although Oxbridge did suffer purges from both the crown and the Cromwellian government. In Scotland, King's College, Aberdeen, had been in decline since the 1610s, and political pressures affected the Scottish universities in the years before the civil wars. Trinity College Dublin also suffered in the military suppression of the Irish Rebellion. In 1641, Richard Washington, its provost, and most of its fellows retreated permanently to Oxford, and a new provost was only appointed ten years later. One educational sector did flourish in the mid-century, but, strangely, the development of girls' schools through the 1620s and 1630s has often been depicted as a symptom of educational decline rather than as a step forward. Still, the shift in the boundaries of education seen there was an ongoing impulse as education and literacy filtered through society.

Increasing levels of male and female literacy emerge in the political radicalism of the civil wars. Print became the arena of competing ideologies in an explosion of pamphlets and newsbooks, rapidly written and printed in great numbers. Such newsbooks were targets for censorship; in the early years of the conflicts crown newsbooks such as *Mercurius Aulicus* rivalled parliamentarian ones, and censorship continued under Cromwell. Apart from a unique newsbook produced in York, the majority were printed in London and Oxford; although *The Scottish Dove* ran from 1643 to 1646, it seems to have been written in London. The first Scottish-printed paper in Scots would not appear until the Restoration.

Newsbooks were accompanied by a rush of political pamphlets written by crown supporters and by radical parliamentarian religious sects, such as the Quakers, Levellers, and Diggers. Interestingly, the Levellers' demand for the franchise for all men (not for women) was accompanied by an unprecedented increase in female opportunity. Women had the freedom to preach, write, and to be involved in the decision-making of these sects. There was an expansion in the number of female prophets and preachers, and unprecedented printed outpourings of women's religious and political fervour from all classes. Such freedoms were seen by conservatives as the direct result of the destruction of the ordained social order in the rebellion against Charles I, and the writings and preachings of such women were countered in other pamphlets, such as the satirical *Parliament of Women* (1646) which attacks both parliament and the female sex. Although radical religious sects were minorities, they were prolific. A London bookseller, George Thomason, collected pamphlets and broadsheets; by 1660, in a far from exhaustive collection, there were over 20,000 separate items. It seems that print had become the battleground for all political persuasions.

Perhaps paradoxically, the radical questionings of power favoured by the Levellers stood in the same tradition of philosophical inquiry as the writings of James VI and I. In the same way, the execution of Charles I and the crisis of political thought which it caused and reflected, were the context for one of the century's most significant works of political philosophy, Thomas Hobbes's *Leviathan* (1651).[18] Famously describing humanity's natural condition as 'nasty, brutish, and short', Hobbes depicts humankind's threatening natural equality as overtaken by the pragmatic need to limit absolute freedom by giving absolute power to a protector, called the Leviathan, which might be interpreted as either the Rump Parliament or Cromwell himself. This bond between circumstance and political thought recurs in John Locke's *Two Treatises of Government*. Written under the patronage of Anthony Cooper, first earl of Shaftesbury during the 1680s Exclusion Crisis (which centred on the exclusion of the Catholic James Duke of York from succession to the throne), Locke's treatise was not published until the more favourable climate of 1690. Setting out the foundations of a liberal tradition of political thought, Locke stresses that humans are born in 'a *State of perfect Freedom* to order their Actions and dispose of their Possessions, and Persons as they think fit ... without asking leave, or depending upon the Will of any other Man'.[19] It seems, therefore, that an ongoing philosophical debate informed the political and military upheaval of the mid-seventeenth century.

The prominence of the cultural agency of women of the radical sects shows that the civil wars did not halt cultural production, but rather changed the conditions in which it was created. However, the

---

18 Thomas Hobbes, *Leviathan* (London, 1651), part I, ch. 13.
19 John Locke, *Two Treatises of Government*, ed. Peter Laslett (Cambridge, 1967), 'The Second Treatise', ch. 2, p. 287.

suggestion that dramatic culture in the British Isles stopped dead in 1642 has only recently been successfully challenged. Critics such as Susan Wiseman have shown that drama did not halt; instead the civil wars created the space for cultural experimentation in the form of a country house performance, or the use of female actors. Performance now centred not on the theatre building (although four London theatres remained open in the winter of 1648–9) but on alternative sites of theatrical display.

The survival of theatre in the British Isles during the closure of the London theatres points to an energetic dramatic tradition beyond that city. Within England alone, the signs were clear. Theatre troupes had always toured as a part of their usual duties, and the journeys of English troupes to Scotland and Ireland were complemented by performances in town halls, private houses, and inns throughout England in a circuit which regularly reached York and Bristol. Furthermore, the country houses of aristocratic families were the locations of masque performances throughout the Jacobean and Caroline reigns. One of the most prominent, the anonymous *Coleorton Masque* danced in 1617 by the earl of Essex, Robert Devereux, celebrates the power of the local nobility. During the civil wars, performance became increasingly politically loaded. However, as the contradictory figure of Essex, the aristocratic parliamentarian, shows, such statements are not simplistic. The masques performed in Cromwell's court and the toleration of Davenant's 1650s performances reject a straightforward alignment between royalist performance and parliamentarian anti-theatricalism. The existence of a tradition of private performance alongside that of aristocratic entertainments and of provincial touring theatre meant that theatrical forms were available to be taken up.

One poet who exploited existing traditions was William Davenant, leader of the Cockpit company in London. In 1656, Davenant's *Siege of Rhodes* was acted at his London home, Rutland House, and again in 1659 at the Cockpit Theatre in Drury Lane. Converted into a permanent indoor playhouse in 1616 by Inigo Jones, the Cockpit was used during the Interregnum and into the Restoration. Despite the official ban, *The Siege* was far from a cloak and dagger affair; Davenant sent the published script to Bulstrode Whitelocke, Cromwell's lord commissioner of the treasury, before the performance. Building on the use of scenery and music in aristocratic entertainments, Davenant's 'operatic drama' was the first to put English female performers on the English public stage. Once again, however, the court masque is a formative influence. The gradual movement of the female masquer towards vocal expression had culminated in Aurelian Townshend's 1632 masque, *Tempe Restored*, in which the role of Circe was sung by one Madame Coniacke. In the late 1620s and 1630s, Henrietta Maria had commissioned pastoral plays, in which the queen and her women both spoke and cross-dressed to perform male roles. These controversial moments, analysed by Sophie Tomlinson, predict the emergence of the Restoration female actor. Yet the developments of these court performances were not replicated on the public stage; Davenant and his composers give their women song but no speech. However, Davenant's productions, complete with scenery and female performers, suggest that we can no longer point to Charles II's 1660 return as the only pivotal influence on Restoration London's theatre.

Another dramatist whose work demonstrates an ongoing theatrical production during this period is Margaret Cavendish, Duchess of Newcastle. Cavendish arranged the publication of her first works, *Poems and Fancies*, in 1653 during her return from exile to raise funds for her husband, the royalist marquis of Newcastle. In the light of seventeenth-century women writers' usual public repudiation of their desire for publication, Cavendish's open acknowledgement of her ambition is striking. Her plays were published in two sets, one written during the Interregnum and the second, *Plays, Never Before Printed* (1688), after the Restoration. Although one collection is ostensibly written without performance in mind and one when performance was possible, Cavendish's work is often generally described by the contested term 'closet drama', which refers to plays written without the intention of a conventional staged performance.

Cavendish was self-taught, and her work argues strongly for women's education. In particular, *The Female Academy* (1662) and *The Convent of Pleasure* (1668) address ideas of women's education and separatism. Dealing with Lady Happy's decision to withdraw from the aristocratic marriage market, *The Convent of Pleasure* attempts to set up an exclusively female society. Based on the model of the Catholic convent, Lady Happy's is, however, one in which pleasure is utmost. Matrimony is rejected not because 'conversation' between the sexes is sinful, but because it denies women both pleasure and opportunity; the separate existence of women is mooted as a viable solution to their perceived marital exploitation. However, this ideal does not survive the play; an interloper, the Prince, enters the convent disguised as a woman and Lady Happy is represented as desiring someone she believes to be another woman. The play's conclusion, the conventional closure of Lady Happy's marriage to the Prince (who has finally revealed his identity as a man), denies both this desire and female independence. *The Female Academy* also denies the possibility of women's separate existence, ending with the negotiation of the women's marriages with the men who have listened in frustration throughout the play. However, the concept of female separatism gives Cavendish the opportunity to explore ideas of women's community and the theatrical tradition of cross-dressing.

The expression of such ideas shifted throughout the seventeenth century as female opportunities changed with time and circumstance. For instance, early in the century, Ben Jonson's *Epicene* had put forward a cynical representation of Lady Haughty and her group of educated women. One character, Truewit, described that female academy as

A new foundation ... here i'the town, of ladies that call themselves the Collegiates, an order between courtiers and country-madams, that live from their husbands and give entertainment to all the Wits and Braveries o'the time, ... cry down or up what they like or dislike in a brain or fashion with most masculine or rather hermaphroditical authority, and every day gain to their college some new probationer.[20]

Cavendish's revival of a radical female separatism as utopian fantasy contrasts with her male predecessor's representation. Jonson, court writer for James I and Anna of Denmark, presented learned independent women in a negative light which would have appealed to the private theatre audience. However, Cavendish's concept was taken up more positively at the very end of the century

---

[20] Ben Jonson, *Epicene,* in *Ben Jonson: The Alchemist and Other Plays,* ed. Gordon Campbell (Oxford, 1995), 1. 1. 67–74.

by Mary Astell in *A Serious Proposal to the Ladies* (1694), which again suggested sequestration as a solution to women's dependent position. The seventeenth century seems, therefore, to have been one in which an increasing number of educated women responded to their society, their position within it, and the ways in which it was possible to be represented and to represent themselves.

Restoration: nation, culture, and identity

With the return of Charles II from France in 1660, British culture entered a new phase. The London theatres officially reopened and with the appointment of James Duke of York as High Commissioner of Scotland (1679) a court returned to Edinburgh. Restoration Edinburgh, however, already had a theatre. Late 1660s and early 1670s Edinburgh housed a Scottish theatre company, managed by Thomas Sydserf in the Tennis Court Theatre, Holyrood. William Clerke's *Marciano* (1663) was published in Edinburgh and its title-page states that it was 'acted … before His Majesty's High Commissioner … at the Abby of Holyrudhouse'.[21] The next Scottish play performed in Edinburgh was Syderf's own *Tarugo's Wiles*, later staged at Lincoln's Inn Fields in 1667 (published 1668), the only Scottish-authored play staged in Restoration London. It is likely that Sydserf, who in 1661 published the first Scots-language newspaper, *Mercurius Caledonius*, managed the company from 1667. The Tennis Court Theatre was patronized by the aristocracy, dominated by English plays and players, and attacked by the Kirk.

The relationship between the stages of London and Edinburgh is perhaps an example of English cultural colonization. Evidence of the primarily one-way trade between these theatres is found in the presence of actors from the English Theatre Royal company in the Scottish capital between 1678–9 and 1682. The poet and playwright John Dryden wrote this satiric description;

> Our Bretheren are, from Thames to Tweed departed,
> And of our Sisters, all the kinder hearted,
> To Edenborough gone, or Coacht, or Carted.

---

[21] William Clerk, *Marciano* (1663).

With bonny Blewcap, there they act all night,
For Scotch half Cron, in English Three-pence hight.[22]

The majority of plays staged in Edinburgh were those which had been successful in London. While English culture performed itself for audiences in both London and Edinburgh, Scottish theatre adopted an Anglocentric model. During the Restoration and the Exclusion Crisis, Scotland was a place of safety for the theatrical playing out of English courtly rule. This does not exclude the performance of plays by Scots to Scots, but it does mean that when that happened the model followed was Anglocentric. *Tarugo's Wiles* itself was Anglicized; Sydserf wrote in English about an English hero. And yet, the experience of watching London-focused plays staged in Edinburgh must have differed substantially from the experience of that play in London.

One play by an Englishman, Sir George Etherege's *The Man of Mode*, was definitely performed in Edinburgh sometime in 1679–80, by a coalition of Syderf's actors and English players. This play is a self-conscious representation of London upper-class life, full of references to its locations and inhabitants. How, then, did this self-aware performance of London life translate to the stage of a nation in such a problematic relationship with that centre of power? After all, a play which represents absence from London as a penance (one character, Harriet, threatens her suitor, Dorimant, with a life in Hampshire) might have looked very different to the Edinburgh audience depending on whether they were English courtiers absent from London or Scottish aristocrats in a restored English court in the Scottish capital.

The Man of Mode was first acted in London in 1676. The London theatre consisted of two licensed playing companies, the King's and the Duke's. The latter was led by Davenant and performed in a new theatre in Lincoln's Inn Fields, and the former by Sir Thomas Killigrew and performed in the converted Gibbon's Tennis Court; Charles II attended both. The Restoration theatre was a politicized performance space. Played in a lighted auditorium, again negating the boundary between audience and performers, this theatre staged

---

[22] John Dryden, 'Prologue to the University of Oxford (1680)', in *The Works of John Dryden*, ed. Edward Niles Hooker and H. T. Swedenberg (Cambridge, 1956), i. 164.

versions of the riotous Restoration court. A sense of social change is represented in the individual and in the change of manners. In *The Man of Mode*, Lady Woodvill speaks of the shift in behaviour since the Restoration in terms of the difference between 'love' in her day and present 'lewdness', putting gender relations centre-stage; 'this is not the women's age, ... Lewdness is the business now; love was the business in my time'.[23] And yet, while satirizing the fashionable behaviour of the female wit Lovewit and the gallant Sir Fopling Flutter, the play also shows the stultifying effect of Lady Woodvill's nostalgia. The politicization of the London Restoration theatre, clear in the work of Aphra Behn and Thomas Otway, makes its transfer to Edinburgh a significant cultural interface.

The Restoration also saw the establishment of the professional female actor. Emerging from domestic and continental traditions, this had a strong impact upon the plays in which women performed. The most obvious changes were in the female roles themselves; actors like Nell Gwynn, Elizabeth Barry, and Anne Bracegirdle now took the roles of active and witty women courted by equally attractive, witty men, in what came to be known as the 'gay couple'. At the same time, drama embarked on a fetishizing of the female body; female actors played roles in which rape, sexual violence, and the exposure of their bodies were commonplace. One way in which the women's bodies were shown was through cross-dressing; 'breeches' parts, in which the old convention of disguise as a boy was used to fit the actor in tight breeches, exposed her legs for the audience's titillation. However, before Charles II licensed women, female actors performed alongside transvestite boys in a mixture of pre- and post-war practice. Samuel Pepys saw Edward Kynaston, one of the last male transvestite actors, very early in the Restoration: 'one Kynaston, a boy, acted the Duke's sister but made the loveliest lady that ever I saw in my life—only her voice not very good'.[24] As Stephen Orgel's work has made clear, the issue in the performance of femininity by men or women is not gender but the quality of the performance: representation, it seems, is all.

[23] Sir George Etherege, *The Man of Mode* (1676), in *Restoration Plays*, ed. Robert G. Lawrence (London, 1997), 4. 1.

[24] Samuel Pepys, *Diary*, ed. Robert Latham and William Matthews (London, 1971), i. 224.

The female actor was accompanied by the professional female playwright, the most well-known of whom was Aphra Behn. A royalist, she challenged women's social position and attacked those still attached to the 'Good Old Cause' in plays such as *The Rover* (1677) and *The Roundheads* (1681). Behn's work also illuminates another discourse, as yet unmentioned in this chapter. Having written *Oronooko* (1688), a prose narrative depicting the slave-trade and colonial experience of Surinam, Behn turned to the American colonies for *The Widow Ranter* (performed 1690). The representation of colonial enterprises demonstrates the impact of these ongoing ventures on the British Isles. The representation of the exotic on the British stage points to the relationship between the colonizing processes which operate inside the British Isles, and the process writ large in the world beyond. This impulse is one of the most significant of the early modern period and is vital to an assessment of British culture.

I return, though, to the British theatre. In February 1663 a female-authored play was performed on the Irish Restoration stage. Katherine Philips, called 'the matchless Orinda' by her quasi-platonic coterie, the Society of Friends, translated Corneille's tragedies, *Le Mort de Pompée* and *Horace* (1669). Although *Horace* remained unfinished when Philips died of smallpox in London, *Pompey* was performed in Dublin at the Theatre Royal, Smock Alley, in the presence of the lord lieutenant of Ireland, James Butler, duke of Ormonde, and perhaps of Philips herself. Born in London and educated in a Hackney woman's school, she married Colonel James Philips, high sheriff of Cardiganshire, where she lived during her marriage, and her work circulated around a coterie in London and west Wales. Philips, a royalist writer married to a Welsh parliamentarian, and the author of a play performed in Dublin, is a good representative of an English cultural model in transit.

Pompey is a coterie work intended for those considered 'sophisticated', for which we can read 'Anglicized'. The prologue which the earl of Roscommon wrote for the Dublin performance makes the dynamics of cultural primacy clear, praising Philips, 'Whose Eloquence from such a Theme deters / All Tongues but English, and all Pens but Hers'. Roscommon's dedication to Ormonde also demonstrates the cultural priorities at play here: in his wish that

'Rome, France, and England join their Forces / To make a Poem worthy of your Ear' there is no trace of Irish influence or identity. The prologue does mention the context of performance, however. Identifying the Dublin audience with the Irish freedom from Roman conquest, the prologue sees the audience as equipped to judge the play: 'And you alone may Boast, you never saw / Caesar till now, and now can give him Law'. Yet while this amalgamation of Irish history and Anglicized aesthetics declares Ireland's favoured status, the careful elision of Ireland from Roscommon's equation suggests that although an Anglo-Irish identity might bestow the ability to judge, it is the culture of the London theatres that is worthy to be assessed. Irish identity is represented as improved by an English presence but also as ultimately irrelevant. In the same process, any traces of Welsh identity surrounding Philips are also elided.

Pompey's politics are apparent in the play itself. Philips presents the distinctions between Pompey, Caesar, Ptolomey, and Cleopatra—between different models of government—for judgement. Clearly, a play which deals with the power struggle between Roman republic and Egyptian monarchy, and colonization by an imperial power—Caesar considers Egypt 'a province won'—can refer to the recent civil wars and to Ireland itself. Furthermore, Achoreus's description of Pompey's off-stage execution is reminiscent of that of Charles I:

> This great Soul fled, his body did expose
> To th'greedy Eyes of his inhumane Foes:
> His head, which tumbled on the blushing Deck,
> (By vile *Septimus* sever'd from his neck)
> Upon *Achillas* Lance we fixed see[25]

Under the cover of translation, Philips reworked the civil war struggle in a performance staged in England's most disputed colony, perhaps showing the extent to which, in these years, theatre was a space of political action.

Although most theatre seems to move from England to its neighbours, there was some two-way traffic between the stages

---

[25] Katherine Philips, *Pompey: A Tragedy* (London, 1669), prologue by the Earl of Roscommon and 3. 1, 2. 2.

of Charles II's kingdoms. In 1677, Ormonde sent the Smock Alley company to perform in Oxford University, sparking off a dispute with Dryden's company. The cruelty with which Dryden responded reveals that the old assumptions of Irish 'barbarity' and English 'civility' are still in place:

> Teg has been here, and to this learned Pit,
> With Irish action slander'd English wit.
> You have beheld such barb'rous Macs appear,
> As merited a second Massacre.[26]

Performing in England demanded performance in the English style. The Dublin players did not give a display of 'Irish' theatre, but a demonstration of their ability to perform 'Englishness'; any slip recalls the brutality of the Cromwellian massacres. However, the experiment was repeated in 1681, when the earl of Roscommon commissioned the Dublin company to perform for the duke of York in Edinburgh. Ogilby was also involved in a performance by the duchess of York's women; Mithridates was staged at Holy-roodhouse with the future Queen Anne in the cast. An imported English theatrical model, staged for an English Dublin coterie and the Anglicized Irish gentry, is successfully transferred to both an English university and the Scottish court. It might be said that English theatre forms a network around Britain, transporting English plays, players, and aesthetics and seemingly remaining relatively unaffected by the cultures to which it is performed.

Some critics argue that the theatrical interests of the English court and the attendance of Charles II alongside a fairly mixed audience is an indication of the popular status of Restoration culture. Others use the same evidence to argue for the theatre's elitism. What can be said, however, is that the years following Cromwell's government see the continued growth of literacy and of a popular readership of chapbooks and romances. Two examples of the period's literary production demonstrate its diverse energies. Although both puritan in outlook and both positioned outside the Restoration mainstream, John Milton and John Bunyan created vastly different works. In Paradise Lost (1667), Milton completed an 'English' epic, steeped in classical learning, at a moment when the

---

[26] Dryden, 'Prologue to the University of Oxford', 165.

nature of England itself was under interrogation. Bunyan, whose autobiography, *Grace Abounding to the Chief of Sinners* (1666), was the result of imprisonment for religious dissidence, created an individual spiritual romance, circulated through the growing popular print culture and drawing on domestic religious debates and dissenting writings. Bunyan's works also attest to the continuing recourse to print and its suitability for the communication of spiritual matters. *Pilgrim's Progress* (1678) again focused on the individual, adapting romance tradition to show the puritan hero who abandons his family to follow his faith. These popular and godly books were also translated into Welsh, circulating as tools of religious education. *Pilgrim's Progress* was published in 1688, the verses of Rhys Prichard were accompanied by a New Testament and Psalms in 1672, and the largest and cheapest edition of the Welsh Bible was published in 1677.

While the democratization of print continued, the diverse British educational systems had very different fates. English university intake slumped following the Restoration, and the social background of students also changed. The number of non-elite students dropped sharply (as too in the grammar schools which once trained them) and there was a decrease in aristocratic sons attending to acquire social polish. The main growth group was the sons of the middle-class professionals, in particular of the clergy. The availability of English university education was narrowing fast, and academic standards were dropping. After the Royal Society was incorporated in 1662, the only scholar associated with both its achievements and the English universities was the Cambridge scholar Isaac Newton. The Royal Society's distinct approach to concepts of scientific, medical, and epistemological investigation involved men such as Christopher Wren, who practically rebuilt London after the Great Fire of 1666, Robert Boyle, who published Boyle's Law in 1662, and Newton who, along with Wren, was later to become the Society's president. The first president of the English Royal Society was in fact a member of the Irish peerage, the mathematician, William Viscount Brouncker. Restoration Dublin saw the foundation of the College of Physicians (1662) and, while Oxford and Cambridge struggled against declining intake and standards, other universities, Edinburgh in particular, were undergoing a period of growth and change. Medical education, which had begun in Britain at Aberdeen in the early sixteenth century, flourished and the Royal College of Physicians of Edinburgh was founded in 1681. This was accompanied by the rise of the legal profession (the Faculty of Advocates Library was set up in 1689) and the growth of a Scottish intelligentsia. In fact, with the patronage brought by the duke of York and the development of the professions, Edinburgh survived the earlier departure of the Stuart court to London and flourished as the cultural and legal capital of Scotland.

Conclusions: reputations and reception

Moving forward from what might seem an almost paradoxical diversity as seen from the twenty-first century, I have attempted to break down the notion of a 'British' culture into its constituent parts to question whether such a cultural composite could really be said to have existed. The dangers of generalizing from individual instances in a period of such transformations in political authority, religious belief, and gender relations are clear. That said, the multiple journeys and meeting points of the cultures of the British Isles, presenting the culture of each nation to the other in the travels of players, playwrights, poets, architects, craftsmen, and royalty, can tell us much about the cultures of these countries and their interactions within Britain. It would seem that, rather than a pervasive Anglicization operating from a London centre, we cannot really identify a single centre for these cultures. They meet on boundaries, but those cultures which may at first seem marginalized resist Anglicization in significant and interesting ways, for instance, in the assertion of the Welsh vernacular or the disapproval Dublin audiences showed for Shirley's English theatre. This assertive national identity does, however, seem to lessen somewhat after the Restoration and the historical differences within the century's chronology should not be lessened. Still, it is in these constant collisions between cultural centres rather than in the performance of a dominant culture to a submissive other that seventeenth-century British culture is found.

And what of Shakespeare, the playwright who polled so well in the BBC's somewhat maligned 'Great Britons' poll of 2002? In a poll in which the only women to feature in the top ten were Elizabeth I and Diana Princess of Wales, both in their own ways in central but difficult relationships to the British monarchy, Shakespeare figured at number five and was represented (perhaps predictably) as the epitome of British culture. It was not often mentioned that 'Britain' itself did not really exist at the time he was writing nor was that seen as an obstacle to his inclusion. Interestingly enough, however, the poll itself, although designed to paper over the cracks in the present-day edifice of Britain and gesture towards an organic national unity, spoke to distinct cultural, national, and regional agendas. For instance, although Winston Churchill was voted the 'Greatest Briton', in Northern Ireland Shakespeare polled twice Churchill's amount of votes. The Northern Irish preference for Shakespeare, clearly wrapped up in present day ideas of Britishness and a fraught sense of national identity, can be seen either as a positive vote for literary creation or as a conservative appeal to Britishness which belies the way that Shakespeare is now often taught in schools and universities. Either way, this result points out the disparities within a poll which sought to disavow local difference in favour of the construct of a 'Britain' which looks as tenuous now as it did when Shakespeare was writing.

The canonization of Shakespeare (even when he does not win such polls) seems to have survived relatively unchallenged. In contrast, my omission of Shakespeare from most of this chapter is, of course, a deliberate reaction to the centrality of a writer who was, after all, only one of many, involved in only one area of cultural production, but whose Englishness has often been taken to stand for Britishness and Britain itself. My hope is that in dealing with a period in which scientific innovation and religious fervour, female oppression and women's negotiation of patriarchy, conspicuous courtly consumption and widespread poverty, absolutist rule and the execution of a monarch were all juxtaposed, a focus on things other than Shakespeare has helped to highlight the prolific and contradictory culture of a problematic grouping of nations in a tumultuous and difficult century.

List of authors and others mentioned in this chapter

Sir William Alexander	c.1567–1640
Anna of Denmark	1574–1619
Mary Astell	1668–1731
John Aubrey	1626–1697
Francis Bacon	1561–1626
William Barlow	d. 1586?
Elizabeth Barry	1658–1713
Aphra Behn	1640–1689
Robert Boyle	1627–1691
Anne Bracegirdle	c.1663–1748
William viscount Brouncker	c.1620–1684
John Bunyan	1628–1688
Margaret Cavendish, duchess of Newcastle	?1624–1674
George Chapman	?1559–1634
William Davenant	1606–1668
Wentworth Dillon, Earl of Roscommon	c.1633–1685
William Drummond of Hawthornden	1585–1649
John Dryden	1631–1700
Sir George Etherege	1636–1692
Nell Gwynn	1650–1687
Philip Henry	1631–1696
Henrietta Maria	1609–1669
Thomas Hobbes	1588–1679
Robert Holland	1557–?1622
Lucy Hutchinson	1620–?
Inigo Jones	1573–1652
Ben Jonson	1573–1637
Sir Thomas Killigrew	1612–1683
Edward Kynaston	c.1640–1706
David Lindsay of the Mount	1490–1555
John Locke	1632–1704
John Marston	?1575–1634
Andrew Marvell	1621–1678

Thomas Middleton	?1570–1627
John Milton	1608–1674
John Napier	1550–1617
Isaac Newton	1642–1727
John Ogilby	1600–1676
Thomas Otway	1652–1685
Samuel Pepys	1633–1703
John Philips, bishop of Sodor and Man	c.1555–1633
Katherine Philips	1631–1664
Rhys Prichard	1579–1644
Edmund Prys	?1541–1624
William Salesbury	?1520–?1600
Alexander Seton	c.1555–1622
William Shakespeare	1564–1616
James Shirley	1596–1666
Sir Philip Sidney	1554–1586
Edmund Spenser	?1552–1500
Philip Stubbes	c.1555–c.1610
George Thomason	d. 1666
John Webb	1611–1671
Christopher Wren	1632–1726

Conclusion

Jenny Wormald

Historiographical warfare: England

Life used to be relatively easy for historians of seventeenth-century England. Put simply, in 1603 a Scottish king emerged from the northern mists to take over the kingdom of the great Elizabeth. Vain, pedantic, overenthusiastic about the theory of kingship by divine right, he was in fact wholly inept at the business of ruling England, that sophisticated and powerful realm which he never understood. Thus began a process which was bound to lead to a collision, helped on by his son who was, if anything, even more confrontational and tyrannical, as was seen all too clearly when he tried, in the 1630s, to rule without parliament: his eleven-year tyranny. The upshot was the collapse into civil war in the 1640s, and, in 1649, his public trial and execution. The failed attempt to create an English republic brought the monarchy back in 1660, with the rule of the more intelligent Charles II. But it lasted for only twenty-eight years, for not enough had been resolved; and when James II in a brief three-year reign showed all the faults of his father and grandfather, and compounded them by his determined Catholicism, another 'revolution' was necessary, and it duly came about with the 'Glorious Revolution' of 1688. Then and only then could the grievous problems of monarchy, Stuart-style, be fully resolved, and England settle down under a constitutional monarchy to all sorts of great things, world power, economic success story, creator of mighty empire. In its way, it was an impressive story. Certainly it impressed a lot of people.

The events of 1688 may not actually have been particularly 'glorious' nor, indeed, 'revolutionary'. Yet the familiar lineaments of the four Stuart kings who reigned between 1603 and 1688–9 can hardly be detected in their immediate successors, Mary II and Anne, 'Stuart' only in that Stuart blood ran in their veins, while William III, himself with Stuart blood, saw his role as king in terms profoundly different from his predecessors, not least because he was the sworn enemy, not the friend, of that greatest of absolutists, Louis XIV. To the 'Whig' historians—Thomas Babington Macaulay, S. R. Gardiner, Wallace Notestein, and others—1603–88 therefore made sense as a coherent period with a coherent theme: the fight against absolutism, spear-headed and ultimately won by those doughty champions of liberty, English members of parliament. It is fair to say that one of the historians mentioned above, S. R. Gardiner, had a vast and impressive knowledge of events throughout the British Isles, which modern historians, struggling with the new demands of the 'British' perspective, might well envy. Nevertheless, the focus of 'Whig' history was very definitely English, as indeed it had to be. Constitutional preoccupations, constitutional ideologies, were, after all, and had long been a fundamental concern and interest of the English, not shared by the more backward, less governed Scots, Irish, and Welsh of previous centuries, and hardly likely to be so in the seventeenth; 'nasty' Irish Catholics and 'horrible' godly Scots had other things to think about.

That approach proved remarkably prehensile; it took a remarkably long time for the problems which it visibly raised to be addressed. Even comparatively recently, for example, it was still possible to read English historians who claimed that the only monarchical skill required in Scotland by the first Stuart king, James VI and I, was the ability to survive in the face of his over-mighty aristocracy. One might have thought that this was hardly the most obvious springboard for that despotic style of divine right kingship—or tyranny—of which James apparently became such a noted exponent after 1603; but then James had condemned himself out of his own mouth, in his two tracts on kingship written in 1598–9, *Basilikon Doron* and *The Trew Law of Free Monarchies*, which certainly espoused divine right theory, and he cheerfully compounded this with his speeches to the English parliament, some of which left his audience in considerable doubt about how far he believed in king-in-parliament, rather than king, as the lawgiver. Perhaps more oddly, by the nineteenth century Oliver

Cromwell had come to stand—literally, as his statue outside the house of commons attests—as the champion of parliamentary liberty, even parliamentary democracy. It did not seem to bother those who cast him in that role that his famous eruption into the commons on 20 April 1653 with soldiers at his back, forcibly to dissolve parliament, makes Charles I's attempt to arrest the Five Members in January 1642, still ritually enacted today at the annual opening of parliament, look positively restrained. Moreover, the inhabitants of England and Scotland appeared to have a lasting enthusiasm for monarchy, or at least a belief in monarchy as the most viable form of government, despite the upheavals of the 1640s. Why else was Oliver Cromwell, already his highness the lord protector, and living in monarchical style (though impoverishing it with his philistine sale of Charles I's glorious art collection) offered the crown? Had he accepted it, he would have created a Cromwell dynasty, its first king—that former minor country gentleman—rejoicing in the somewhat unlikely sounding name of King Oliver. Why else, even after he had rejected the offer, was there a retreat, in this period of the republic, back to the apparently greater security of that traditional monarchical principle, hereditary succession?

Moreover, those stalwart champions of liberty in the English house of commons surely cut a very poor figure as the crisis mounted in 1640–2. Conrad Russell's famous 'billiard ball effect' put great weight on the fact that the English civil war trailed in third, only after—and made possible by—the Scottish civil war (the bishops' wars) of 1639–40, and the Irish Rebellion of 1641; and even the example of the Scottish parliament of June 1640 which met, like its predecessor the Reformation parliament of 1560, without the authority of the king, and decisively rejected his innate assumptions about the nature of monarchy, did not save the Long Parliament from opening, as John Morrill has pointed out, in an atmosphere of dither, muddle, and uncertainty. This may only reflect the fact that, in England at least, Charles I had to work extremely hard to stir up rebellion against him, even having to start the English civil war himself in order to get it going.

Likewise, for all the fears and worries about James VII and II, the 'Glorious Revolution' was hardly a decisive English blow against tyranny. It was made possible by the armed intervention of a Dutch prince, William of Orange, his help sought by a few people in England. He himself was helped by the fact that the wind favoured him in bringing him to England, by a royal nosebleed, and by James's willingness to run away. James's reception by the cheering crowds in London when he was caught in his first attempt to flee by these embarrassing fishermen of Rochester, who recognized him and sent him back to his capital, can hardly be rated as glorious or revolutionary in the Whig sense; and his second and this time successful flight, through doors carefully left unlocked in the hope that he would make the attempt, suggests a measure of desperation rather than a determined onslaught on the would-be absolutism of the king. Indeed, the outcome of 1688 might be seen as much in terms of that vein of Stuart lack of political common sense, sometimes amounting to political coma, first evident in Mary, queen of Scots, and surfacing again in her grandson Charles I and her great-grandson James VII and II. It is surely instructive to compare James's flights, which allowed him to get to France and live in palatial comfort, with that of Louis XVI's flight to Varennes and its aftermath a century later. The unfortunate Louis, apparently conscious of, and deeply worried by, the fate of Charles I, was living through and dying because of a revolution which set out to change the world—*inter alia*, changing the meaning of the word from revolving back to a mythical past to seeking to destroy the past. But that was manifestly not the aim of the 'revolutionaries' of 1688. Moreover, although the Whig emphasis on the English preoccupation with matters constitutional has undoubtedly much to be said for it, it was scarcely well directed and focused. The first preoccupation, in 1688–9, was whether William should be regent or king; months were wasted on this issue, wasted because William had no intention of being anything other than king. By contrast, it took a remarkably long time for the English parliament to get round to passing that Act which guaranteed the existence of parliament, whether the king willed it or no, the Triennial Act, first mooted in 1693, and enacted in 1694. Yet this had been seen as the fundamental safeguard by both English and Scots in the mid-seventeenth century, and indeed had its origins in a widely known tract written as early as the second decade of the century, somewhere between 1614 and 1621, urging the even more extreme measure of annual parliaments. And yet again, it was the Scots who took the more radical political line, if this time after rather than before events in England. The English, keeping rather quiet about their fight for liberty and parliamentary sovereignty, preferred the fiction that James had abdicated. The Scots bluntly said that they had booted him out. And despite a certain amount of short-lived Jacobite sword-rattling north of the border, it was only the Irish who really tried—and failed—to save him.

Today, we can be certain of one thing about the seventeenth century. The old certainty has gone, and gone for good, just as has that even older idea, the 'Whiggish' religious ideology of seventeenth-century Scotland. No longer is it seen as the period in which the would-be absolutism, even tyranny, of the Stuart kings would twice dash itself against the massive rock of English love of liberty, and twice come to grief, the second time fatally. Yet it was not until the 1960s that were there the first signs of a really serious and direct challenge to the 'Whig interpretation', with G. R. Elton's article of 1964, 'A High Road to Civil War?', which, by reinterpreting the Commons' Apology of 1604, dented the Whig assumption that it was James VI's accession to the English throne as James I in 1603 which put England firmly on to that high road. There had, however, been earlier attempts to find alternative explanations for that century which departed from the Whig line. The mid-twentieth century was enlivened by two of them: the Marxist interpretation, most notably associated with Christopher Hill; and the so-called 'Storm over the Gentry', whose exponents, R. H. Tawney, Lawrence Stone, J. H. Hexter, and others, settled down to count manors, assess peerage and gentry incomes, identify rising and falling peerage and gentry, in an effort to explain the line-up in the English civil war, with all the passion of that civil war recreated, except that they fought it with pens dipped in vitriol rather than swords dipped in blood. In the first case, the attempt to pit the 'feudal' against the 'bourgeois' offered too many hostages to fortune; as with Whig history, it forced the seventeenth century into a model built in the nineteenth century. The second was no doubt great fun in its day, especially for those with a head for figures, but even before Christopher Thompson's *coup de grâce*, the arguments and disagreements between the practitioners of this art meant that it was impossible to make a clear link between this approach and the English civil war.

Much more fruitful was the new attention given to local studies. Originally conceived in too crude a form—court versus country—real advances were made when attention was given to individual counties by T. G. Barnes, Alan Everitt, Morrill, Anthony Fletcher, Clive Holmes, Richard Cust, Ann Hughes, and others. These immediately showed up the fatal flaw in any attempt to find an overarching explanation for the events and the crises of the seventeenth century, especially as the studies themselves became increasingly nuanced and sophisticated, exploring the layers within the various counties which made it increasingly difficult simply to set 'county' against 'centre'; rather, local and national concerns were interwoven. The more diversity and division were stressed, the more detailed attention was given to the responses of individuals and groups to the sometimes too forceful imposition of royal authority and then its breakdown, the more the sheer complexity of the seventeenth century became insistently apparent. Analysis of local responses to ship money, for example, makes it easier to understand, why Charles I initially thought that, far from being the infamous and dubiously legal arbitrary act of an autocratic king, it was a success, for to begin with it was. It might be unfortunate that England was not at war in the 1630s, which raised doubts about whether it was necessary at all; and no doubt the inhabitants of the inland counties, taxed for the first time, did not appreciate the king's desire to make defence a national issue rather than putting the whole burden on the coastal shires, as had traditionally been done. But what was really wrong was that, as so often, Charles utterly failed to see the fragility of the success, choosing to ignore the fact that many of his subjects were increasingly hungry for information, and getting it, in the form of pamphlets, copies of speeches in parliament, newsletters, and so on, available to those who could read and those to whom they could be read. He was, therefore, dealing with considerable political awareness in the localities. This was by no means wholly new, even if by the seventeenth century it had come to depend increasingly extensively on the written as well as the oral word. The same phenomenon has been analysed for the fourteenth century, based round the county court, and it undoubtedly goes back a lot further than that. England had long had the demanding and invasive government which provoked political awareness and political response, and its relative geographic smallness, compared to the vast and sprawling dominions of Spain, France, the Empire, meant that its counties could operate in a more integrated form, as the astonishing inter-county organization of the Peasants' Revolt of 1381 had dramatically demonstrated. That did not mean, a necessarily integrated response, but rather a huge range of varying and conflicting responses, as well as changes of heart; those who complained about Charles I in the 1630s were not always to be found on the parliamentarian side in 1642. And of course 'information' could be misinformation: that fascinating thing, gossip. As Sir John Coke wrote in March 1642, 'so many false reports are spread abroad that a man knows not what to believe'; and that was not only true in the tense years of the 1640s.

Nevertheless—to pluck out a single example—the delightful diary of William Whiteway of Dorchester, written between 1618 and 1635, does give a strong sense of a world slipping out of control, and forcing men to react to unpalatable directions from London. Whiteway was intensely interested in his family affairs; in the men elected to parliament and chosen as baillies, sheriffs, and under-sheriffs; in local and sometimes national events, such as a comet in 1618, grim herald of the Thirty Years' War, and an eclipse of the sun in 1621, James's spectacular hunting accident in 1622, the weather, including great storms and the number of people drowned in them, the price of corn, births, marriages, and deaths; in the spectacular, including the murder of the tapster of the George in Dorchester in 1623 and other crimes and executions, the birth of a seven-toed baby in 1634, and the arrival of a Frenchwoman in Dorchester in the same year 'that had no hands, but could write, sow, wash and do many other things with her feet'; in the amounts of money he gave to his wife; and of course in news from Europe, including a false report in January 1623 that the Spanish match was concluded. But a new note intrudes itself from 1625 onwards. Whiteway tended to be simply factual in reporting high political actions under James, and neutral in his comments on James himself, though the king might well have been pleased that this southern Englishman, recording his death, referred to him as 'king of great Britain'. Yet 'god be praised' for his recovery from his hunting accident. There was no mention of God, but merely the cold statement that in 1634 Charles, also having a hunting accident, recovered. And from 1625, political comment and an account of men's reactions to the contentious issues of Charles's early years began to creep in. In August 1625, he describes the Oxford parliament's absolute refusal of Charles's demands for further supply, and its dissolution 'with great dislike of both sides'. In May 1626, parliament was 'resuming courage' in questioning Buckingham although the king had forbidden it, and in June parliament took 'offence and dislike' when Buckingham was made chancellor of Cambridge, while in the same month London twice refused Charles's demands for a loan of £100,000, having no money 'by meanes of the deadness of trade', though the aldermen did eventually produce £2,400. In January 1627 he tells us about hostile reactions to the Forced Loan, and in January 1635 writes at unusual length about ship money, the unfairness of the rating of Dorchester, and the 'much grudging' with which it was paid.

When historians began to move out from the centre to investigate the localities, the Whig waters were certainly very muddied. And this might make the study of the seventeenth century a great deal more difficult. But it also made it a great deal more interesting, as the worried subjects of the Stuart kings became three-dimensional. And then in the 1970s came the explosion of 'revisionism'. It is more accurate, of course, to speak of 'revisionists', for 'revisionism' was not a school. Indeed, it is not always clear which historians are, or would see themselves as, revisionists; some are revisionists and then not revisionists; some, like Pauline Croft, whose contribution to modern seventeenth-century scholarship is equally notable, hardly fit in at all. Perhaps it can better be regarded as a methodology. In 1978, Kevin Sharpe made his striking plea for 'a return to the drawing board, rather than a repair of the old [Whig] canvas'. What he meant by this was that historians should allow the sources to speak directly to them, rather than being refracted through the imposed assumptions of later centuries. And when historians like Conrad Russell, whose name towers over early seventeenth-century studies, John Morrill, Mark Kishlansky, Sharpe himself, and many others did so, it became clear that the old canvas was beyond repair. What emphatically did not replace it was a new canvas; the most one could say is that it was a patchwork quilt.

The very absence of a new school is in itself a measure of the importance and success of returning to the drawing board. For the first time, the idea of parliamentary 'opposition', redolent of modern party politics, was decisively rejected; there was no party ideological line-up in early seventeenth-century parliaments. Indeed, it could now be emphasized that, far from sticking to entrenched positions, men were very capable of changing their minds, even men like the notorious 'royalist', Thomas Wentworth, who became earl of Strafford, and the notorious 'parliamentarian', Sir John Eliot. Attention was focused away from constitutional conflict to structural problems in government—the creaking machinery of the state, the burgeoning desire for office to the extent that demand far outstripped supply, the mounting fiscal problems, of which kings and MPs were uneasily, sometimes dimly, aware without having any real solutions to offer, and which were hardly resolved under Charles II and James VII and II. James VI and I himself complained repeatedly about English MPs' habit of talking endlessly rather than acting, which was not a good way of getting things done; he unblushingly compared the English parliament with the Scottish one, in his profoundly misleading account of that supposedly cooperative and subservient body in 1607—a rare example of an attempt to portray Scotland as more governable than England. But not only James was aware of the point; men talked, and issues were ducked or postponed, even in cases such as the highly contentious monopolies where there was in fact a measure of consensus in attacking them. Moreover, there was a very real sense in which the kingdom by now could no longer afford the king by using traditional methods of financing him, certainly in time of war. But it was easier to blame a spectacularly extravagant king, James I, than try to address that more fundamental problem. What was not in evidence, however, was the use of the weapon whose existence Whig historians so firmly believed in: refusing supply until grievances had been redressed. In the parliament of 1610, John Savile objected to the linking of supply and redress on the grounds that if the link were admitted redress would henceforth be bought. This, of course, in itself shows that supply and redress were linked in men's minds. What that did not mean, however, was that they thought it appropriate, in effect, to blackmail the crown. Even in the two fraught parliamentary sessions of 1625, it can be argued that the problem arose from Charles I's demand that, such were his needs in time of war—by no means an unreasonable point, especially given the enthusiasm for war of the parliament of 1624—supply must be granted, while redress could be discussed on some other occasion, and then, having got supply in the first session, asked for more in the second.

As with local studies, all this muddied the waters. Moreover, the revisionist attack went well beyond its initial preoccupation with crown and parliament. It had the distinct advantage of showing an awareness of the importance of the British perspective as crucial to the understanding of the problems of the seventeenth century, whether in England or in the multiple kingdoms of the British Isles. England, to invoke *1066 and All That*, was no longer necessarily 'top nation', and certainly not the only nation. Again, it added to the complexity. It also had the great merit of making sense. Scottish, Irish, and English historians began to talk to one another; it was notable, for example, that it was John Morrill, an English historian who had espoused the British cause, who was invited to edit the essays in *The Scottish National Covenant in its British Context, 1638–51*. Of course there remain many historians who concentrate on their particular kingdoms. The difference is that they are now more inclined to trust one another. The charge of 'Anglocentricity' still exists, but it has become less shrill; and it has shifted from being the defensive response of the underdog to the more positive awareness that the seventeenth century simply does not make sense in English terms alone.

No one today doubts the importance of 'revisionism'. But the very fact that not all 'revisionists' sang the same song meant that, although there would be a backlash, 'post-revisionism', far from being monolithic, showed the same strengths as revisionism itself. Ideological positions came back in, and convincingly so. Consensus and continuity were undoubtedly sought, in a world in which change was readily equated with threat. Actually—if unfortunately—the world had changed, and in its new circumstances political, religious, and constitutional ideas were certainly up for grabs, forcing questioning and dissent. Moreover, there was unease about the fact that 'revisionism' could be seen as Whig history with the roles reversed. As Christopher Thompson trenchantly said, in 1989,

The new model of seventeenth-century Parliamentary history ... has the appeal of novelty. But many of its features, particularly its characterization of James and Charles and its view of the House of Commons, are recognizable as those of the Royalists in the Civil War and of the Tories who succeeded them. It is, in fact, the mirror image of the old Whig view dispelled by S. R. Gardiner. Unfortunately, this new analysis of the Parliamentary politics of the period is just as misleading.

As there was no single characterization of James and Charles, or a drive to turn kings into good guys, MPs into bad ones, this is surely going too far. Nevertheless, there is certainly something in it, and it very much makes the point that creating models and using labels for groups of historians can have its own considerable dangers. That is a historiographical habit perhaps particularly associated with seventeenth-century English historians, who appear to have a special need for the protecting umbrella of a 'school'. But too much attention is still being given to labelling, as the excellent introductions to the recent *Festschriften* for Conrad Russell and Nicholas Tyacke demonstrate; when is a revisionist a revisionist and when is he not is, in the last resort, not really the most helpful approach, and carries the risk of a new form of straitjacketing. Thirty years after the explosion of what has been called the 'full-fig revisionism' of the 1970s, it can be urged that 'revisionism' and its associated terms are now redundant. What really matters is that in recent decades historians, whatever their views, have engaged in exceedingly fruitful debate, and at last released us from the old Whig straitjacket. We 'understand' the seventeenth century less clearly than the Whigs did; it is now possible to discuss whether the civil war was inevitable, and if it was, when it became inevitable; and the inevitability of Charles I's execution is now being pushed further and further towards the decisive date of 30 January 1649. Confusion, muddle, fearfulness are now the order of the day; and infinitely more rewarding it is.

Religion, and the Scots and the Irish

It is, of course, quite wrong to separate out religious tensions and doubts and fears from the political and constitutional issues discussed in the previous section. Keith Brown, in his essay in this book, tartly concludes his analysis of secular Britain, 1603–37, by pointing out that missing from his discussion is 'the issue that more than any other fired political debate, hardened divisions, and inspired men to take those dangerous steps that turned them from dutiful subjects into rebels: religion'—the subject of John McCafferty's chapter. I sympathize with his frustration. In no way does it reflect any critique by me of John Morrill's *dictum*, that the civil wars were 'the last wars of religion'; and I have long been puzzled by the claim that the 'revisionists' 'hermetically' separated religion and politics. It should rather be said that, in rethinking the seventeenth century, focused rather than sweeping interpretation was desperately needed; and it has certainly had it in the religious sphere. Ever since Nicholas Tyacke, in the 1970s, dropped his bombshell onto the prevailing orthodoxy on religion, the idea that there were the Anglicans of the mainstream church, and in opposition to them, the disruptive, dissenting puritans, with their enormous talent for making life difficult—which was, indeed, a very Elizabethan and Caroline, though not Jacobean, view of the matter—the religious history of the seventeenth century has not only never been the same again, but infinitely more exciting. Patrick Collinson, in his seminal study *The Elizabethan Puritan Movement* (1967), had convincingly attacked the over-simplistic and neat picture for the late sixteenth century. Tyacke, whose initial research was contemporaneous, though publication came later, equally destroyed that picture for the early seventeenth century, arguing instead for a moderate Calvinist consensus under James, which incorporated the 'puritans'; what broke that consensus, and reactivated the puritans was the Caroline attempt to push the English church away from Calvinism towards Arminianism. What followed was a flood of fascinating scholarship, by Peter Lake, Christopher Haigh, Diarmaid MacCulloch, Kenneth Fincham, Felicity Heal, Anthony Milton, Michael Questier, Alexandra Walsham, Peter McCullough, and many, many others—the list is seemingly endless—extending and refining the Collinson and Tyacke insights, as indeed they themselves were doing, and sometimes challenging them. Easy assumptions, as for example an English irrational and knee-jerk hatred of popery, or, for that matter, a ready dislike of Archbishop Laud, were gone for good. As in the 'state', so in the church: the polar approach no longer satisfied. And religious issues, as much as political ones, became the stuff of local and central studies.

The sheer wealth of scholarship in itself provides a pragmatic explanation for the divisions in this book: trying to fit every-thing into a single chapter on 1603–37 was virtually impossible. But there is more to it than that, simply because of the 'British' approach of the essays published here. For neither English consti-tutional/political preoccupations nor religious ones can be readily transferred to Scotland and Ireland; nor, of course, can Scotland and Ireland be slotted together. To be sure, the National Covenant of 1638 does look very 'constitutional', laboriously rehearsing a list of acts of parliament as it does. When one thinks of the fifteenth- and sixteenth-century bonds so familiar to Scottish society, and which had fed their way into religious bonds and covenanting theology, of which the Covenant, in concept at least, was the most remarkable example, it is immediately apparent that, in the form it took, the Scots were doing something new. Hitherto, their interest in constitutional matters had been casual to the point of indifference. There was no Scottish equivalent to the English tracts on the nature of parliament, no real discussion of ways of financ-ing the king; not until 1681, for example, did Sir George Purves produce his *Revenue of the Scottish Crown*, and that was little more than a turgid list of valuations of royal lands. And in Scotland only George Buchanan and James VI were interested enough to write extensively about the nature and source of sovereignty, and then for a very different purpose. Possibly the way in which the Covenant was cast reflects the awareness of its devisers that they were acting on an international stage and seeking to influence a very Anglicized king with a distinct taste for English-style rhetoric, and a distinct distaste for the Scottish-style religion which he had been seeking to undermine in the 1630s; it has much in common with the way in which Buchanan had been wheeled out to justify the deposition of Mary, Queen of Scots, for Elizabeth's benefit, as opposed to following on any Scottish tradition of justification for the removal of individual monarchs for home consumption. If so, the Covenanters encouraged a trend, for it is from this period on that Scottish intellectuals would turn their attention to issues of 'state', even if initially at least they were ministerial intellectuals such as Samuel Rutherford. Here we do have a brief flash of what might be called British, or at least Anglo-Scottish, history. For this is an underplayed example of the way in which the immediate

'British problem' of the 1620s and 1630s made Charles's Scottish critics see real value in a 'British' approach, or, more specifically, one which would have greater resonance with Charles's English critics.

However, in historiographical terms, there was a profound difference between England and Scotland. For there was one area in which the 'Whiggism' of nineteenth- and twentieth-century English and American historians was alive and well in late sixteenth- and seventeenth-century Scotland, in its powerful religious ideology. To an extent John Knox, and certainly Andrew and James Melville and these doughty presbyterian ministers and historians of the reformed kirk David Calderwood and John Row, all enthusiastically espoused a teleological approach in their accounts of that kirk, with sufficient success for James VI to encourage John Spottiswoode, archbishop of St Andrews, to write the alternative and pro-royal version. It was unfortunate that Spottiswoode simply did not write so well, lacking the fire and passion of the presbyterians, who made themselves the major (true, as they saw it) sources for the history, and the very considerable myths, of the late sixteenth and seventeenth centuries, myths so powerful that they are only now being unpicked. For the triumph of English parliamentary liberty over royal tyranny, the Scots of the post-Reformation era created in their own day the triumph of the godly kirk over the ungodly prince, once God had relieved his sinful people in 1560. It is a sobering thought that as late as 1961 an Aberdeen professor of theology, J. S. MacEwen, could publish a book called *The Faith of John Knox* (trailing in a year late for the quatercentenary celebrations of the Reformation) in which, with all the vigour of Knox himself, he thundered forth about the 'black terrors of the soul' suffered collectively by medieval and early-modern Scots until in 1560 they were dispelled by a Calvinist God and the pure light of the Calvinist faith. It is a perhaps even more sobering thought that it was still possible to extol 1560 as The Year of the Scottish Reformation. Fortunately, there was hope. Getting the year 'right', Gordon Donaldson published his magisterial *The Scottish Reformation* in 1960, and this was followed up two years later by an excellent collection, *Essays on the Scottish Reformation*, edited by David McRoberts. The subject was taking off—though such was Donaldson's grip that it took rather too long to break away from the parameters he set, and much of the work on the Jacobean church remained in the realms of high ecclesiastical politics, even if enlivened by a fight between Donaldson and James Kirk over the polity of the Kirk and the place of the 'godly' prince worthy of James VI and Andrew Melville themselves. Although far removed from the emotional approach of MacEwen, they were, in other words, still fighting in Whig terms, although it is fair to say that in order to move the subject forward, they had to do so.

Since then, Scottish ecclesiastical history has changed out of recognition. The very absence of sects within the kirk, in complete contrast to those in the English church, gave the kirk the appearance of a starker, more monolithic institution, its members—or many of them—made miserable by the ferocious discipline imposed by the church courts, and especially the local ones, the kirk sessions, with their obsession with morality and their shame punishments. Contemporaries were all too aware of this. 'Quhair is the blyithnes that hes beine?' sadly asked the poet and government official Sir Richard Maitland of Lethington, now that 'kirkmen cled lyik men of weir [war]' were on the rampage? In an anonymous 'Admonition to the Antichristian Ministers in the Deformit Kirk of Scotland', blame for the new dismal Scotland was put squarely on the shoulders of that great hero of Scottish history, John Knox:

> For sen the time that fals Apostat preist
> Enemie to Christ and mannis salvation
> Your maister Knox, that vicked, venemous beist
> Vas chaiisit from the Inglish nation
> And come to you to preiche abhomination
> In Scotland, sumtyme realme of renoun
> Extreme has been that desolation
> Ye have sustenit in citie, tour and toun.

But such responses were drowned out in the paeans of praise for Calvinist Scotland, whether in the hands of the presbyterian historians of the time, rhapsodizing on the sufferings and persecution of the godly—persecution being, of course, the hallmark of godliness—or later historians, themselves often ministers, basking in their ultimate triumph. Certain things became axiomatic: 'the Scots' wanted presbyterianism; 'the Scots' hated episcopacy. Only in the second half of the twentieth century did these begin to be seriously questioned. Now, thanks to the work of Kirk, Michael

Lynch, Ian Cowan, Margo Todd, Michael Graham, Louise Yeoman, Alan MacDonald, and many others, old certainties have gone, new debate has begun, whether at the level of high politics or parishioners in the localities, and ecclesiastical history has thereby become much more fascinating, both in its own right and in the insights it offers into the tensions which led to the crisis of the late 1630s. We have even been asked recently by that energetic revisionist of just about everything, Mark Kishlansky, whether we should re-evaluate Charles I in Scotland, and allow more to be said for the religious policy which created the crisis. Concurrently, in Alan MacDonald's work and that of Laura Stewart, we are being encouraged to contemplate the heresy that James VI, in his later years, did much to anticipate the problems associated with Charles, especially because of his infamous Five Articles of Perth, now once again an issue for debate. And that period when the godly Covenanters determined events not only in Scotland but even to an extent in England—a most unusual position for the Scots—is now seen as a very brief period, with the Covenanters less firmly in control than used to be thought.

Despite fears of popery, that 'structure of a prejudice' beautifully analysed by Peter Lake, and certainly helped on in its day by Henrietta Maria, aided by misunderstanding of Charles I, it is within the parameters of Protestant faiths—puritan, presbyterian, Arminian, Laudian, and so on—that the troubles of Scotland and England can be set. That does not mean that it is an easy matter. But it is less horrendously complex than trying to fit into the problems of composite monarchy the third of the three kingdoms of the British Isles, Ireland. To put it at its simplest, Scotland and even England saw advantages in the union of the crowns, with the exception of the republicans of 1649, who would willingly have allowed Scotland to retain its monarchy in the person of Charles II and thus broken the union. The same cannot be said of Ireland, struggling with the prevailing English belief in Irish barbarism and colonial status, and a country in which Catholicism impressively survived and flourished. The spine-chilling views expressed by Edmund Spenser, secretary to the late Elizabethan Lord Deputy Arthur Grey of Wilton, in his *View of the present state of Ireland* (1596) and by Sir John Davies, speaker of the Irish parliament of 1613–15, in his *Discovery of the true causes why Ireland was never entirely subdued ... until the beginning of his majesty's happy reign* (1612), both of whom saw the only solution to Ireland in suppression of Irishness and the forcible imposition of English language, law, and custom, at least for the moment remained confined to the written word; it was Cromwell who would translate theory into violent reality, when he forcibly redrew the map of Irish landholding in favour of the Protestants, in a policy which John Morrill describes as 'a terrifying and unreversed revolution ... perhaps the greatest exercise in ethnic cleansing in early modern Europe'. It was not one which could readily have been predicted when Davies penned his treatise. Ironically his title, while overoptimistic, does have something to be said for it. For James, inheriting the crowns of England and Ireland at the tail end of the disastrous Nine Years' War, 1594–1603, was enough of a Scot to take a more favourable and less fearful view of Ireland than his predecessor had done, and certainly regarded himself as king rather than colonial ruler. Indeed, it has been suggested that, had it not been for their flight in 1607, he might have established a working relationship with the earls of Tyrone and Tyrconnel along the lines of that which he had had with those Scottish magnates on whom he relied to maintain local control. Instead, he turned to another Scottish policy, even if not one which had had noted success: plantation. As he had tried to plant lowlanders in the Western Isles, so now he planted English and Scotsmen in Ulster. (It is distinctly hard that there are those who thereby attribute to him the problems of present-day Ulster, not least because those whom he planted did include some Catholics, and in any case the plantation policy had begun under Elizabeth.) He was also helped by his confident and ecumenical approach; despite his harsh anti-papal language to his parliament, Catholics did in fact get more concessions than they might have expected.

Where it went wrong was in Charles's reign. Like his father, Charles did not press down heavily on Irish Catholics. Indeed, in the interests of getting men and money, in 1626 the king offered 'matters of grace and bounty to be rendered to Ireland', which offered considerable concessions to the Catholics. But Charles was to succeed, where James did not, in turning this into a three kingdoms matter. How far James tried to bring 'congruity' between the churches of England and Scotland remains a matter of debate. Charles left no doubt about his intentions, going far beyond 'congruity'. From his point of view, religious schizophrenia was impossible for a king with responsibility for the souls of his subjects, and that was not necessarily an untenable position. What made it entirely untenable, for Scottish Calvinists seeing creeping Anglicanism being steadily forced on them, was that their religion was being undermined while Charles did not show the same determination to bring Irish Catholics into line. In fact, Strafford did want to bring Ireland into line with England and Scotland and establish the church acceptable to Charles I and Laud, but his way of going about it was distinctly less strident than Charles's in Scotland, and men could be forgiven for failing to see the point. On the other hand, it did not sweeten Irish Catholics when Strafford failed to deliver the 'graces'.

But there is a more basic problem about Ireland's place as one of the multiple kingdoms of seventeenth-century Britain. In the case of Ireland, historians are up against a quite different difficulty from those of England and Scotland. Irish history, unlike Scottish or internal English, cannot stand in its own right because Ireland unlike Scotland had not been a separate and independent entity before 1603. If one is going to 'blame' anyone for the Irish problem, it is not James VI and I with his Ulster Plantation, but the medieval English monarchs who failed to follow up on and consolidate Henry II's initial settlement, turning their attention instead to different prizes: Scotland, Wales, and above all—and most ludicrously—France. Tudor attempts to resolve the problem foundered on the fact that Henry VIII's 'kingdom' of Ireland was an English appanage, and no really successful way of governing Ireland was ever discovered. Even more disastrously, England failed to impose Protestant Reformation. The reasons for this have been the subject of much nuanced debate between Brendan Bradshaw, Nicholas Canny, Alan Ford, and others, just as the problems of finding a workable form of government have exercised the minds of Irish historians such as Ciaran Brady and Aidan Clarke; it should of course be added that there is not a fixed demarcation line between the two groups. So in Ireland, in stark contrast to England and Scotland, there was a groping Protestant 'official' church and a vibrant Counter-Reformation Catholic one.

This means that Russell's 'billiard ball effect' must be used with a certain caution. It is certainly the case that the Scottish and Irish troubles between the Prayer Book riots of 1637 and the Irish Rebellion of 1641 anticipated and in some measure made possible the outbreak of civil war in England in 1642. But there was a profound difference between the Scottish and English crises and the Irish one. A certain type of Protestant and, in England, constitutional ideology underpinned and might be seen to dignify the Scottish and English crises, and even, if very temporarily, provided their protagonists with a measure of common cause. It was altogether different in Ireland. From the Anglo-Scottish point of view, that was bloody and terrifying Catholic revolt, with neither justification nor dignity. That is a forcible reminder that, whatever difficulties other multiple kingdoms experienced, the British version faced the particularly intractable and long-lived problem of fundamental and unresolved religious division.

The lull before the next storm?

Any actor playing Charles I, be it Sir Alec Guinness in the film *Cromwell* or Jeremy Clyde in the television series *By the Sword Divided*, can hardly fail to play to stunning effect the scene of the king's trial, such is the brilliance of the script provided for him by Charles himself, and the execution, such was Charles's awesome calm and courage. For his opponents, it was hardly an auspicious beginning for the rule of the Saints. In Scotland, and even more in Ireland, the harsh imposition of military rule worked, up to a point. Indeed, it used to be fashionable for older generations of Scottish historians to praise Cromwell for bringing order to an ill-governed land, with considerable indifference to how the Scots of the 1650s might have regarded the matter. How long it could have lasted is another question. Where the republican experiment clearly failed was in England. Indeed, the 1650s suggest the supreme paradox that Cromwell, more than any monarch, was crucial to the survival of the republican state, or rather, a state with many of the trappings of monarchy under the guise of republicanism. It is, of course, highly problematic to attribute the fate of any historical event to one individual, just as it is dangerous to be determinist to the extent of seeing the Restoration as necessarily inevitable. Yet the great examples of republican states in the seventeenth century, Venice and the Dutch republic, are hardly successful role models. In the first case, the constraints put on the *doge* still left something approaching individual rule; in the second, the effective fight-back of the house of Orange paved the way for a prince of Orange available to take over not an English republic but the English throne. Morrill's 'weak republicanism' in practice as opposed to the 'strong republicanism' of theory makes very good sense. The trouble was that no way had been found to make it 'strong' enough.

And so, when hereditary succession in the house of Cromwell produced the ineffective Richard, the better chosen name for a monarch *manqué* did not save him. Charles II, acknowledged king since 1649, came back, to much rejoicing; an overenthusiastic gunner even managed to fire himself off the battlements of Edinburgh castle amid the general celebrations, and already the maypoles were once again standing. There was, apparently, a palpable lightening of the atmosphere, even a blessed taste for immorality after two decades of intense godliness, with the return to the desired *status quo*. Monarchy was restored. Charles famously vowed never to go on his travels again (which actually included a distinct distaste for travelling to Scotland), and therefore offered a different and more relaxed style of kingship; restoration comedy—with women appearing on stage—got going, as did royal mistresses; the Royal Society was founded; and even the follies of James VII and II only managed to provoke a 'revolution' which was infinitely more low-key than the wars of the 1640s, if more long-lasting in its results.

It therefore used to be possible to think that, after all the drama of the first half of the seventeenth century, the second was an anti-climax, even a comparatively neglected postscript, with much less to offer. In fact, the wealth of recent scholarship which has opened up the period makes it very clear that the later seventeenth century had every bit as much drama as the earlier; continuity of old concerns, old worries, old obsessions was far more prevalent than the euphoria of a new age, with problems solved. Charles II was wildly overoptimistic when he expressed the hope, in the Declaration of Breda of 4 April 1660, 'that the memory of what is passed may be buried to the World' and that 'all Notes of discord, separation and difference of Parties, be utterly abolished among all our Subjects'. Indeed, new notes of discord were already being sown in the Declaration itself. Charles was manifestly less intransigent in religious matters than his father. But his offer of religious toleration in the Declaration went down to defeat in the face of the ruthless intransigence of the Anglican Church, on the surface perhaps less visibly harsh than its godly predecessor, but as relentlessly intolerant; all that happened was that the persecuted changed places with the persecutors, but the persecuting mentality was, to say the least, no less strong than it had been in the days of Charles and Laud in the 1630s and the godly in the 1640s and 1650s. And in Scotland, the Covenanting murder of Archbishop James Sharpe in the presence of his daughter in 1679 in brutal response to increasingly draconian legislation against and repression of conventiclers was followed by the notorious 'killing times' which reached their peak in the mid-1680s. The savagery passed into Covenanting myth, and was certainly exaggerated, but equally certainly not invented; the level of bloody repression was higher than at any other time in the seventeenth century.

Indeed, wherever one looks, religious and political tensions and conflicts appear to have been no less a feature of this period than the earlier one. Even the Cavalier parliament, when it met in 1661 in a mood, apparently, of excessive enthusiasm for and generosity to the new king, was hardly a model of subservient cooperation. For it adopted the exclusive Anglicanism which Charles and Clarendon so disliked. MPs, for example, had to take the sacrament and kneel at communion—something which would cause potential problems some forty-five years later, in the proposals for uniting the English and Scottish parliaments. Charles II's second attempt to introduce toleration, the Declaration of Indulgence of 1672, was equally unsuccessful, defeated a year later by a parliament resolutely opposed to it; and a worrying echo of earlier fears was heard in the doubts expressed about the king's prerogative use of his suspending power, in order to give his Declaration sub-stance, just as there were fears about his freedom of action as supreme governor of the church. And while the idea of organized

244 | JENNY WORMALD

opposition in parliament under the first two Stuarts is no longer accepted, the Exclusion Crisis of 1679–81 produced it, creating a whole new level of campaigning and disputed elections now that there had come into being 'parties'—Whigs and Tories—even if certainly not anything approaching party government. In the same years, the Test Act and the monstrous Popish Plot dreamt up by Titus Oates reflected an unparalleled and hysterical degree of anti-Catholicism; even if his subjects knew nothing about the secret part of the Treaty of Dover of 1670, Charles's enthusiasm for that nightmare figure to all good Protestants, Louis XIV, produced a dangerous concatenation of absolutism and Catholicism in men's minds, far greater than had existed in the years immediately before the civil war, despite the myths surrounding Charles I. These highly problematic questions, when did the civil war/Glorious Revolution become 'inevitable', will no doubt go on being debated. But whereas the inevitability of civil war can be pushed nearer and nearer to its outbreak, the final downfall of the Stuarts now appears to be pushed further and further back. As Jonathan Scott memorably wrote, fear of popery, fear of arbitrary government, fear for the survival of the monarchy, meant that 'by 1667, with 100,000 Londoners dead of plague, much of the city in ashes and a return to the condition of Stuart military failure [with the second Dutch war], the party was over'.

And yet people seemed remarkably reluctant to leave the party. Uncertainty rather than direction, combined with solid backing for the monarchy, ensured that it went on. Indeed, Charles and James got away with something which had been one of the flashpoints under their father: the militia. There were standing armies in each of the three kingdoms, and an apparent acceptance, in stark contrast to the earlier fears of an army in one kingdom being turned against another which had helped to bring down Strafford, that these armies were not nationally confined. In Scotland, a new note crept in to discussion about monarchical power, with strongly royalist ideas now being advanced, shorn of the old religious divisions. And in this movement lawyers had a new prominence. Sir George Mackenzie—'Bloody Mackenzie', Scottish equivalent to the English Judge Jeffries—was a passionate defender of divine right monarchy; for him, it was tantamount to treason to question the mythical antiquity of the Scottish monarchy, on the eve of the final destruction of that myth by that most remarkable Catholic priest and scholar, Fr Thomas Innes. Moreover, within a very few years of the high-point of anti-Catholicism, James VII and II was having some success in getting a better deal for Catholics; there were even some fashionable conversions in a Scotland largely hostile to episcopacy and committed to presbyterianism. Like Charles I before him, James had to work very hard to dissipate the practical and ideological support for his monarchy which eased his passage to the throne in 1685. Thanks to the existence of an all too willing William of Orange, the time-scale was just shorter.

Was there any fun in the seventeenth century?

Perhaps more than any other century, a long pall of gloom hangs over this one, certainly as far as historians are concerned; even the century of the Reformation is not so agonized, so confused, as this one. It is a measure of the necessary preoccupations of historians in seeking to understand the traumas of this age that discussion of its religious and political history tends to look particularly bleak: things seemed to be going wrong, did go wrong, and why? But of course the answer is yes. James VI and I and Charles II certainly had a marked taste for pleasure. Charles I himself was, in 1637, the self-proclaimed 'happiest king in Christendom', thoroughly enjoying practising his dance steps for that year's court masque. And one can no doubt hope that the stiffest and most humourless of the Stuarts, James VII and II, did get some fun out of life, if only in sharing with his brother an enjoyment of sex.

More generally, however, it is to the chapters on economy and society and on the cultures of the three kingdoms in this book to which one has to turn for some mitigation of the gloom. Inevitably that on the economy is the more ambivalent. There was certainly no fun in being a witch, in England and even more in Scotland—though not in Wales or Ireland—for much of the century, although witch-persecution was markedly in decline by its end. Plague also died out. And despite the horrific economic distress in Scotland in the 1690s, incidence of famine was lessening, 1623 being in general the last truly grim year; the most appalling famines in Ireland lay far in the future. But there was a very positive side. Lavish building by nobility and gentry, on either side of the civil war; the spectacular rise of London, with its social and cultural advantages as well as its economic problems, and similar developments in other cities, including Dublin and Edinburgh, if on a smaller scale; lower down the social scale, the beginnings of a consumer society which could ameliorate living conditions; all these offer a welcome corrective to the prevailing political and religious picture, and feed in to the development of 'the polite and commercial society' of the eighteenth century. Indeed, there was far more continuity here, less disjunction than was necessary for that development in political assumptions and aspirations.

And there is no doubt at all about the vitality of cultural life. Inevitably much of it was shot through with the prevailing concerns and worries of the age. But 'fun' takes on a new dimension when one thinks about that great new source of it, the public theatre, in its various manifestations, again on both sides of the civil war. Just as the greater number of news-sheets and pamphlets were feeding and encouraging greater political involvement, so did the political satire available on the stage, though, as James VI and I shrewdly appreciated, political satire in witty and enjoyable form—like the political satire of today—could help to take the sting out of grievance and complaint. And if one were feeling less politically minded, Jacobean black drama had plenty to satisfy the ghoulish-minded, while comedy throughout the period provided enjoyment for those in more light-hearted mood. Drama, medieval romance and derring-do, godliness, were increasingly on offer, as pedlars took the chapbooks round the country, those chapbooks which reached their most marvellous culmination in Bunyan's *The Pilgrim's Progress*. And particularly in the later seventeenth century, the theatre became a 'British' phenomenon, if primarily English-driven, whatever the problems of 'Britishness' in other areas of life, while at the same time, not only actresses but female authors began to make their mark on the stage. It would be far too much to expect that the inhabitants of the British Isles spent the period 1603–88 in a constant state of worry and perplexity, or in initially confident and ultimately despairing godly righteousness, and it is a great relief to find that they did not.

The seventeenth century explained?

Well, hardly. But it can be urged that the contributors to this book have made it more explicable. Certain themes do emerge, with clarity and coherence. Of Glenn Burgess's three tests for the successful writing of 'British History', outlined in the Introduction, it is the comparative which is seen to produce the most interesting results, highlighting as it does the differences in the three kingdoms which were now forced to interact under a single monarchy. The crucial importance of the personalities and abilities, or lack of them, of the four kings who tried to preside over the multiple kingdoms of the British Isles is fully demonstrated, and this remained true, as Toby Barnard convincingly shows, in what might at first sight appear to be the calmer, less fraught world of the post-Restoration era. If that era lacked the drama of the execution of a king and the confused and confusing attempts to create a wholly different state, it was still the follies of Charles II and, even more, James VII and II, so fatally like his father in his talent for turning friends into enemies, which brought the final collapse. It was the seventeenth century as a whole which was a different world from that ushered in with the 'Glorious Revolution' of 1688, which brought to the throne the Dutch Prince William who was much less exclusively concerned with his British realms, war with Louis XIV being his major interest, and twenty-six years later the German prince who became George I, arriving in England without bothering to learn the language of his new subjects. It was in that same period that the tired and creaking structure of the personal union of the crowns finally collapsed, and a new solution was found to the problems of keeping together at least the Anglo-Scottish part of the multiple monarchy. When that happened, with the union of the parliaments of 1707, the Scottish parliament went into abeyance: the 'end o' an auld sang', as the earl of Seafield said. In a much wider sense, with its style of kingship, its political muddles and aspirations, its religious tensions and passions, it was the seventeenth century itself which was the 'end o' an auld sang'.

Further Reading

Introduction

There is an increasingly vast literature on 'British History'. The starting point is J. G. A. Pocock's famous essay 'British History: A Plea for a New Subject', *New Zealand Journal of History*, 8 (1974), reprinted in *Journal of Modern History*, 47 (1975), 601–28; also 'The Limits and Divisions of British History: In Search of the Unknown Subject', *American Historical Review*, 87 (1982), 311–36. For the writings of the many historians who have answered the plea and embarked on the search, see H. Kearney, *The British Isles: A History of Four Nations* (Cambridge, 1989), and the following collections of essays: R. G. Asch (ed.), *Three Nations: A Common History? England, Scotland, Ireland and British History, c.1600–1920* (Bochum, 1993); S. G. Ellis and S. Barber, *Conquest and Union: Fashioning a British State* (Harlow, 1995); A. Grant and K. J. Stringer, *Uniting the Kingdom? The Making of British History* (London, 1995); B. Bradshaw and J. Morrill, *The British Problem, c.1534–1707: State Formation in the Atlantic Archipelago* (Basingstoke, 1996); B. Bradshaw and P. Roberts, *British Consciousness and Identity: The Making of Britain, 1533–1707* (Cambridge, 1998); G. Burgess (ed.), *The New British History: Founding a Modern State, 1603–1715* (London, 1999); J. Smyth, *The Making of the United Kingdom, 1660–1800* (Harlow, 2001); N. Canny, *Making Ireland British, 1580–1650* (Oxford, 2001). See also the works on the union of the crowns listed in the Further Reading for Monarchy and Government in Britain.

Monarchy and Government in Britain, 1603–1637

Good introductions are R. Lockyer, *The Early Stuarts: A Political History of England 1603–1642* (London, 1989) and D. L. Smith, *A History of the Modern British Isles 1603–1707* (Oxford, 1998). There is a very good short biography of James VI and I by P. Croft, *King James* (2003), and a valuable collection of essays by M. Lee jr., *Great Britain's Solomon: James VI and I in his Three Kingdoms* (Urbana, Ill., 1990). See also M. Lee jr., *Government by Pen: Scotland under James VI and I* (Urbana, Ill., 1980). On Charles I, K. Sharpe's massive *The Personal Rule of Charles I* (New Haven, 1992), which makes a case for the king, and A. I. Macinnes, *Charles I and the Making of the Covenanting Movement 1625–1641*, which is much less sympathetic, as is P. Donald, *An Uncounselled King* (Cambridge, 1990), and M. Lee jr., *The Road to Revolution: Scotland under Charles I,*

1625–1637 (Urbana, Ill., 1985). The impact of the Anglo-Scottish union is discussed by B. Galloway, *The Union of England and Scotland 1603–1608* (Edinburgh, 1986), B. P. Levack, *The Formation of the British State: England, Scotland and the Union 1603–1707* (Oxford 1987), K. M. Brown, *Kingdom and Province: Scotland and the Regal Union 1603–1715* (Basingstoke, 1992), R. A. Mason (ed.), *Scots and Britons: Scottish Political Thought and the Union of 1603* (Cambridge, 1994), T. C. Smout (ed.), *Anglo-Scottish Relations from 1603 to 1900* (Oxford, 2005), G. Burgess, R. Wymer, and J. Lawrence (eds.), *The Accession of James I: Historical and Cultural Consequences* (Basingstoke, 2006), and R. G. Houlbrooke (ed.), *James VI and I: Ideas, Authority and Government* (Aldershot, 2006); see also K. M. Brown, 'The Scottish Aristocracy, Anglicization and the Court, 1603–38', *Historical Journal*, 36 (1993), 543–76, and J. Wormald, 'James VI and I: Two Kings or One?', *History*, 68 (1983), 187–209. For Ireland, C. Brady and R. Gillespie (eds.), *Natives and Newcomers: The Making of Colonial Society 1534–1641* (Bungay, 1986), N. Canny, *Making Ireland British 1580–1650* (Oxford, 2001) and H. S. Pawlisch, *Sir John Davies and the Conquest of Ireland: A Study in Legal Imperialism* (Cambridge, 1985). A somewhat neglected aspect of British foreign relations is splendidly rescued by S. Murdoch, *Britain, Denmark–Norway and the House of Stuart, 1603–1660* (East Linton, 2002). Another area is fully opened up by A. I. Macinnes, *Clanship, Commerce and the House of Stuart, 1603–1788* (East Linton, 1996). On aspects of English politics and government, D. Newton, *James VI and I and the Government of England, 1603–1605* (Woodbridge, 2005); D. L. Smith, *The Stuart Parliaments 1603–1689* (London, 1999) and C. Russell, *Parliament and English Politics 1621–1629* (Oxford, 1979); J. Crampsie, *Kingship and Crown Finance under James VI and I 1603–1625* (Cambridge, 2002); L. L. Peck, *Court Patronage and Corruption in Early Stuart England* (London, 1990); R. Lockyer, *Buckingham: The Life and Political Career of George Villiers, First Duke of Buckingham 1592–1628* (Harlow, 1981). Scottish politics and government are analysed by J. Goodare, *State and Society in Early Modern Scotland* (Oxford, 1999) and *The Government of Scotland 1560–1625* (Oxford, 2004).

The Churches and Peoples of the Three Kingdoms, 1603–1641

A great deal has been written about religion, religious matters and ecclesiastical politics in Britain and Ireland in the first decades of the seventeenth century. Readers who wish to learn more might begin with some of the books mentioned below and afterwards make use of the free service provided online by the Royal Historical Society Bibliography at http://www.rhs.ac.uk/bibl.

No one has yet attempted a book-length treatment of the various churches on both islands after 1603 but F. Heal's *Reformation in Britain and Ireland* (Oxford, 2003) covers the ground from Henry VIII to the death of Elizabeth I. For the reign of James VI and I there are P. Collinson's accessible Ford lectures in the *Religion of the Protestants* (Oxford, 1982) which are usefully read in conjunction with K. Fincham's treatment of the Jacobean episcopate in *Prelate as Pastor* (Oxford, 1990). Fincham's book uses the bishops as a way of understanding the entire English Church in the period and it is complemented by A. R. MacDonald, *The Jacobean Kirk 1567–1625* (Aldershot, 1998). *The Protestant Reformation in Ireland 1590–1641* (Dublin, 1997) is A. Ford's survey of the predominantly colonial enterprise that was the Church of Ireland.

Since religious policy in England played such an important part in the confessional life of the other two kingdoms those looking for a clear and concise narrative of events and trends will find a guide in P. Marshall, *Reformation England 1480–1642* (London, 2003). Marshall's book also offers an analysis of some of the recent debates in the field, which in turn serves as an introduction to two key essay collections. The first of these is *The Early Stuart Church* (London, 1993) edited by K. Fincham and the second, titled *Conformity and Orthodoxy in the English Church* (Woodbridge, 2003), was edited by P. Lake and M. Questier. Both have an impressive range of articles on key questions by leading scholars. For a wider European perspective on what was happening there is W. B. Patterson's *King James VI and I and the Reunion of Christendom* (Cambridge, 1997) and A. Milton's seminal *Catholic and Reformed: Roman and Protestant Churches in English Protestant Thought, 1600–1640* (Cambridge, 1994).

Most general political and social histories of the early Stuart reigns offer some account of church affairs and religious practices but a number of titles open up other dimensions of the story. M. Todd's *The Culture of Protestantism in Early Modern Scotland* (New Haven, 2002) uses the kirk session to chart the transformation of one national culture, while *The World of Geoffrey Keating* by B. Cunningham (Dublin, 2000) investigates the creation of a self-consciously Catholic culture in Ireland which sought to transcend historic ethnic differences. M. Questier's *Catholicism and Community in Early Modern England* (Cambridge, 2006) reconstructs the mental and social world of English Catholics through an examination of one aristocratic family. The early chapters of Tadhg ÓhAnnracháin, *Catholic Reformation in Ireland* (Oxford, 2002), give an account of the implementation of the Tridentine reforms which when taken together with D. G. Mullan's *Episcopacy in Scotland: The History of an Idea* (Edinburgh, 1986) and J. Davies, *The Caroline Captivity of the Church of England* (Oxford, 1994) give three overlapping perspectives on bishops and their enduring influence over religious matters on both islands. Accounts of another strand of Christian thinking are to be found in J. Spurr, *English Puritanism, 1603–1689* (London, 1998) and D. G. Mullan's *Scottish Puritanism, 1590–1638* (Oxford, 2000), as well as in several chapters of A. Ford's *Protestant Reformation in Ireland*. Those interested in the religious issues which contributed to the war of the three kingdoms will find G. Donaldson's *The Making of the Scottish Prayer Book* (Edinburgh, 1954) helpful. Two more recent publications, J. S. Morrill (ed.), *The Scottish National Covenant in British Context* (Edinburgh, 1990) and A. Ford and J. McCafferty (eds.), *The Origins of Sectarianism in Early Modern Ireland* (Cambridge, 2005), contain collections of relevant essays.

The Rule of Saints and Soldiers: The Wars of Religion in Britain and Ireland 1638–1660

Over the centuries, historians have fluctuated in the significance they have attached to seeing events in England, Scotland, and Ireland as necessarily interdependent. For a review of this story see J. Morrill, 'The War(s) of the Three Kingdoms', in G. Burgess (ed.), *The New British History: Founding a Modern State 1603–1715* (London, 1999). Recent books which stress that interdependence include A. Woolrych, *Britain in Revolution 1625–1660* (Oxford, 2002), J. P. Kenyon, and J. Ohlmeyer (eds.), *The Civil Wars: A Military History of England, Scotland and Ireland 1638–1660* (Oxford, 1999), and M. Bennett, *The Civil Wars Experienced: Britain and Ireland 1638–1661* (London, 2000), all strong as military and political narratives. D. Hirst, *England in Conflict 1603–1660: Kingdom, Community, Commonwealth* (London, 1999) is less concerned to narrate the wars than to analyse their political and religious dynamics. C. Carlton, *Going to the Wars: The Experience of the British Civil Wars 1638–1651* (London, 1992) seeks to analyse how the war was fought—how many combatants there were, how they were trained and supplied, how many were killed and maimed, etc.; and it pays some attention to the distinctiveness of the war in its English, Irish, and Scottish theatres. Many of the important articles by J. Morrill have been published in a welcome collection, *The Nature of the English Revolution* (Harlow, 1993). Three-kingdom approaches to the Interregnum include R. Hutton, *The British Republic 1649–1660*

(2nd edn. London, 2000), strong on narrative, and B. Coward, *The Cromwellian Protectorate* (London, 2002) or J. Morrill (ed.), *Revolution and Restoration: England in the 1650s* (London, 1992), strong on analysis. For specific aspects of the Scottish and Irish dimensions, D. Stevenson, *King or Covenant: Voices from the Civil War* (East Linton, 1996), and J. Ohlmeyer, *Ireland from Independence to Occupation 1641–1660* (Cambridge, 1995) are recommended. The best biographies of Oliver Cromwell are by R. S. Paul, *The Lord Protector* (London, 1955), P. Gaunt, *Oliver Cromwell* (Oxford, 1996), and C. Davis, *Oliver Cromwell* (London, 2001). There has been much rethinking and rewriting the importance of the literary revolution that accompanied the political revolution. For an excellent guide, see N. H. Keeble (ed.), *Cambridge Companion to Writing of the English Revolution* (Cambridge, 2001). The pivotal moment in the story with which this chapter is concerned is analysed from many angles in J. Peacey (ed.), *The Regicides and the Execution of Charles I* (London, 2001). Books appearing too late to be incorporated in this study, but highly relevant to it, include S. Armstrong, *Protestant War: The 'British' of Ireland and the Wars of the Three Kingdoms* (Manchester, 2005), P. Little, *The Cromwellian Protectorate* (Woodbridge, 2007), P. Little, *Lord Broghill and the Cromwellian Union with Ireland and Scotland* (Woodbridge, 2005), and C. Holmes, *Why was Charles I Executed?* (London, 2006).

Restoration or Initiation?

An ambitious recent attempt to write an integrated history of all three kingdoms is T. Harris, *Restoration: Charles II and his Kingdoms, 1660–1685* (London, 2005). R. Hutton's *Charles II: King of England, Scotland and Ireland* (Oxford, 1989) attempts the same feat. Of the accounts of James VII and II that by J. Miller, subtitled *A Study in Kingship* (Hove, 1978), explores both politics and personality. The earliest phase of Charles's reign is thoroughly investigated in R. Hutton, *The Restoration: A Political and Religious History of England and Wales, 1658–1667* (Oxford, 1985) and P. Seaward, *The Cavalier Parliament and the Reconstruction of the Old Regime, 1661–1667* (Cambridge, 1989). Briefer analyses of the period are offered by T. Harris, *Politics under the Later Stuarts* (London, 1993); P. Seaward, *The Restoration, 1660–1688* (Basingstoke, 1991); and J. Spurr, *England in the 1670s: 'This Masquerading Age'* (Oxford, 2000). Popular responses concern T. Harris in *London Crowds in the Reign of Charles II: Propaganda and Politics from the Restoration to the Exclusion Crisis* (Cambridge, 1987). The crisis of 1678 to 1681 is analysed by J. P. Kenyon,

The Popish Plot (Harmondsworth, 1974); M. Knights, *Politics and Opinion in Crisis, 1678–1681* (Cambridge, 1994); and J. Miller, *Popery and Politics in England, 1660–1688* (Cambridge, 1973). For events outside London, A. Coleby, *Central Government and the Localities: Hampshire, 1649–1689* (Cambridge, 1987); L. K. J. Glassey, *Politics and the Appointment of Justices of the Peace, 1675–1720* (Oxford, 1979); P. D. Halliday, *Dismembering the Body Politic: Partisan Politics in England's Towns, 1650–1730* (Cambridge, 1998); V. Slater, *Noble Government: The Stuart Lord Lieutenancy and the Transformation of English Politics* (Athens, Ga., and London, 1994); and P. Gaucci, *Politics and Society in Great Yarmouth, 1660–1722* (Oxford, 1996) are all illuminating. Parliament is scrutinized by A. C. Swatland, *The House of Lords in the Reign of Charles II* (Cambridge, 1996), and B. D. Henning (ed.), *The House of Commons, 1660–1690*, 3 vols. (London, 1983). Valuable collections covering many aspects of affairs are L. K. J. Glassey (ed.), *The Reigns of Charles II and James VII and II* (Basingstoke, 1997); T. Harris, P. Seaward, and M. Goldie (eds.), *The Politics of Religion in Restoration England* (Oxford, 1990); and J. R. Jones (ed.), *The Restored Monarchy, 1660–1688* (London and Basingstoke, 1979). Military matters are treated in J. Childs, *The Army of Charles II* (London, 1976) and J. Childs, *The Army, James II and the Glorious Revolution* (Manchester, 1980); naval in J. D. Davies, *Gentlemen and Tarpaulins: The Officers and Men of the Restoration Navy* (Oxford, 1991). Foreign policy is considered in S. P. Pincus, *Protestantism and Patriotism: Ideologies and the Making of English Foreign Policy, 1650–1688* (Cambridge, 2000).

Biographies range from the massive—K. H. D. Haley, *The First Earl of Shaftesbury* (Oxford, 1969) and A. Browning, *Thomas Osborne, Earl of Danby and Duke of Leeds*, 3 vols. (Glasgow, 1951)—to the more succinct: J. P. Kenyon, *Robert Spencer, Earl of Sunderland* (London, 1858); R. C. Paterson, *King Lauderdale: The Corruption of Power* (Edinburgh, 2003). On the Irish counterpart of Lauderdale, there is T. Barnard and J. Fenlon (eds.), *The Dukes of Ormonde, 1610–1745* (Woodbridge, 2000). Another who—unusually—operated in all three kingdoms is the subject of a fine study: P. Little, *Lord Broghill and the Cromwellian Union with Ireland and Scotland* (Woodbridge, 2004).

Religious life can be followed in J. Spurr, *The Restoration Church of England, 1649–1689* (London and New Haven, 1991); M. R. Watts, *The Dissenters: From the Reformation to the French Revolutions* (Oxford, 1978). Ideas and ideologies are dissected in R. Ashcraft, *Revolutionary Politics and Locke's 'Two Treatises of Government'* (Princeton, 1986); M. Hunter, *Science and Society in Restoration England* (Cambridge,

1981); and J. Scott, *Algernon Sidney and the Restoration Crisis, 1677–1683* (Cambridge, 1991).

Events in Wales can be followed in G. H. Jenkins, *The Foundations of Modern Wales: Wales 1642–1780* (Oxford, 1987). Local detail is offered by P. Jenkins, *The Making of a Ruling Class: The Glamorgan Gentry, 1640–1790* (Cambridge, 1983). For a succinct introduction to events in Ireland, D. Dickson, *New Foundations: Ireland, 1660–1800* (new edn. Dublin, 1997). There is also T. Barnard, *The Kingdom of Ireland, 1641–1760* (Basingstoke, 2004). More detailed are L. J. Arnold, *The Restoration Land Settlement in County Dublin, 1660–1688: A History of the Administration of the Acts of Settlement and Explanation* (Dublin, 1993); A. Clarke, *Prelude to Restoration in Ireland: The End of the Commonwealth, 1659–1660* (Cambridge, 1999); and J. G. Simms, *Jacobite Ireland, 1685–1691* (London, 1969). On Scotland, a brief guide is K. M. Brown, *Kingdom or Province? Scotland and the Regal Union, 1603–1715* (Basingstoke, 1992), and a fuller one, C. Jackson, *Restoration Scotland, 1660–1690: Royalist Politics, Religion and Ideas* (Woodbridge, 2003). Also useful are J. Buckroyd, *The Life of James Sharp, Archbishop of St Andrews, 1618–1679* (Edinburgh, 1987); J. Buckroyd, *Church and State in Scotland, 1660–1691* (Edinburgh, 1980); I. B. Cowan, *The Scottish Covenanters, 1660–1688* (London, 1976).

Two diarists throw vivid light on the period: R. C. Latham and W. Matthews (eds.), *Diary of Samuel Pepys*, 11 vols. (London, 1970–83) and E. S. de Beer, *The Diary of John Evelyn*, 5 vols. (Oxford, 1955). Written by a disgruntled provincial royalist, A. Browning (ed.), *Memoirs of Sir John Reresby*, in a 2nd edn. by M. K. Geiter and W. A. Speck (London, 1991) offers numerous insights into the attitudes of his kind. At the other end of the spectrum, the distress experienced by Protestant dissenters is conveyed by one of the most prolific of the kind: Richard Baxter's *Reliquiae Baxterianae*, in an abridgement by J. M. Lloyd Thomas, ed. N. H. Keeble (London, 1974).

The Social and Economic Context

There are a number of general surveys covering or including the seventeenth century. Among them are J. A. Sharpe, *Early Modern England 1550–1760: A Social History* (2nd edn., London, 1997); K. Wrightson, *English Society 1580–1680* (London, 1982); K. Wrightson, *Earthly Necessities: Economic Lives in Early Modern Britain* (New Haven and London, 2000); R. Gillespie, *The Transformation of the Irish Economy, 1550–1700* (Dublin, 1991): C. Brady and R. Gillespie (eds.), *Natives and Newcomers:*

Essays on the Making of Irish Colonial Society 1534–1641 (Dublin, 1986); I. D. White, *Scottish Society in Transition c.1500–c.1760* (Basingstoke, 1997); R. A. Houston and I. D. Whyte (eds.), *Scottish Society 1500–1800* (Cambridge 1989); T. C. Smout, *Food and Wages in Scotland 1550–1780* (Cambridge, 1995); and J. R. Dickinson, *The Lordship of Man under the Stanleys: Government and Economy in the Isle of Man 1580–1704* (Chetham Society, 3rd ser. 41; 1996). No comparable overview exists for seventeenth-century Wales, but there is much useful information on economic and social matters in G. Williams, *Recovery, Reorientation and Reformation: Wales c.1415–1642* (Oxford, 1987) and G. H. Jenkins, *The Foundations of Modern Wales: Wales 1642–1780* (Oxford, 1987). Most of the works cited above discuss agriculture, but agricultural change and agricultural life are central to M. Overton, *Agricultural Revolution in England: The Transformation of the Agrarian Economy, 1500–1850* (Cambridge, 1996), a broad study which can be contrasted with the microhistorical approach of K. Wrightson and D. Levine, *Poverty and Piety in an English Village: Terling 1525–1700* (2nd edn. Oxford, 1995). K. Wrightson and D. Levine, *The Making of an Industrial Society: Whickham, 1560–1765* (Oxford, 1991) examines what was probably the fastest growing industrial zone in the British Isles. For urban life, see P. Borsay and L. Proudfoot (eds.), *Provincial Towns in England and Ireland: Change, Convergence and Divergence* (Proceedings of the British Academy, 108; 2002). More specifically, the experiences of two British capital cities are discussed in P. Griffiths and M. S. R. Jenner (eds.), *Londonopolis: Essays in the Cultural and Social History of Early Modern London* (Manchester, 2000), and R. A. Houston, *Social Change in the Age of Enlightenment: Edinburgh 1660–1760* (Oxford, 1994). P. Slack, *Poverty and Policy in Tudor and Stuart England* (London, 1988) is an excellent guide to poverty, attitudes to poverty, and poor relief. There is an extensive literature on witchcraft in the British Isles, but C. Larner, *Enemies of God: The Witch Hunt in Scotland* (London, 1981) remains the classic study of the subject in the part of the British Isles which experienced the heaviest witch-hunting, and can now be complemented with J. Goodare (ed.), *The Scottish Witch-Hunt in Context* (Manchester, 2002). For England, J. A. Sharpe, *Instruments of Darkness: Witchcraft in England, 1550–1750* (Harmondsworth, 1996) and his more detailed study *The Bewitching of Anne Gunter* (London, 2000). Similarly, a solid body of publications now exists dealing with the history of women in this period: for a good pioneering example see M. MacCurtain and M. O'Dowd (eds.), *Women in Early Modern Ireland* (Edinburgh, 1991).

'What ish my Nation?': The Cultures of the Seventeenth-Century 'British Isles'

For introductory and primary texts: S. Deane *et al.* (eds.), *The Field Day Anthology of Irish Writing* (Derry and London, 1991–2002), i–iii, and A. Bourke *et al.* (eds.), *The Field Day Anthology of Irish Writing, iv and v. Irish Women's Writing and Traditions* (New York and Cork, 2002) are essential reading for anyone interested in Irish literature, especially following the highly significant intervention of the volumes on women's writing. C. Morash, *A History of Irish Theatre, 1601–2000* (Cambridge, 2002) is highly scholarly and intensely imaginative in its close study of 'nights at the theatre'. The first chapter is particularly relevant to this period. R. Geraint Gruffydd (ed.), *A Guide to Welsh Literature c.1530–1700* (Cardiff, 1997) is an important overview of the literature of the period. M. Glendinning, R. MacInnes, and A. MacKechnie, *A History of Scottish Architecture from the Renaissance to the Present Day* (Edinburgh, 1996) is a valuable overview of architectural developments in Scotland. R. D. S. Jack (ed.), *The History of Scottish Literature; i. Origins to 1660 (Medieval and Renaissance)* (Aberdeen, 1988) and A. Hook (ed.), *The History of Scottish Literature; ii. 1660–1800* (Aberdeen, 1987) are two collections of essays introducing the earlier periods of Scottish literature: this important introductory reading can be usefully supplemented with B. Findlay (ed.), *A History of Scottish Theatre* (Edinburgh, 1998). *The Records of Early English Drama* volumes from A. F. Johnston and M. Rogerson (eds.), *REED: York*, 2 vols. (Toronto, 1979), to D. N. Klausner (ed.), *REED: Wales* (Toronto, 2005) provide invaluable primary records of theatrical activity all over the British Isles; the publication of these volumes, with a forthcoming volume ed. J. McGavin, *Records of Early Drama: Scotland*, has changed the shape of early theatre studies. I. Rivers, *Classical and Christian Ideas in English Renaissance Poetry: A Student's Guide* (2nd edn. London, 1994) is an extremely thorough introduction to classical and Christian allusions and images in the poetry of the English Renaissance and a valuable introductory text.

In terms of literary and cultural analysis, a vast range exists, but the following are recommended. S. Greenblatt, *Renaissance Self-Fashioning: From More to Shakespeare* (Chicago and London, 1984) is the seminal text on the relationships between culture and identity, and remains essential reading. See also B. Bradshaw and P. Roberts (eds.), *British Consciousness and Identity: The Making of Britain, 1533–1707* (Cambridge, 1998), especially the chapters by Caball and Jenkins. P. Allen Brown and P. Parolin (eds.), *Women Players in Early Modern England, 1500–1660* (Burlington, Vt., 2005) is a lively collection on women's contribution to theatre and theatricality which shows how English theatrical culture is intimately connected to that of early modern Europe. It supplements work by Karen Britland, Elizabeth Howe, Clare McManus, and Sophie Tomlinson. M. Butler, *Theatre and Crisis, 1632–1642* (Cambridge, 1984) is a significant study of Caroline court theatre and its political connections. A. Fletcher, *Drama, Performance, and Polity in Pre-Cromwellian Ireland* (Toronto, 2000) is a significant book, which analyses a wealth of information from the same author's *Drama and the Performing Arts in Pre-Cromwellian Ireland: A Repertory of Sources and Documents from the Earliest Times until c.1642* (Woodbridge, 2001). S. Dunnigan, *Eros and Poetry at the Courts of Mary Queen of Scots and James VI* (Basingstoke, 2002) provides an important context for studies of seventeenth-century culture and a sophisticated reading of the literature of the Marian and Jacobean courts. A. Gurr, *The Shakespearean Stage, 1574–1642* (3rd edn. Cambridge, 1992), revised several times, remains the essential first resource for information on the Elizabethan and Jacobean London theatres. S. Orgel, *Impersonations: The Performance of Gender in Shakespeare's England* (Cambridge, 1996) is a study of gender, theatre, and culture in seventeenth-century England and Europe. T. N. Corns (ed.), *The Royal Image: Representations of Charles I* (Cambridge, 1999) is an interdisciplinary collection examining the representation and self-representation of the king. T. F. Healey and J. Sawday, *Literature and the English Civil War* (Cambridge, 1990) although the title acknowledges its predominantly English focus, is a wide-ranging collection of essays on the cultures of the 1640s and 1650s and their aftermath. S. Wiseman, *Drama and Politics in the English Civil Wars* (Cambridge, 1998) is a study of the theatre and politics of the 1640s and 1650s. And see J. Loxley, *Royalism and Poetry in the English Civil Wars: The Drawn Sword* (Basingstoke, 1997). D. Rankin, *Between Spenser and Swift: English Writing in Seventeenth-Century Ireland* (Cambridge, 2005) discusses English writing in Ireland in a range of genres and modes through the seventeenth century. H. Ostovich and E. Sauer (eds.), *Reading Early Modern Women: An Anthology of Texts in Manuscript and Print, 1550–1700* (London and New York, 2004). J. Todd, *Aphra Behn* (Basingstoke, 1999) collects the most important recent critical essays on Behn's poetry, theatre, and prose writings.

Conclusion

The bibliographies for the individual chapters provide a wealth of reading on the seventeenth-century British Isles. To this should be added the works of that most magisterial figure among the revisionists, Conrad

Russell: see his *Parliaments and English Politics 1621–1629* (Oxford, 1979), *The Causes of the English Civil War* (Oxford, 1990), *The Fall of the British Monarchies 1637–1642* (Oxford, 1991), and his collected essays in *Unrevolutionary England, 1603–1642* (London, 1990). Another early call for a new approach was K. Sharpe (ed.), *Faction and Parliament: Essays on Early Stuart History* (Oxford, 1978). The 'revisionist' approach has come under fire, notably in R. Cust and A. Hughes (eds.), *Conflict in Early Stuart England: Studies in Religion and Politics 1603–1642* (London, 1989). See also the introductions to T. Cogswell, R. Cust, and P. Lake (eds.), *Politics, Religion and Popularity: Early Stuart Essays in Honour of Conrad Russell* (Cambridge, 2002) and K. Fincham and P. Lake (eds.), *Religious Politics in Post-Reformation England: Essays in Honour of Nicholas Tyacke* (Woodbridge, 2006); the articles in these two splendid collections should also of course be read. On the 'state' see the works on 'British History' cited in the Further Reading for the Introduction, and those of J. Goodare in Monarchy and Government in Britain. A 'must' for this and much else besides is J. Scott, *England's Troubles: Seventeenth-Century English Political Instability in its European Context* (Cambridge, 2000), which offers a new way forward for thinking about England and, indeed, the other components of the composite monarchy. In general, as this whole section on Further Reading shows—even when it can only offer a selection—seventeenth-century scholarship is in a highly flourishing and vital state.

Chronology

1583   Founding of Edinburgh university

1592   Founding of Trinity College Dublin

1598   James VI, *The Trewe Lawe of Free Monarchies*

1599   Globe theatre opens in London
William Shakespeare, *Henry V*
James VI, *Basilikon Doron*

1600   William Shakespeare, *Hamlet*

1601   Poor Law Act, building on previous legislation of 1598, sets pattern for poor relief in England and Wales which will survive until 1834

1603   Death of Elizabeth and accession of James VI to English throne, 24 Mar.
James VI and I crosses Tweed into England, 6 Apr.
Basilikon Doron and *Trewe Lawe of Free Monarchies* reprinted in London
earl of Tyrone surrenders to Lord Mountjoy, 30 Mar.; end of Nine Years' War
England's war with Spain ended by royal proclamation, 23 June
Bye Plot and Main Plot discovered, June–July
Millenary Petition in England
recusancy plots in Ireland
severe outbreak of plague in London and other parts of the British Isles

1604   James VI and I's ceremonial entry into London
English parliament opens, 19 Mar.; king's plans for union unveiled, 22 Mar.
Scottish parliament opens, 10 Apr. (to 11 July)

James adopts title of king of Great Britain, France, and Ireland by proclamation, 20 Oct.

Hampton Court conference; 'preachers for Ireland' mentioned there

English canons issued

Richard Bancroft becomes archbishop of Canterbury

peace with Spain, by treaty of London

passing of Witchcraft Act in England, supplanting previous 1563 Act

1605   Gunpowder Plot discovered, 5 Nov.

tariffs between England and Scotland abolished

'Mandates' attempt to impose recusancy fines in Ireland

Ben Jonson, *Masque of Blackness*

George Chapman, Ben Jonson, and John Marston, *Eastward Ho!*

Francis Bacon, *The Advancement of Learning*

1606   Gunpowder Plotters executed

new recusancy laws in England with oath of allegiance

Scottish presbyterian ministers brought south, imprisoned, exiled; Scottish parliament rescinds 1587 Act of Annexation

'Mandates' continued in Ireland

Irish commission established to investigate defective land titles

earliest documentary reference to cultivation of potatoes in Ireland

union flag proclaimed, 12 Apr.

Treaty of Paris with France

John Day, *The Isle of Gulls*

1607   Colony established at Jamestown in Virginia

flight of the earls of Tyrone and Tyrconnel, opening way for plantation of Ulster

1608   Calvin's case establishes Anglo-Scottish naturalization

tanistry outlawed in Ireland

Book of Common Prayer published in Irish
new book of rates introduced in England, first since 1558
Scottish parliament recognizes king as supreme governor
of church
James VI and I's project for the union of England and
Scotland rejected by the English parliament
Treaty of The Hague with the United Provinces

1609   Plantation of Ulster begins
survey of Ulster reports
Statutes of Iona
Virginia company receives royal charter
James VI and I, *A Premonition to all Christian monarchs,
free princes and states*
Ben Jonson, *Epicene*

1609–10   Comprehensive plan for commissioners of the peace in
Scotland

1610   English and Scottish undertakers assigned land in Ireland
consecration of Scottish bishops in London
high commission re-established in Scotland, general
assembly and parliament held
King recognized by general assembly as supreme governor of the Kirk; this ratified by parliament, 1612
Great Contract proposed; defeated by English house of
commons
assassination of Henry IV of France

1611   Scots law imposed on Orkney and Shetland
Scotland reintroduces customs rates on English exports
James VI and I's 'orders' for the Irish church; Catholic
bishop and priest executed
death of earl of Dunbar
George Abbot becomes archbishop of Canterbury
theological controversy between king and Conrad Vor-
stius, Dutch Arminian
Robert Carr created Viscount Rochester, then earl of
Somerset 1613

publication of *Authorized Version of the Bible* or *King James's Bible*

William Shakespeare, *The Tempest*

1612 Death of earl of Salisbury

death of Henry, Prince of Wales

Scottish parliament meets, 12–23 Oct.

1613 marriage of Princess Elizabeth to Frederick Elector Palatine

Irish parliament held

appointment of Diego de Sarmiento de Acuña, later count of Gondomar, as Spanish ambassador

divorce between earl of Essex and wife Frances Howard who marries Somerset

murder of Sir Thomas Overbury

tobacco imports from Virginia to England begin, despite king's disapproval and attempt to ban smoking (at court); royal policy takes nearly 400 years to implement

Elizabeth Cary, *The Tragedy of Mariam*

performance of *The Irish Masque at Court*

1614 English parliament sits from 5 Apr. to 7 June: the Addled Parliament

John Napier discovers logarithms

1614–17 Cockayne Project, aimed at remodelling English cloth trade, provokes severe economic depression

1615 Royal visitation of Church of Ireland; convocation produces the Irish Articles

execution of earl of Orkney

arrest of earl and countess of Somerset

1616 Trial of earl and countess of Somerset

George Villiers created Viscount Buckingham, afterwards earl 1617, marquis 1618, and duke 1623

Scottish confession of faith issued

Marco Antonio de Dominis, Archbishop of Spalato,

arrives in England; given benefices in the Church of England; returns to Roman Catholic Church, 1622

publication of the *Workes* of King James

publication of Ben Jonson's *Workes*

death of William Shakespeare

death of Francis Beaumont

1617   James VI and I returns to Scotland

Scottish parliament sits during his visit, 27 May–28 June

Five Articles of Perth introduced and rejected by general assembly at St Andrews

1618   Five Articles of Perth passed by general assembly at Perth; last assembly of the kirk until 1638

James VI and I's *Book of Sports* published in England

Irish ordered to leave lands owned by British undertakers

execution of Sir Walter Raleigh

Bohemian revolt; beginning of Thirty Years' War

1618–19   Ben Jonson travels to Scotland, stays with William Drummond of Hawthornden

1619   Death of Queen Anna

Inigo Jones builds third Banqueting House in Whitehall

Synod of Dort held; success of Calvinists over Arminians

Frederick Elector Palatine elected king of Bohemia

1620   Pilgrim Fathers found settlement at Plymouth, New England

Frederick loses Bohemia; imperial forces invade the Palatinate

1621   English parliament meets; revives impeachment; attack on monopolists; Lord Chancellor Bacon found guilty of corruption

Scottish parliament passes Five Articles of Perth and introduces new form of taxation, on annual rents

border commission disbanded

William Laud becomes bishop of St David's
Robert Burton, *Anatomy of Melancholy*

1622   Investigation into corruption in Ireland
death of Chancellor Dunfermline
'Direction to preachers' in England

1623   Prince Charles and Buckingham go to Madrid in lurid
attempt to secure the Spanish match; fail
publication of Shakespeare, *First Folio*

1623–4   Harvest failure throughout British Isles, particularly
severe in Scotland

1624   Search for bride for Prince Charles shifts from Spain to
France
English parliament: war party dominant
Lord Treasurer Cranfield dismissed
Treaty of London with United Provinces
marriage treaty with France, Nov.
Richard Montagu, *A new gagg for an old goose*

1625   Death of James VI and I and accession of Charles I,
27 Mar.
marriage of Charles and Henrietta Maria, May
English parliament opens, 17 May; dissolved, 12 Aug.
further anti-Catholic legislation, Sabbath Act
commencement of war with Spain, Sept.
return of Buckingham's failed Cadiz expedition, Nov.
Act of Revocation proclaimed in Scotland
Scottish convention of estates meets, 27 Oct.–2 Nov.
James Ussher becomes archbishop of Armagh
severe plague in London and other parts of the British
Isles
Francis Bacon, *Essays*

1626   English parliament meets, 6 Feb.; dissolved 15 June
commencement of hostilities with France, Apr.
Forced Loan imposed in England, Sept.

proclamation for 'the peace and quiet of the church of England'; York House conference

teind (tithe) commission established in Scotland

'Graces' drawn up in Ireland

1627
Expedition to La Rochelle defeated, Oct.

arrest of the five knights, Nov.

1627–9
Period of intense witch-hunting in Scotland

1628
King's declaration forbidding controversies

English parliament meets, 17 Mar.; prorogued, 26 June

king accepts Petition of Right, June

Buckingham assassinated, Aug.

king offers 'Graces' to Irish delegation

1629
Second session of English parliament opens, 20 Jan.; Speaker held forcibly in chair to prevent announcement of dissolution, 2 Mar.; dissolved, 10 Mar.

English Commons look for ratification of Thirty-Nine Articles with Irish Articles

Treaty of Susa with France, Apr.

1629–31
Severe trade depression

1630
Birth of Prince Charles

convention of estates meets in Scotland, 28 July–12 Nov.

Treaty of Madrid with Spain

Guinea Company established

plague in Scotland

1631
Hamilton's expedition to Germany

death of John Donne

1632
Thomas Wentworth appointed lord deputy of Ireland

Aurelian Townshend, *Tempe Restored*

1633
Charles I crowned in Edinburgh, 18 June

Scottish parliament in session, 18–28 June

Charles I's *Book of Sports* published in England
Laud's instructions for Canterbury province

1634   Irish parliament meets
Irish convocation meets; new canons
ship money tax introduced to maritime counties in England
Archbishop Spottiswoode appointed chancellor in Scotland
plague and famine in Scotland
Rubens completes 'the apotheosis of James VI and I' for the ceiling of the Banqueting House at Whitehall

1635   Lord Balmerino convicted of treason
ship money writs issued in inland English counties

1635–7   The Werburgh Street theatre opens in Dublin under Wentworth's patronage

1636   William Juxon bishop of London appointed lord treasurer
arrival of George Con, papal envoy, in England
canons published in Scotland
new High Commission sits in Ireland

1637   Trial and conviction of Burton, Bastwicke and Prynne: their ears are sliced off for libelling the bishops
Prayer Book riot in Edinburgh
the 'Tables' set up as alternative government in Scotland

1638   Majority of Scottish political nation subscribe to the National Covenant to withstand religious innovations
general assembly at Glasgow annuls canons, liturgy, and Five Articles, deposes bishops, and abolishes court of High Commission
verdict in Hampden's case (ship money): narrow victory for king

1639 King plans to use English, Irish, and Scottish troops to impose his policies on the Scots: first Bishops' War; king loses, with no fighting.

Pacification of Berwick

Scottish parliament summoned but prorogued

1640 Short Parliament meets, April–May; no supply voted

second Bishops' War; English forces defeated by Scots

king forced to summon Long Parliament, as money needed to pay off the Scottish army occupying north-east England

Laud and Strafford impeached

Scottish parliament meets in defiance of king's prorogation: passes Triennial Act, abolishes the clerical estate in parliament, makes the committee of the articles optional, and ratifies the Acts of the Glasgow assembly

William Davenant, *Salmacida Spoelia*

James Shirley returns to England

1641 Long Parliament passes Triennial Act, abolishes Star Chamber and High Commission, and ship money, impeaches ministers and judges, Feb.–Aug.

Root and Branch petition

Strafford attainted and executed, May

Treaty of Edinburgh leads to Scottish army being withdrawn

king's visit to Scotland, Aug.–Nov.

outbreak of Irish rebellion, Oct.; widespread massacre of Protestants

Grand Remonstrance passed by 159 votes to 148, Nov.

Werburgh Street theatre closed

1642 Attempt to arrest the Five Members, Jan.; king leaves London

militia ordinance passed by Lords and Commons

military and political provocations escalate

king raises standard at Nottingham, Aug.

first battle of civil war, Edgehill, indecisive, Oct.

Eastern Association established

Scottish army sent to Ulster

Adventurers Act paves way for massive subsequent land redistribution in Ireland

parliament orders closure of all theatres, though some in London and the regions remain open

1643   Solemn League and Covenant: English parliamentarians and Scottish Covenanters form alliance: Scots promise to send 20,000 troops into England and English promise a federal union between England and Scotland and a single system of church government

success in the war lies with the royalists

1643–52   Westminster assembly

1644   Battle of Marston Moor, largest of all civil war battles, won by parliamentarians and Scots: first massive defeat of the royalists

parliamentary trial of Laud, leading to his attainder and execution in Jan. 1645

committee of both kingdoms established

new directory of worship approved by Westminster assembly

John Milton publishes defence of intellectual liberty, *Areopagitica*

1644–5   Campaign of Montrose in Scotland

1645   New Model Army created; wins battle of Naseby

new directory of worship authorized by parliament; use of Prayer Book prohibited

1645–7   Period of severe witch-hunting in eastern England

1645–9   Serious plague outbreak in Scotland; but the last experienced there

1646   King surrenders to Scottish army and first Civil War ends

parliament orders a presbyterian church system to be set up throughout England rise of the Levellers calling for more accountable government

1647 Failure of many attempts at peace
Scots hand king over to parliament, Jan.
king seized by the army, June
Heads of the Proposals presented by the army to the king, Aug.
army grandees and Levellers debate the fundamentals of the constitution in Putney church, Oct.–Nov.
king escapes and flees to the Isle of Wight, Nov.

1648 King agrees the Engagement with dissident Scottish nobles
second Civil War breaks out: Scottish army invades on behalf of the king, and is defeated at Preston
Pride's Purge of English parliament, leaving the Rump
peace of Westphalia ends Thirty Years' War

1649 Public trial and execution of Charles I and abolition of monarchy in England and Ireland
Scottish estates proclaim Charles II king of Britain and Ireland
publication of *Eikon Basilike* begins cult of Charles I as martyr-king
witch-hunt in Scotland

1649–50 Cromwell leads army against the Irish confederates; massacres at Drogheda and Wexford

1650 Cromwell invades Scotland; defeats a covenanting army purged of all considered ungodly, at Dunbar
Western Remonstrance, banning compromise with king, royalists, and English Independents, issued in Scotland

1651 Charles II crowned king of Britain and Ireland at Scone
Scots invade England and are defeated at the battle of Worcester

Charles II flees to France

Scotland incorporated into English commonwealth

failed Anglo-Dutch negotiations for a federal union of the two republics

most important of series of Navigation Acts aimed at Dutch carrying trade seeks to enhance English mercantile marine

Thomas Hobbes, *Leviathan*

1652   First Anglo-Dutch war breaks out; ends 1654

Act of Settlement threatens to expropriate most Irish landowners and confine the Catholic population in the western fastnesses of Connacht between the Shannon and the Atlantic; it is partially realized

Gerrard Winstanley, *Law of Freedom*

1653   Cromwell expels the Rump, Apr.

Barebones Parliament, July–Dec., includes MPs from Scotland and Ireland; abolishes chancery and lay patronage of benefices

army council summons a constituent assembly of 144 hand-picked men to prepare a longer term settlement for Britain and Ireland, July

assembly resigns power back into Cromwell's hands, Dec.

Cromwell is installed as lord protector of England, Scotland, and Ireland under *The Instrument of Government*, a written constitution for 'Britain'; MPs from all three countries to sit in Westminster parliament

Margaret Cavendish, *Poems and Fancies*

1653–5   Glencairn's rising and highland campaign in Scotland

1654   Union of Scotland and England formally proclaimed

first protectorate parliament meets, attempts to restrict religious toleration

Cromwellian state church created by ordinance

treaty of Westminster: peace with United Provinces and defensive alliance

treaties with Sweden, Portugal, and Denmark
expedition against Spanish colonies in West Indies and
mainland America
Nova Scotia captured from French

1655 Failure of Penruddock's rising in England, royalist attempt to overthrow Cromwell
Cromwell dismisses parliament; appoints the major generals
Cromwell's army and navy fail to capture Hispaniola, but capture Jamaica
Jews admitted to England

1656 Second protectorate parliament, further attempts to restrict religious toleration
Cromwell declares war on Spain and makes a treaty with France
persecution of the Quakers peaks with public torture of James Naylor, convicted by parliament of 'horrid blasphemy'
performance of William Davenant's *Siege of Rhodes*

1657 Rule of major-generals ended
Cromwell refuses an invitation to become king, but accepts a revised written constitution, *The Humble Petition and Advice*
offensive alliance with France against Spain
failed attempt to establish university of Durham

1657–9 Extensive witch-hunting in Scotland

1658 French and English forces defeat Spanish army
death of Oliver Cromwell, Sept.
son Richard becomes lord protector

1659 collapse of the Protectorate; restoration of the Rump; political and military disintegration; year ends in anarchy

1660 George Monck, general of the army in Scotland, marches south, occupies London, and calls free elections

Long Parliament dissolves itself, Mar.

Convention parliament meets, Apr.; initially plans to recall Charles II on terms, but after Charles's Declaration of Breda, Apr., promising to leave all disputed issues to be settled by parliament, recalls him unconditionally

Charles proclaimed and returns to London, May

English Navigation Act excludes direct Scottish trade with the American colonies; Glasgow continues to import tobacco

theatres reopen and first professional English actresses appear onstage

Samuel Pepys begins his diary

1660–80   Charles II rules Scotland through the earl of Lauderdale, secretary and, from 1663, commissioner

1661   Savoy conference between Anglicans and presbyterians fails to produce compromise on forms of worship

new English parliament seeks a more partisan Cavalier and Anglican settlement

king guaranteed income—though not an adequate one

Scottish parliament passes Act Recissory annulling all legislation since 1633

Mercurius Caledonius, first Scots-language newspaper, published by Thomas Sydserf

1661–2   Major witch-hunt in Scotland

1662   Act of Uniformity restores Anglican church worship and order 'lock stock and barrel'; king's attempts to secure liberty for tender consciences by prerogative action stymied

episcopacy restored in Scotland, and lay patronage in the kirk

export of Irish wool prohibited by English parliament

Act of Settlement and Removals attempts to regulate and limit provision of poor relief in England and Wales

Charles II establishes Royal Society by charter; Boyle's Law published

founding of the College of Physicians in Dublin
Charles II outlaws transvestite boy actors

1663   William Clerke, *Marciano*
Katherine Philips, *Pompey*, performed in Theatre Royal, Dublin

1664   First Conventicle Act lays penalties on those attending illegal Protestant services other than those established by law in the Act of Uniformity
second Dutch war, ends 1667

1665   Great Plague hits London and Eyam in Derbyshire; marks end of large-scale outbreaks of bubonic plague in England
Five Mile Act bans the clergy who resigned or were ejected in 1662 from living in or even visiting their former parishes

1666   Great Fire of London destroys much of the city
unsuccessful Pentland rising in Scotland
John Bunyan, *Grace Abounding to the Chief of Sinners*

1667   English fleet destroyed in battle of the Medway
Lord Chancellor Clarendon goes into exile under threat of impeachment
sale of Irish cattle and meat prohibited in England and Scotland
Robert Sibbald founds physic garden in Edinburgh, later the Royal Botanic Garden
John Milton, *Paradise Lost*; another version, 1674

1669   Indulgence granted to presbyterian ministers in Scotland, repealed 1672

1670   Secret Treaty of Dover, for Anglo-Dutch alliance to dismantle the Netherlands and for French help to assist Charles II to remain in power after declaring himself a Catholic

Second Conventicle Act increases penalties on those attending illegal Protestant services other than those established in the Act of Uniformity

| 1671 | Publication of Jane Sharp's *The Midwives Book*, the only such book written by a practising midwife in the period |

1672   Third Dutch war, ends 1674
king issues the Declaration of Indulgence allowing dissenters to hold licences to worship outside the Anglican church
Royal Africa Company receives charter
Act passed by Scottish parliament reducing privileges of the royal burghs

1673   English parliament pressures king to withdraw the Declaration, and passes first Test Act, imposing new and stringent oaths designed to prevent Catholics from remaining in public offices

1674   Corn bounties introduced as England enters new era as net exporter of grain

1674–5   Harvest failure in Scotland

1676   George Etherege, *The Man of Mode*

1677   Marriage of James Duke of York's elder daughter Mary to William of Orange, stadtholder of the Netherlands
Aphra Benn, *The Rover*

1678   Titus Oates launches the Popish Plot
the 'Highland Host': highland soldiers quartered in south-west Scotland, marking end of Lauderdale's policy of moderation
John Bunyan, *Pilgrim's Progress*

1679   Danby impeached
the Exclusion Crisis begins
James Duke of York appointed high commissioner in

Scotland; remains in Scotland for much of the time
until 1682

murder of Archbishop Sharpe of St Andrews by Covenanters

armed rising in south-west Scotland suppressed at Both-
well Brig

Covenanters declare Charles II to be the enemy of God

1681   King's opponents in England over-reach themselves;
popular concern about the Popish Plot wanes; king
launches 'Tory reaction'

Scottish parliament passes Test Act and Act acknowledging royal supremacy in all matters, secular and ecclesiastical

Royal College of Physicians founded in Edinburgh

James Dalrymple, Viscount Stair, *Institutions of the Law
of Scotland*

Aphra Benn, *The Roundheads*

1683   The Rye House plot in England: assassination attempt
on king, fails and costs the lives of several leading republicans, including Algernon Sidney

renewal of East India Company's charter

1684   Scottish colonies founded in East New Jersey and
Charlestown, Carolina

1684–8   The 'Killing Times': savage persecution of Covenanters
(though accounts somewhat exaggerate)

1685   Death of Charles II; accession of James II of England and
Ireland and VII of Scotland

rebellions of earl of Monmouth in south-west England and earl of Argyll in south-west Scotland brutally
suppressed

1686   King launches programme to achieve full religious and
civil equality for Catholics; Anglicans refuse to cooperate

1687   James attempts to 'woo the Whigs': appoints them to office, begins campaign to pack English parliament with supporters of religious liberty, issues Declaration of Indulgence

two indulgences proclaimed in Scotland, granting complete religious toleration

1688   Seven bishops tried for claiming the king's Declaration illegal; acquitted of the charge of seditious libel

birth of a son to James II after eleven years of marriage, opening up prospect of Catholic dynasty

Edinburgh university given new charter: 'king James's university'

William of Orange invades England to procure a free parliament, an Anglo-Dutch military alliance, and an inquiry into the legitimacy of the prince of Wales

James flees to France

Margaret Cavendish, *Plays, Never Before Printed*

Aphra Benn, *Oronooko*

1689   English convention declares that James's flight is an act of abdication and the throne is vacant; invites William and Mary to be joint rulers

Scottish parliament deposes James for tyranny

Bill of Rights, England; Claim of Right, Scotland

Battle of Killiecrankie ends Scottish Jacobite attempt to restore James

James goes to Ireland

Advocates Library formally inaugurated in Edinburgh

1690   Battle of the Boyne ends James's chance of restoration; king flees back to France

John Locke, *An Essay concerning Human Understanding* and *Two Treatises of Government*

1694   Mary Astell, *A Serious Proposal to the Ladies*

Maps

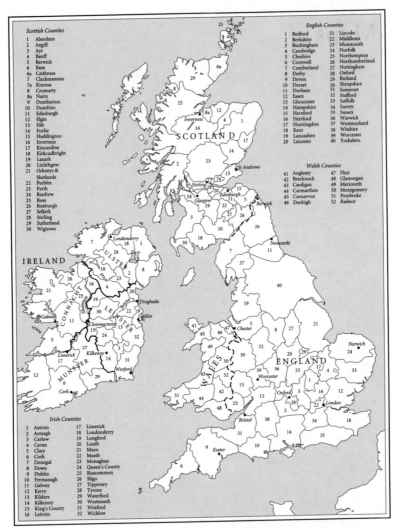

Map 1 The counties of England, Scotland, and (from the 1540s) Wales and Ireland

1   Raphoe
2   Derry
3   Down and Connor
4   Dromore
5   Armagh
6   Clogher
7   Kilmore
8   Elphin
9   Achonry
10 Killala
11 Mayo, Annaghdown,
    Tuam
12 Ardagh
13 Clonmacnoise
14 Meath
15 Dublin
16 Kildare
17 Clonfert
18 Kilmacduagh
19 Kilfenora
20 Killaloe
21 Cashel
22 Ossory
23 Leighlin
24 Ferns
25 Waterford & Lismore
26 Emly
27 Limerick
28 Ardfert &
    Aghadoe
29 Cloyne & Cork
30 Ross

In this period, the only later changes were the creation of a seperate diocese of Edinburgh out of the diocese of St Andrews in 1634 & the reestablishment of Clayne as a seperate diocese in 1638.

Map 2 The dioceses of the Churches of England, Scotland, and Ireland, 1603–1641

Map 3 The civil wars in the three kingdoms (1642–1651)

Index